HEALTH, SAFETY AND WELFARE LAW IN IRELAND

Health, Safety and Welfare Law in Ireland

Second Edition

JOSEPH KINSELLA

GILL & MACMILLAN

Gill & Macmillan
Hume Avenue
Park West
Dublin 12
with associated companies throughout the world
www.gillmacmillan.ie

978 07171 5263 6

Index compiled by Rachel Pierce
Print origination by Carrigboy Typesetting Services
Printed by GraphyCems, Spain

*The paper used in this book is made from the wood pulp of managed forests.
For every tree felled, at least one tree is planted, thereby renewing natural resources.*

A CIP catalogue record for this book is available from the British Library.

Dedicated to my family

Contents

Foreword

Health, safety and welfare have increasingly become core themes in the life of every professional in the course of their policy development, planning and initiatives, irrespective of their field of expertise. More than ever it is imperative that people be well-versed not only in the legislation pertaining to the area, but in the practicalities and realities of these issues as they exist in the workplace. It is right that these concerns be central to our endeavours to keep workers out of danger and protect them in the course of their duties.

Much has been written about health, safety and welfare in legislative environments, in ergonomics, psychology and related fields, but it is rare to find such a practical and comprehensive book written in an engaging and down-to-earth fashion covering not only the background information and legislation, but also substantial and practical advice on how these things are operationalised and implemented in a variety of workplaces. This book integrates theory and practice in a competent and fruitful manner, inspiring confidence in the reader that once they have reached the last page, that they are equipped with everything they need to move forward knowledgably in their plans.

The questions following each chapter sharpen and refine our thinking in each area before we move on to the next and make this an ideal reference guide for all students of Health and Safety. This revised edition of what is a very successful book continues to provoke our thinking and inspire us to take an integrated approach to the topic in the light of problems that confront us within working environments on a daily basis. The chapters draw our attention to the manner in which health, safety and welfare issues dovetail in a variety of work environments while representing different facets of the same broad concerns.

This is a most welcome revised edition; it is informative and encouraging, and brings colour and clarity to an area that has inspired fear in many as they struggle with tomes of legislative procedures. It grounds us in reality and makes the relevant topics concrete and aims achievable for all who need to merge theory and practice in the course of their work. I commend the author on his vision for this text and have no doubts about the positive and valuable contribution it makes to the field.

Helen Ryan
Principal
Cork College of Commerce
Morrison's Island, Cork

Acknowledgments

I wish to thank my principal Helen Ryan for her beautifully crafted foreword; my deputy principal Ger Crowley for his invaluable contribution on optical radiation; my colleague Ann Fanning for her contribution to the provisions on revision of childcare; and finally, my daughter Anne Marie for her excellent advice and assistance in the presentation of this work.

1

Health, Safety and Welfare Legislation in Ireland

This chapter traces the development of health, safety and welfare practice in Ireland since the enactment of the Health, Safety and Welfare at Work Act 1989.

HEALTH, SAFETY AND WELFARE AT WORK ACT 1989

The 1989 Act was the first piece of legislation to cover all places where work activities are carried on; prior to that there was only limited safety legislation covering factories and office premises. The purpose of the legislation and its aims can be said to be:

- placing a legally based responsibility on employers and employees and independent contractors with regard to safety, health and welfare in their respective places of work
- setting out legal standards for the management of safety at work
- stressing the importance of accident prevention in the workplace
- establishing a basis on which consultation can take place between employers and employees on matters affecting safety, health and welfare in the workplace.

GENERAL DUTIES OF EMPLOYERS TO EMPLOYEES

The general duties of employers to employees are set out in Section 6 of the 1989 Act. They reflect the common law principles that an employer must adopt a preventive approach to work-related accidents by providing a safe place of work, a safe system of work and competent staff.

To meet the required standard of care, the employer must take all reasonably practicable steps to protect the health, safety and welfare of his/her employees. It should be noted at this early juncture that there really is no such place as an accident-free environment and to achieve such a standard (which the law does not impose) would be humanly impossible.

A legal onus is placed on employers with regard to the provision of adequate training, including induction and ongoing safety training. Where, despite the use of best safety practice, the employer is unable either to eliminate the hazard or to provide a safer substitute, the employer must provide suitable personal protective equipment for use by any employee exposed to that hazard. Employers are obliged to plan for emergencies such as fire, flooding or major spillages and to hold emergency fire drills at least once each year but preferably every six months. Employers are obliged to provide adequate welfare facilities, including clean and well-ventilated toilet and washing facilities. Where necessary, the employer is obliged to obtain the services of a competent person from outside the workplace to ensure the health, safety and welfare of his/her employees.

GENERAL DUTIES OF EMPLOYERS TO OTHERS

Employers have duties under Section 7 of the 1989 Act to persons other than their employees, for example to self-employed contractors who come onto their premises and use their equipment. A legal duty is imposed here with regard to the safety of the equipment supplied.

Also, where premises are shared with other business activities, a duty will be owed to persons such as those delivering or collecting goods from the premises. A duty is imposed on employers to ensure that exit and entrance points to their premises are kept clear of obstruction and maintained in such a manner as to minimise as far as possible the incidence of workplace accidents.

DUTIES OF EMPLOYEES

Duties of employees, as set out in Section 9 of the 1989 Act, may be summarised as follows: an employee must take reasonable care of his/her own safety and ensure that his/her activity is not a danger to the safety of fellow employees. The Act requires cooperation on the employee's part to enable the employer to comply with any statutory requirement. Examples of this cooperation would include the maintaining of guards on machinery, using personal protective equipment when and in the manner prescribed, participating fully in the holding of emergency evacuation drills and any training courses intended to enhance safety at work. Employees must report to either their employer directly or their immediate supervisor any defect discovered in equipment which might adversely affect health or safety. Misuse of or any interference with plant or equipment which might cause a risk of injury to anyone in a place of work is strictly prohibited.

GENERAL DUTIES OF DESIGNERS AND MANUFACTURERS

Section 10 of the 1989 Act imposes a general duty on all designers and manufacturers to ensure as far as reasonably practicable that articles designed or manufactured by them do not pose a hazard when used in a place of work. Under this section there is a legal obligation to provide adequate information when supplying articles for use in the workplace, this information includes conditions relative to its proper use and information concerning its safe dismantling and disposal. If the information initially supplied is found to be inadequate, additional information must be supplied on request.

Research by manufacturers and designers is crucial with regard to the safety of articles supplied and this section imposes an obligation with regard to carrying out that research. The purpose of any such research must be to either eliminate or at least minimise any hazard arising from the use of that article.

Those who import articles from outside the Irish state have a similar duty to that of designers and manufacturers as to the safety of the article imported. A specific duty is imposed by the Act on those who design places of work to ensure as far as practicable that they are safe and impose no risk to health; a similar duty is imposed on those who construct such places of work.

SAFETY STATEMENTS

Safety in the workplace is primarily the employer's responsibility and the safety statement is the employer's commitment in writing to the proper management of health, safety and welfare in the workplace (see Section 12 of the 1989 Act). The Health and Safety Authority, which has statutory authority to enforce health and safety legislation, has issued detailed guidelines for the preparation of safety statements. This matter will be addressed later in detail, suffice it to say at this point that the preparation of the safety statement is based on the carrying out of a risk assessment by the employer in consultation with his/her employees.

The objectives of a safety statement can be said to be to:

- demonstrate the commitment of management at the highest level to a programme of good health, safety and welfare practice
- identify workplace hazards and make recommendations for action to address those hazards
- identify positions of responsibility in relation to health, safety and welfare

- ensure adequate financial resources are allocated by law (this must be part of the organisation's annual budget)
- ensure commitment by all concerned to the aims of the safety statement.

If a health and safety inspector finds the safety statement to be inadequate, he/she may order it to be revised.

Safety statements are a legal requirement and it is a criminal offence not to have one. There is a legal obligation on employers to bring the contents of the safety statement to the attention of their employees. This obligation extends to seasonal and part-time employees. With the increasing number of non-national workers there may be an onus on the employer to have the statement printed in more than one language. Usually copies of the statement are posted adjacent to the workplace notice board; another method is to supply the principal features of the statement to new employees during induction training, explaining them in practical terms.

WORKPLACE CONSULTATIONS AND SAFETY REPRESENTATIVES

Section 13 of the 1989 Act imposes a duty on all employers to ensure that measures are in place in the workplace to facilitate both consultation and cooperation with employees on all matters relevant to their safety, health and welfare. All employees have the legal right to make representations to and consult their employer on all health, safety and welfare issues pertaining to them.

With this objective in mind, employees may from time to time select and appoint one of their fellow workers to represent them in consultations with the employer. Safety representatives so selected have a right to be kept informed about all issues concerning safety, health and welfare in the place of work.

A safety representative has the following rights and duties:

- to represent the views on health, safety and welfare issues of his/her fellow employees to the employer
- to investigate accidents and dangerous occurrences, however this right may not interfere with investigations by bodies with legal authority to do so
- to be informed by the employer when a health and safety inspector is visiting the premises
- to make representations to an inspector and receive advice from him/her
- on request, to accompany an inspector on a tour of the premises. This right however does not include occasions where an inspector is investigating an accident at the place of work.

Employers are under a legal obligation to consider and if necessary to act on representations made to them by a safety representative concerning the health, safety and welfare issues of any employee represented. A safety representative must be allocated sufficient time to discharge his/her functions without loss of remuneration, and must be afforded an adequate opportunity to acquire knowledge in order that he/she may better discharge the function. Any employee who undertakes the role of safety representative should not in any way be disadvantaged with regard to advancement within the organisation as a result of his/her position. The Health and Safety Authority has advised that this role should be discharged by an experienced worker and should be held for a period of at least three years, with the opportunity for employees to review the position on an annual basis.

SAFETY, HEALTH AND WELFARE AT WORK ACT 2005

The Safety, Health and Welfare at Work Act 2005, which replaces the earlier 1989 Act, applies to employers, employees and the self-employed. It updates and repeals provisions of the earlier legislation and of the Safety, Health and Welfare at Work (General Application) Regulations of 1993 (as amended in 2001 and 2003). The 2005 Act can be said to develop further the concept of modern hazard identification begun by the 1989 Act and is aimed at the prevention of dangers to health and safety at work.

The 2005 Act includes provisions to improve the safety and health at work of both temporary and fixed-contract employees. The principles of prevention set out in the third schedule to the Act can be said to be the very basis of this legislation and may be summarised as:

- avoidance of risks
- evaluation of risks that cannot be avoided
- dealing with risks at their source
- design of places of work to suit the worker and in particular the adoption of measures to relieve monotonous work
- using new technology to adapt the place of work
- replacement of the dangerous with the less dangerous
- giving priority to safety measures designed to protect the workforce as a whole over measures designed to protect the individual worker
- development of prevention strategies that are designed to take account of the organisation, new technology, working conditions and factors affecting employees on a social level
- provision of adequate training for employees.

This Act defines the term 'reasonably practicable' as meaning that an employer has exercised all reasonable care by putting in place the necessary protective and preventive measures, having identified the hazards and evaluated the risk likely to result in injury to health and safety, and where the putting in place of any additional measures would not be justified having regard to the unforeseen or exceptional nature of an incident at the place of work that may result in injury to health or safety. It should be noted that in any prosecution for failure to take all steps reasonably practicable to prevent injury in the workplace, it is up to the defendant to prove that it was not practicable to do more than was done or that there existed no better practical means to satisfy this legal requirement.

A competent person is defined under the 2005 Act as a person having sufficient training, experience and knowledge to perform the task required to be performed.

COMPENSATION CLAIMS

Under the 2005 Act, breaches of any of the duties imposed may be the subject of both criminal proceedings by the Health and Safety Authority and civil compensation claims by injured parties. The Civil Liability and Courts Act 2004 reduces the limitation period from three years (as contained in the Civil Liability Act 1991) to two years under the 2005 Act. The period of limitation within which civil proceedings may be taken commences from the date of the accident or the date on which the illness is diagnosed. Within two months of the incident arising, the defendant must be notified in writing giving details of the nature of the claim and of the intention to commence legal proceedings. Legislation enacted in 2003 now requires all persons seeking compensation for injuries to be referred to the Personal Injuries Assessment Board before commencing court proceedings. This legislation encourages parties in civil compensation claims to take possible steps to settle the claim before going to court; the court of trial under this legislation has the power to convene pre-trial conferences with a view to shortening the trial; final offers of settlement must be exchanged before the case goes to trial. Courts are empowered to appoint suitably qualified assessors to assist in any matter relating to expert evidence.

MANAGING WORKPLACE SAFETY

Under Section 8 of the 2005 Act employers have legal duties to:

- manage and conduct work, as far as is reasonably practicable, in such a manner as to protect the health, safety and welfare of employees
- prevent any improper conduct or behaviour likely to put employees at risk
- design and maintain machinery in a condition that its use poses no significant risk of injury to employees
- prevent injury to the health of employees from any substance in use in the workplace and, in particular, from exposure to noise, vibration or radiation
- plan, revise and organise systems of work that, as far as practicable, are safe and pose no risk to health
- provide and maintain adequate welfare facilities for the use of employees
- provide appropriate instruction and training
- determine and implement all necessary health, safety and welfare measures to protect employees, ensuring that measures taken as a result of risk assessment take account of the principles of prevention and of changing circumstances in the place of work.

The Act places a major onus on employers to manage workplace safety and prohibits them from imposing on employees any costs arising from the implementation of safety measures.

The duties imposed under this legislation extend to independent contractors, their employees and members of the public likely to be affected by work activities. Protective measures here would include conducting a safety audit on the work of specialist contractors. Employers sharing a common place of work are required to cooperate with each other in preparing and implementing health, safety and welfare strategies for their respective workplaces.

INFORMATION FOR EMPLOYEES

Section 9 of the 2005 Act sets out the types of information required to be given on health, safety and welfare issues to employees. This information must be in a manner and language understood by employees and it must include details of workplace hazards, the risks arising from those hazards and the preventive measures put in place by the employer to combat them. Where employees of another company or employees of independent contractors are employed in the place of work they must be similarly informed. Employees must be informed of the names of persons designated to act in emergencies and the names of persons selected to act as safety representatives.

Information on risks associated with their employment must be given to those employed on either a fixed-term or temporary basis. An employer who hires employees through a temporary employment agency or labour supplier must give to that body details of any necessary occupational skills required for that position and the specific features of that employment. It is the duty of the employer to ensure that this information be passed on to the prospective employee. The employment agency or supplier is obliged to give the same information to employees.

EMERGENCY PLANNING TO DEAL WITH SERIOUS DANGERS

Section 11 of the 2005 Act sets out measures to be adopted to deal with emergencies in the workplace such as fire, explosion or emissions of toxic gas. Any measure taken by the employer must be suitable for the place of work and cover such matters as first aid, fire fighting, contact with emergency services, medical care and rescue. The selection of personnel to implement the emergency plan and the training and equipment necessary to deal with emergencies will depend on the nature of the undertaking.

When an emergency occurs, workers must be informed immediately of the risk and protective measures proposed, and they must be allowed to leave the place of work and not be required to return until the danger is at an end. Employees so affected may not be at any financial loss as a result of their temporary absence from the place of work. Where a specific danger exists in a particular part of the workplace, the employer must ensure that only those with the proper training have access to that area. In this regard an area of the workplace where there exists a high level of danger may be designated a danger zone and only those with either permits to work therein or adequate training in the use of relevant safety equipment may enter that zone.

GENERAL DUTIES OF EMPLOYERS TO PERSONS OTHER THAN THEIR EMPLOYEES

Section 12 of the 2005 Act sets out the duty owed by employers to those who are not employees arising from work-related activities. It applies to places of work that are occupied by more than one employer. The section can be said to take on even greater significance when independent contractors are brought into the place of work. A legal onus is placed on the employer here to carry out an assessment of the competence of the particular contractor to undertake a particular task where there exists a potential for exposure to risk. This issue is developed further when the Health, Safety and Welfare at Work Construction Regulations 2006 are being assessed. The employer here may have to give specific instructions to the independent contractor on the specific safety features of the workplace, whether for example a permit to work system exists in part of the undertaking or when isolation procedures are in place in the vicinity of electrical installations. A consultant engineer would also need to assess the implications of this section in relation to any advice he/she might have given in relation to the structure of the building. Another issue, which will be further developed in Chapter 5, is that of public access to places of work and measures required to be taken to prevent unauthorised access by members of the public.

Section 12 does not apply to:

- non-hazardous noise or noxious smells associated with the place of work
- issues involving either clinical judgment or the level of clinical care provided
- road traffic accidents except those involving road works or arising from excessive debris or mud left on the roadway as a result of construction work
- public consumer health and safety issues.

Duties of Employees

The duties of an employee under Section 13 of the 2005 Act may be summarised as:

- to comply with all relevant legislation
- to ensure that he/she is not under the influence of an intoxicant to the extent that he/she is a danger to his/her own safety or that of others
- if reasonably required to do so by an employer, to submit to appropriate tests by a competent person
- to cooperate as far as it is necessary to do so with the employer to ensure compliance with all relevant legislation
- not to engage in any improper conduct that is likely to pose a risk to health, safety and welfare in the workplace
- to attend such training as is reasonably necessary in relation to either work or health, safety and welfare issues at work
- to report to his/her employer any work carried on in a manner likely to endanger that workplace and any breach of statutes that are likely to endanger the health, safety and welfare of employees.

The duty not to be under the influence of an intoxicant, which is defined as including any chemical substance, requires the making of a ministerial regulation to implement it. This area poses particular difficulties for both employers and employees and any regulation would have to address the following matters:

- what constitutes a reasonable belief on the employer's part as to what constitutes a danger through intoxication
- how is the test to be carried out and by whom
- the need to produce a list of safety-critical occupations, including driving motor vehicles and operating machinery
- whether the regulation should ban all intoxicant consumption for these safety-critical occupations
- what employment sanctions should be imposed on those found to have breached the regulation.

The issue of any such regulation would require widespread consultation between the Health and Safety Authority, employer and employee bodies and the minister. Supervisors and line managers have an important role to play in ensuring that any known problem in the area of health, safety and welfare is brought to the attention of senior management as soon as possible.

Violence, bullying and horseplay at work come under the generic term of improper conduct. When working with potentially dangerous machinery, horseplay can have serious consequences and all varieties of this type of conduct are prohibited under Section 13.

Interference with, damage to or misuse of any item of protective equipment without reasonable cause is also prohibited under this section.

GENERAL DUTIES OF OTHER PERSONS

Under Section 16 of the 2005 Act, a general duty imposed on any person who designs, manufactures, imports or supplies any article used at work is that the article is designed and constructed so that it may be used with safety at work and is properly tested and examined to ensure its safety whilst in use. Persons who supply such articles are obliged to provide and update as necessary information on their safe installation, use, maintenance, cleaning and dismantling or disposal without risk to health or safety; the entire life cycle of the article must be covered from initial installation to final disposal. Designers and manufacturers of articles must carry out adequate research aimed at eliminating or minimising risk to health and safety posed by the use of the article.

Those who erect, install or assemble any article for use in a place of work must endeavour to ensure that when that article is assembled, installed or erected that it will not constitute a risk to the health or safety of employees in that undertaking.

Similar rules apply to the supply of substances for use in the place of work with the exception that information supplied about a substance must include:

- its identification
- details of any risks arising from the properties in that substance
- results of any tests that are relevant to its safe use
- details of conditions necessary to its handling.

Persons who either design or construct places of work must design or construct that place of work in a manner that does not pose a danger to others.

PROTECTIVE AND PREVENTIVE MEASURES

Section 18 of the 2005 Act deals with protective and preventive measures. Employers may need to appoint one or more competent persons to assist them in complying with health, safety and welfare provisions. Depending on a number of factors, including the level or degree of risk involved, the size of the place of work and the number of its employees, a competent person would be a person qualified to give technical advice on health, safety and welfare matters, including management strategies in safety, electrical installation and handling of loads. Such a person, where appointed, must demonstrate a detailed knowledge of best practice in his/her particular discipline, be fully cognisant of such matters as a perceived gap in training and be in a position to fill that gap. The number of competent persons appointed will reflect the size of the undertaking and the difficulty of the problems encountered.

The employer in the appointment of a competent person must first give consideration to appointing a competent person as an employee, because an employee is considered to be more familiar with the working of a particular undertaking. A small- to medium-sized business is less likely to have an employee with the necessary expertise and it makes sense to hire an individual or company with the relevant expertise. A company may also require temporary assistance to deal with a specific problem and in this instance an outside specialist will be employed. The competent person when appointed must be supplied with all relevant data pertaining to health, safety and welfare at the place of work. Cooperation between safety representatives and the competent person appointed must be ensured by the employer. It should be noted that the appointment by the employer of a competent person does not relieve him/her of legal responsibility imposed by the legislation.

Identification of Hazards and the Assessment of Risk

A legal duty is imposed on employers to identify hazards in the workplace, to assess the risks from those hazards and to prepare a written risk assessment of those hazards as they apply to the workforce (see Section 19 of the 2005 Act). In this regard attention must be paid to the needs of particular groups of workers such as the young or inexperienced, expectant mothers and those who work alone or at night. A hazard in this context is any substance, article, machine or manner of working with the potential to cause harm. The degree of risk of harm is likely to be determined by the likelihood of harm, its potential severity and the number of workers exposed.

The level of detail required in a risk assessment depends on the size of the workplace and the number of significant hazards identified. For example, a small- to medium-sized undertaking with relatively few identifiable hazards only requires a simple risk assessment, a large undertaking with a wide range of hazards would require a far more detailed approach. Employers are only expected to provide for reasonably foreseeable hazards; they are not expected to provide for the unforeseen. Guidance on the preparation of risk assessments is available from the Health and Safety Authority, suppliers' and manufacturers' manuals should also be used as well as specialised independent advice if required. The risk assessment should include:

- any hazard that is foreseen as posing a significant risk of injury in the place of work
- all aspects of work, including shift and night work and work outside the workplace
- all work-related tasks, including occasional maintenance.

A duty of consultation with employees is imposed on employers when carrying out a risk assessment.

Using the information obtained through the risk assessment, the employer should be in a position to make informed decisions on the management of risks to health, safety and welfare in the workplace.

A risk assessment is not intended to last forever and must be reviewed and updated where found necessary. The assessment needs to be reviewed where significant change has taken place, for example if the workforce has increased significantly or the type of work conducted has changed. Incidents of ill health, an accident or a dangerous occurrence could also necessitate a review of the original risk assessment.

The employer must take all steps reasonably practicable to implement any changes found to be necessary by the most recent risk assessment. The general principles of prevention outlined earlier must be taken account of in the conduct of any risk assessment. It is important to note that the legal requirement to review imposed on employers only applies in the circumstances outlined earlier; as long as the original assessment remains valid, there is no legal obligation to review it.

It should be noted that the legislation also imposes a duty on persons in control of places of work to carry out a risk assessment in relation to those other than employees likely to be affected by the undertaking. In this regard those undertaking work experience, those delivering supplies and members of the public may have to be considered, as well as adjoining places of work.

Safety Statements

Every employer is required to have a written safety statement (see Section 20 of the 2005 Act). This statement must be based on the hazards identified in the risk assessment and must set out how the employer proposes to manage the health, safety and welfare of employees. As with the risk assessment, the general principles of prevention must be taken into account when preparing the safety statement.

The safety statement should:

- set out the hazards previously identified and the degree of risk assessed from those hazards
- outline emergency procedures
- set out employees' duties of cooperation and compliance in health, safety and welfare matters
- include the names and job titles of those assigned specific health, safety and welfare duties
- set out the arrangements for safety consultation.

The aims of the safety statement can be summarised thus:

- to involve management at the highest organisational level by assigning clear responsibilities in the control of safety, health and welfare at work
- to ensure that appropriate steps are taken to comply with legal requirements and to monitor and review where necessary any such steps taken
- to identify hazards and evaluate risk
- to allocate sufficient resources to the management of safety
- to ensure the involvement of employees in workplace safety management
- to ensure that problems as they arise are dealt with in an efficient manner.

The contents of the safety statement must be brought to the attention of all employees in a form, manner and language that is clearly understood. The contents of the statement must be brought to the attention of all new employees at the commencement of their employment. If persons other than employees are exposed to risk by the place of work, such persons must also be informed of the statement's contents. Those exposed to special risk, such as people working in confined spaces, must be informed of the details of the specific risk assessment carried out in relation to their circumstances and the protective measures proposed to be adopted. A copy or extract of the safety statement must be available to a health and safety inspector at or near to the place of work. Despite the generality of this provision, employers with three or fewer employees comply with Section 20 by observing a code of practice for the industry concerned; these codes are available for public inspection at the offices of the Health and Safety Authority.

HEALTH SURVEILLANCE

The risk assessment should identify circumstances in the workplace where health surveillance may be necessary. Health surveillance is designed for the early detection of adverse health effects in order to prevent further harm (see Section 22 of the 2005 Act). Continued health surveillance can be said to:

- monitor the effectiveness or otherwise of existing methods of control
- identify vulnerable employees
- consolidate the risk assessment.

A health surveillance programme is appropriate in the following circumstances:

- a particular type of work activity either has associations with an identifiable disease or is generally speaking adverse to health
- there exists a reasonable likelihood of a disease occurring
- valid techniques exist that are capable of detecting the health-related condition
- it is likely to provide further protection to employees
- it may be required by safety legislation, for example where an employee may be exposed to a substance likely to cause cancer such as asbestos or lead.

Where the employer proposes to adopt health surveillance procedures, all relevant information should be given to both safety representatives and the employees affected as part of safety and health consultation. Decisions concerning health surveillance should only be made by a competent person and in some cases this may mean a qualified medical practitioner.

SAFETY CONSULTATIONS AND REPRESENTATIVES

Employees are entitled to select and appoint a safety representative, the role of this representative being to bring to the attention of the employer matters affecting the health, safety and welfare of his/her fellow employees. While the safety representative is usually a member of a joint safety committee, where appointed, his/her role is in no way diminished by the existence of that committee.

The rights and duties set out under Section 25 of the 2005 Act are similar to those under the 1989 Act but confer in addition a right to make an immediate inspection where an accident or dangerous incident has occurred, or where there is a threat of imminent danger to the health, safety and welfare of employees. A safety representative has the right to investigate accidents and dangerous occurrences in the workplace but not in a manner that interferes with an investigation by a health and safety inspector.

Prior to the enactment of the 2005 legislation a discussion had arisen as to whether safety representatives should be compulsory in places of work. An example of the compulsory representative can be found in the Construction Regulations 2001 which require the selection of a mandatory safety representative for every construction site with twenty or more employees. The consensus at that time favoured the appointment of the safety representative on a voluntary basis, leaving it to the minister to regulate for the appointment of mandatory representatives where it was deemed necessary to do so.

Another discussion concerned the powers of safety representatives and whether they should have the power to order stoppages of work in certain circumstances. Safety representatives in some jurisdictions have this power, the idea however was opposed by employers' bodies on the basis that such a power interfered with the employer's duty to make decisions concerning health and safety issues. Viewed from another perspective, however, this would open safety representatives to legal responsibility and the possibility of being sued by aggrieved parties. The 2005 Act does not place this legal responsibility on safety representatives. It is suggested that if such a change was envisaged in the future any legal change contemplated would have to lift responsibility in tort from safety representatives, something the Industrial Relations Act 1990 has done for trade unions that authorise picketing of places of work.

RESOLUTION OF DISPUTES

The 1989 Act took the general view that the existence of a formal dispute procedure for dealing with health, safety and welfare issues would result in the matter being looked at as an industrial relations problem, something considered to be undesirable at the time. Guidelines issued by the Health and Safety Authority in 1994 contained useful information as to how disputes in this area could be informally resolved.

Sections 27 to 30 of the 2005 Act bring health and safety dispute resolution straight into mainstream human relations. The legislation simply states that an employer may not in any way penalise or threaten to penalise any employee for performing his/her duty as a safety representative, complying with safety legislation or refusing to work in a place of imminent danger. Appeals against any such action may be taken to a rights commissioner in the Labour Relations Commission. A decision on any such matter by a rights commissioner may be taken to the Employment Appeals Tribunal. This system may in the future establish guidelines for dealing with disputes.

CRIMINAL OFFENCES

Section 78 of the 2005 Act introduces significant changes in penalties imposed for breach of duty under the legislation. There is a potential on conviction in the District Court to a term of imprisonment of not more than six months and/or a maximum financial penalty of €3,000. In the Circuit Court, on indictment, the maximum penalty is two years' imprisonment and/or a fine of up to €3 million. Under the 1989 legislation a maximum fine of €1,900 was possible for breach of general duties imposed under Sections 6 to 11 of the Act and there was no possibility of a custodial sentence; on indictment, an unlimited fine was possible, but a custodial sentence was only possible for breach of a prohibition notice. Under the 2005 Act a wide range of offences now carry the increased penalties.

The issue of corporate killing was addressed by the Law Reform Commission in a report to the government in 2003. The Commission recommended that a new offence be created where gross recklessness in the workplace was found to have caused death, and that the offence should carry a maximum custodial sentence of five years' imprisonment. While the government appeared broadly to favour this recommendation, it was not included in the 2005 Act. The concept of on-the-spot fines was introduced by the 2005 legislation and is to be prescribed by ministerial regulation. At the time of writing no such regulation has been introduced but perhaps it could be used where, for example, there has been a failure by employees to use personal protective equipment when required to do so, or where employers have failed to report workplace accidents.

The Health and Safety Authority issues, on an annual basis, details of prosecutions it has taken both summarily in the District Court and on indictment in the Circuit Court. For the year ending December 2006 the Authority published details of twenty-eight prosecutions dealt with summarily in the District Court, twenty of which involved convictions and sentencing by the District Court, eight were subject to appeal to the Circuit Court; forty-six cases were tried on indictment in the Circuit Court, resulting in forty-three convictions, two appeals against the severity of sentence and one appeal against a conviction to the Court of Criminal Appeal.

OFFENCES COMMITTED BY CORPORATE BODIES

The responsibility of those in senior management for managing health, safety and welfare in the workplace is set out in the 1989 Act and provides that where a body corporate has been found to have committed an offence with the help or knowledge or neglect of a director, secretary or other similar corporate officer, he/she as well as the body corporate shall be proceeded against for the offence alleged. The decision of the Circuit Court in the DPP *v* Roseberry Construction and McIntyre in 2001 demonstrates the use of this section to impose substantial penalties on corporate officers. In this case the court imposed a fine of €50,600 on the managing director, which was confirmed on appeal to the Court of

Criminal Appeal. This prosecution was taken based on the provisions in the 1989 Act.

Section 80 of the 2005 Act includes some important changes with regard to company officer responsibility. Under the 2005 Act it shall be presumed that a director, or other officer with responsibility for the management of the undertaking, authorised, consented to or connived at the acts constituting the offence with which the body is charged, unless he/she can prove to the contrary. Some limited protection is provided by this part to those who give professional advice, because giving professional advice does not for the purposes of this section amount to acting in a management capacity.

GUIDANCE ON PENALTIES IMPOSED BY THE COURTS

The Court of Criminal Appeal in DPP *v* Roseberry Construction and McIntyre, in rejecting the appeal against the severity of the sentence, adopted the list of aggravating and mitigating circumstances set out by the English Court of Appeal in the 1999 decision of R *v* Howe in deciding on the level of fine to be imposed. The aggravating factors to include:

- death as a result of the breach of legislation or regulation
- a refusal or failure to heed warnings
- risks run in order to save money.

The mitigating factors to include:

- an early plea with admission of responsibility
- an effort made to remedy the problem complained of
- an otherwise good safety record.

The Court of Criminal Appeal, in confirming the fine imposed by the Circuit Court, was of the view that if the defendants had had a safety statement in place then risks arising from work-related hazards would have been assessed and necessary remedial action would have been taken, thus avoiding what beyond doubt in this case was an unnecessary loss of life.

The issue of legal duties owed to persons other than employees arose in the decision of the Court of Criminal Appeal in DPP *v* O'Flynn Construction Company Limited. The defendant company had pleaded guilty in Cork Circuit Court to two offences: a legal breach of duty to a person other than an employee under Section 48 of the 1989 Act and a failure under the Construction Regulations to sign and identify the perimeter of a building site properly. The Circuit Court imposed a fine of

€200,000 on the first offence charged and ordered that the second offence be taken into account; an appeal was taken against the severity of the sentence. In dismissing this appeal the Court of Criminal Appeal agreed with the trial judge's finding that the company either knew or ought to have known that children from the adjoining housing estate regularly came onto the site and that, while the company was not reckless in its behaviour, it was indirectly culpable with regard to the death of a young boy from severe burns as a result of wood preservative being spilled and set alight, subsequently causing an explosion. On the date of the fatal accident there was evidence that indicated the presence of several children on the building site, none of whom were challenged by security staff. The most serious lapse found by the court was leaving a container of hazardous material in a position where unauthorised persons, in this case children, could gain access to it. In those circumstances the Court of Criminal Appeal found that the trial judge was entitled to take a serious view of this legal breach by the company because it had played a significant part in a series of events which led to the death of the child. The trial judge had also been mindful of the previous unblemished safety record of this company. Having balanced both sets of circumstances, the judge had imposed a proportionate penalty which could not be said to be either too severe or wrong in legal principle.

REVISION QUESTIONS

1 What are the general duties imposed by the Health, Safety and Welfare at Work Act 1989 on employers in relation to their employees?
2 Under the 1989 Act, to whom do employers have duties other than employees?
3 List the duties imposed by the 2005 Act on employees.
4 Under the 2005 Act, who has primary responsibility for preparing, updating and reviewing the safety statement on an annual basis?
5 Outline the role and function of the safety representative under health, safety and welfare legislation.
6 List five of the principles of prevention as set out in the 2005 Act.
7 What information must an employer give to his/her employees to satisfy the legal requirements set out in the 2005 Act?
8 Define the following workplace terms: 'hazard' and 'risk'.
9 List the circumstances in which a health surveillance programme may be necessary in the workplace.
10 Outline the changes in penalties introduced by the 2005 Act for those committing offences.

REFERENCES

DPP *v* O'Flynn Construction Company Limited, Court of Criminal Appeal, 2006

DPP *v* Roseberry Construction and McIntyre, Court of Criminal Appeal, 2003

Health, Safety and Welfare at Work Act 1989

R *v* Howe, English Court of Appeal, 1999

Safety, Health and Welfare at Work Act 2005

Safety, Health and Welfare at Work (General Application) Regulations 1993 (as amended in 2001 and 2003)

2
Safety, Health and Welfare at Work (General Application) Regulations

This chapter is concerned with the promotion of safety in the workplace, in particular accident prevention, and examines the role of the Regulations made under the Acts of 1989 and 2005 in promoting a safe place of work.

On 22 February 1993, the Safety, Health and Welfare at Work (General Application) Regulations came into force. These Regulations were made by virtue of the powers conferred on the Minister for Enterprise and Employment by Section 28 of the 1989 Act. The 2005 Act provides that breaches of any Regulation made under this legislation shall be considered a breach of that Act and treated accordingly.

The Regulations provide a number of important definitions. For example:

- *fixed-term employee*: an employee working for a fixed period of time or employed to perform a specific function of limited but imprecise duration
- *personal protective equipment*: designed to be worn to protect an employee against hazards to health and safety in the workplace, it includes overalls or uniforms not specifically designed to provide protection at work
- *temporary employee*: an employee in a temporary employment business who is assigned to work under the control of another undertaking.

These provisions apply to members of the permanent Defence Forces except when engaged in active service. The Regulations apply with equal force to self-employed, temporary, fixed-term and full-time workers.

GENERAL PRINCIPLES OF PREVENTION

Part 2 of the Regulations sets out the general principles of prevention, now incorporated in the 2005 Act, as follows:

- avoid risks
- evaluate unavoidable risks
- combat risk at source
- adapt and design places of work to suit the individual worker
- avail of technical progress
- substitute the less dangerous for the dangerous
- develop a policy and ethos of accident prevention
- give priority to collective prevention measures
- suitably train all employees
- adequately cater for emergencies.

EMERGENCY PLANNING

It is essential that planning for emergencies take place. An example of this would be properly planned emergency evacuation procedures, the appointment of competent persons to plan and coordinate emergency evacuation and ensuring that such persons be properly trained and equipped for this purpose. Steps must be taken to warn employees of imminent danger, to stop work and to leave the premises by the nearest and safest emergency exit. Employees should not be requested to return to work until all danger has passed. Only employees who have been specifically trained to do so should be allowed access to an area where danger exists.

VENTILATION

Under Regulation 17 of the General Application Regulations 1993 (as amended in 2001 and 2003), a working area must be properly ventilated. If natural air is not sufficient to provide adequate ventilation in the place of work, then artificial ventilation must be provided. In most cases natural air provided by windows is sufficient, however ventilation will be required in working conditions that involve constant dust or high temperatures. The following factors are relevant in deciding on ventilation systems:

- processes, substances and materials involved
- space involved
- number of occupants, where relevant animals to be included
- physical activity involved
- location within the building.

Mechanical systems, where used, must be maintained in good order. In this regard regular cleaning and maintenance of the system is vital; dirt deposits in the system should be removed before they in turn pose an additional hazard for the workforce.

ROOM TEMPERATURE

The temperatures required in indoor places of work depend on a number of factors, such as level of physical activity and radiant heat. Special working conditions are faced by those who work in very hot or cold temperatures, such as those working with either furnaces or refrigeration, and in those situations localised heating or cooling may be necessary. It is essential in this regard that the danger from contact burns and fume emission be addressed.

With regard to light physical work, the recommended room temperature is 16 degrees Celsius which should be reached within one hour of the commencement of activity. Sedentary occupations such as office work require a room temperature of 17.5 degrees Celsius, again to be reached within one hour of activity commencing. The recommended room temperature for manual work is 10 degrees Celsius but issues such as frequency and location of work involved plus physical effort required will have to be taken into account.

LIGHTING

Natural light is the preferred option but all places of work must be fitted with adequate artificial lighting. The type of lighting fitted should not of itself cause a hazard to workers through glare. In order to make maximum use of natural light, all windows must be cleaned internally and externally on a regular basis. Levels of shading and brightness should be arranged to avoid reflecting the glare from the light into workers' eyes. The standard of lighting provided obviously depends on the type of work activity involved and if any doubt exists as to the quality of lighting required for a particular work activity the advice of an appropriate professional should be sought.

FLOORS, WALLS AND CEILINGS

Floors and traffic routes must be kept free from holes, uneven surfaces and slopes and not be the source of a slip hazard thereby causing a worker to slip and fall, or cause instability in a load carried thereby causing loss of vehicle control. Slopes in traffic routes, where they exist, should be no steeper than absolutely necessary. Where steep slopes exist, a handrail must be provided. Floor surfaces wherever possible must be of the non-slip variety, and should be easy to clean and refurbish. Walls and ceilings need regular cleaning to maintain high standards of hygiene in the building. Walls and ceilings also need regular repainting. Cleaning when conducted should not itself pose a hazard and warning signs in strategic places must be utilised to warn of the cleaning activity.

Use of Warning Signs

In any area of the workplace where there exists an increased risk of injury to a worker exposed to that risk, prominent signs must be erected adjacent to the place of danger warning employees of the threat posed. These signs are especially apt in areas where there are fragile roofs; working on or in the vicinity of such roofs is prohibited unless that employee is specially trained to do so.

Loading Bays and Ramps

Loading bays and ramps must be suitable in size for the loads being transported. Loading bays need at least one exit point to allow any employee in danger of being struck by a vehicle to escape, and the provision of a ladder to a higher area or a side opening will satisfy this requirement. Larger loading bays need an exit point at each end. To avoid accidents, a one-way traffic system is recommended.

Room Dimensions

Overcrowding is a major health and safety concern and in order to reduce the problems associated with it, adequate provision must be made both to access and exit the place of work and a minimum amount of space must be provided for each worker. For example, in the case of an office worker the minimum space required including the office chair is 4.65 metres squared. For employment that is not office-related, the minimum requirement is 11.3 cubic metres per person in any room at any given time. The measured space should not take account of any space more than 4.3 metres from the floor.

USE OF WORK EQUIPMENT

The proper use of work equipment is dealt with under Part IV (18 and 19) of the 1993 Regulations. The range of work equipment in use is almost infinite and the precautions necessary will depend on the type of equipment used and the manner of its use. Equipment can pose a danger to workers in one of two ways: moving machine parts or the actual use of the equipment. All places of work are covered by these Regulations regardless of the work activity conducted.

Accidents in the workplace involving machinery may occur for any one of the following reasons:

- machinery was not properly guarded
- machine guards were not properly maintained
- machine guards were poorly designed
- workers did not receive adequate training
- shortcuts were taken in work practice
- supervisors turned a blind eye to potentially hazardous practices.

In choosing work equipment, health and safety must be a priority; work equipment must be adapted to ensure safe use, all routine maintenance must be carried out and instruction and information on the safe use of the equipment must be provided.

European Community Directive 95/93 imposes additional obligations on employers in regard to the safe use of mobile machinery including fork-lift trucks. The use of lifting equipment now requires more stringent examination as to its safety, and full instruction must be provided in the use of lifting equipment.

Danger zones mean any areas where an employee is subject to any risk to his/her health or safety and in the case of moving machinery this includes the immediate area of that machine. Where gases or vapours are emitted by work equipment a risk assessment is necessary to determine the parameters of the danger zone. In this context an exposed employee is defined as an employee wholly or partially in a danger zone. It is important to note that workers can be at risk from work equipment from start-up time right through its use to servicing and maintenance.

When purchasing work equipment employers must match that equipment to the work required to be done. In this context suitability of equipment means suitable in every foreseeable way and not likely to pose risks to the health and safety of employees.

As part of normal on-the-job training, written, easily understandable instructions will be given on the safe use of equipment. Written instructions on the safe use of equipment should take account of three basic issues:

- the conditions under which the equipment will be used
- foreseeable abnormal conditions
- conclusions where appropriate to be drawn from previous use of similar equipment.

In some instances it may also be necessary to consult manuals supplied with that equipment. If highly technical language is used in instruction manuals, the employer must supply an easily understood interpretation of those instructions.

The European Community Machinery Regulations 1994, in force in Ireland since 1 January 1995, require all machinery to be safe in its design and not to pose a health risk whilst in use. All equipment carrying the European Community safety logo meets the requirements of these Regulations. The National Standards Authority of Ireland will, on request, issue information on the safety standards required for the safe use of equipment. The 1994 Regulations also apply to equipment imported into the European Community. Employers are required under these Regulations to show due diligence in sourcing only equipment that complies with the European Community Safety Standard.

Work equipment must be maintained efficiently and kept in a state of good repair at all times. Experience shows that lack of essential maintenance has caused many work-related accidents. A maintenance log should be kept that should record all servicing and repairs carried out on the equipment. It is essential that all equipment should continue during its working life to meet safety standards. Because of the wide range of work-related equipment, not all safety standards will apply in each case, only those relevant to the particular work equipment will apply.

Control Devices on Machinery

All control devices on machinery must be clearly visible and marked where necessary (see Fifth Schedule, Regulation 20). Such devices, if possible, should be located outside danger zones and must not give rise to any additional risk by virtue of unintentional operation. Control devices essential to the operation of equipment must not pose any risk to the operator by reason of the use of the incorrect control or for any other reason. The preferred aim in locating controls is to position them so that the operator of the equipment is able to see from the control position that nobody is at risk when the equipment is started up, and has a clear view of the part of the workplace likely to be affected by the use of that equipment. Direct sight is the best option but may need to be supplemented by mirrors, television monitors or sensing equipment such as mats which give off warnings. In some instances an audible and/or visible warning device may be more practical, these devices may give warning on start-up and continue for as long as deemed necessary.

Control systems fitted to equipment must be safe and failure of any part of the system should not be a source of danger but should either shut down the equipment or alternatively continue its safe use. It should be possible to start up equipment only by the deliberate act of the operator. The ideal situation is for all equipment to be fitted with fail-safe devices which would result in a failure to start up equipment manually without all safety devices in place.

All equipment should have a device to restart them after stoppage and a device to control a significant change in operation. Neither of these controls should place employees at additional risk. It is crucial that the stop device fitted to equipment have priority over the start-up system. Localised and readily accessible stop controls must be provided at each work station. Where appropriate an emergency stop control should be fitted to equipment, depending on the hazard presented and the normal stopping time of that equipment. Emergency controls, where fitted, must be easily reached and activated; common types in use are mushroom head buttons, bars or levers and sometimes pressure-sensitive cable.

Work equipment presenting hazards due to falling objects or flying projectiles should be fitted with suitable safety devices. If the equipment is emitting gases, vapours or dust, a suitable mechanical extraction system should be fitted to the equipment.

All equipment in use in the workplace should be stabilised if necessary before use. Where items such as abrasive wheels or pressurised containers are in use, and there is a likelihood that while in use the wheel or container will either disintegrate or burst, the supplier's instructions should be fully followed when in use. When dealing with pressurised containers, pressure-release valves may be necessary. Appropriate personal protective equipment must be worn and the abrasive wheel, when in use, must be either fitted with a suitable guard or encased. Regular inspection and maintenance of this type of equipment is essential.

MACHINE GUARDING

Where a risk of injury could arise from contact with the moving parts of machinery, guards should be fitted and regularly checked. Any measure taken must prevent access to danger and stop the movement of a part before danger is posed by the employee reaching that part. As a protective device, a machine guard must:

- be robust
- not give rise to more hazards
- not be easily overcome
- be at a sufficient distance from the danger zone
- not unduly restrict operation
- allow, if possible, for replacement without removal
- be sufficiently strong to take account of both normal and abnormal wear and tear
- in the case of fixed guards, require a deliberate act to remove them.

In certain situations it may be necessary to introduce a viewing window into the guard.

SAFETY IN WORK OPERATIONS

It is essential to operate equipment only in the conditions that it is suitable for. Areas where work is carried out must have adequate lighting, and work equipment operating at high and low temperatures must be protected against operator contact. There are two main methods of addressing this problem:

- reduce surface temperature, insulate the equipment and/or erect screens or barriers
- use easily understood warning signs or signals.

If possible, maintenance on machinery should only be carried out when the machine has been shut down. Any maintenance log supplied with machinery must be updated as necessary; a log is recommended where machinery requires regular maintenance. A clearly identifiable means to isolate equipment from its energy source must be fitted; any reconnection to the energy source must present no risk of injury to the operator. All work equipment shall carry warnings essential to ensure the health and safety of the operator. Those operating, adjusting or maintaining equipment must have safe access to it. All employees must be protected against risk of fire and/or explosion from equipment.

PERSONAL PROTECTIVE EQUIPMENT

The five principles for eliminating work-related hazards are:
- eliminate the risk
- reduce the exposure to risk
- isolate the risk
- bar access to risk source
- use of personal protective equipment.

As a general principle, personal protective equipment should only be used when all other methods of accident prevention have failed. The safety, health and welfare of employees must be protected by measures that eliminate workplace hazards at source through technical or organisational means that provide protection to the entire workforce. Measures provided to protect the workforce as a whole are known as collective safety measures and must be given priority over individual safety measures. It is only where collective measures either prove impossible to implement or are inadequate that individual safety measures are needed.

Personal protective equipment only affords protection to the wearer. Furthermore, the theoretical level of protection provided is never reached in practice. For example, the level of protection afforded by a face mask depends on such matters as facial contour and hair. It is therefore very important that when personal protective equipment is being purchased that more than one size be ordered. The use of personal protective equipment will always restrict the wearer to some extent – movement, visibility, hearing and breathing may all be affected – or the equipment may simply be uncomfortable to wear. Finally workers may feel psychologically more protected than they actually are, which may lead to risk-taking behaviour.

The legislation imposes a duty on employers to supply suitable personal protective equipment and a duty on employees to use that equipment correctly. Part V of the Regulations emphasises the importance of selection and training of the workforce and enforces the duty on employees to make full and proper use of personal protective equipment, to use it as directed, to return it when not in use or to store it correctly. Employees should always be consulted about personal protective equipment. Where provided, personal protective equipment shall be appropriate for the level of risk involved and shall not of itself increase that risk in any way. Such equipment must take account of existing work practices and of the employee's physique and state of health and it must fit properly. When selecting personal protective equipment both the physical features of the workplace and the health of the employee must be taken into account.

Factors to be considered include:

- *movement*: some equipment can be both cumbersome and heavy thereby restricting movement
- *visibility*: ventilated goggles could overcome misting – a perennial problem with goggles – but the field of vision could still be restricted
- *breathing apparatus*: the filters may clog thereby causing breathing difficulties and necessitating frequent change. Workers with sensitive skin may experience skin problems and it may be necessary to change to a different apparatus
- *earplugs*: employees suffering with ear infections will be unable to wear earplugs
- *special needs*: workers suffering from diseases such as asthma, bronchitis and heart-related illnesses need to take special care with the use of personal protective equipment and employers are required to seek medical advice when informed of these complaints by employees.

SAFETY AND DESIGN

Personal protective equipment must conform to European Union safety standards and must contain the necessary design approval (see Part V, Regulation 21). Employers are obliged to assess the suitability of equipment before purchase. This assessment must include an analysis of the level of risk present that cannot be avoided by other means. It must consider what characteristics the personal protective equipment must have to render it effective as well as possible hazards created. A simple test is to compare the characteristics of available equipment with the risk attendant in the place of work. Any assessment that takes place must be reviewed if a significant change in work practices takes place. The level of actual risk must be determined so that the performance required of the equipment can be established. Account needs to be taken of:

- physical effort required
- visibility
- mobility
- duration of use
- possible discomfort – proper fitting is imperative and employees should be consulted.

ASSESSMENT

Personal protective equipment needs periodic review, particularly where there may be reason to believe the original assessment is no longer valid (see Part V, Regulation 22). Replace personal protective equipment when necessary. The conditions for the use of the equipment depend on seriousness of risk, frequency of exposure, characteristics of workstations and duration of use. It is essential that personal protective equipment only be used for the purpose specified. Depending on the level of risk exposure, the employer may be obliged to rearrange work processes in order to reduce the length of workers' exposure. Personal protective equipment selected must have the characteristics necessary to combat the risk during the exposure period. Workers who are required to wear several items of equipment, for example firemen, must be issued with equipment designed to fit properly together, otherwise additional hazards may be created.

STORAGE AND MAINTENANCE

Employers, through proper storage, maintenance, repair and replacement, must ensure that equipment is in good working order and is not a hygiene hazard (see Part V, Regulation 24). Personal protective equipment must be subject to regular examination by trained personnel before being issued for use. In this regard the supplier's instructions should always be followed. Health, safety and welfare legislation requires suppliers of such equipment to provide additional information on its care and use if requested; if in doubt employers should simply request additional information. The wearer of such equipment should also check it before use and report defects found. Defective equipment should not be used but should be repaired or replaced as appropriate.

As a general rule, the more frequent the use, the more frequent the maintenance. Very often maintenance will simply involve cleaning or disinfecting the equipment, and such simple maintenance can be carried out by the user. Equipment supplied for high-risk use should only be maintained by properly trained personnel.

Personal protective equipment due for repair or cleaning should be clearly identified by markings and separated from other such equipment. Where a risk of contamination exists, those items should be stored separately in waterproof bags to provide containment of the hazard; the markings on the bags should clearly indicate hazardous waste.

USE

Personal protective equipment is mostly issued for use by a single individual, however in some cases, particularly for more expensive items such as respirators, it is issued to more than one user. In such cases, the equipment must be properly cleaned after each usage and disinfected after use by each user. The employer has a twofold duty in relation to personal protective equipment (see Part V, Regulation 25):

- to warn employees of the risks that the equipment is issued to combat
- to instruct properly on, and if necessary to demonstrate, correct use.

Two issues are paramount: the reasons for the supply of the equipment and the level of protection that it affords the wearer.

TRAINING AND INSTRUCTION

Where necessary, training and instruction must include the following:

- an in-depth knowledge of the type of risk present and why personal protective equipment is necessary
- an understanding of the factors that affect the equipment such as working conditions, bad fitting, accidental damage, wear and storage
- practice in the correct use of the equipment, inspection, testing and maintenance where the user can do this.

See Part V, Regulation 26.

LIST OF AVAILABLE EQUIPMENT

- *Protective helmets*: used mainly in the construction industry, they should be worn always when overhead work is in progress.
- *Safety shoes with puncture-proof soles*: particularly suitable in warehouses and builders' yards and for scaffolding work.
- *Safety shoes without puncture-proof soles*: suitable for maintenance work, metal assembly, shipbuilding, transport and ceramics businesses.
- *Protective shoes*: suitable for work with very hot or cold materials (insulated).
- *Easily removable shoes*: suitable for any work where there is a risk of penetration by molten metal.
- *Protective goggles and screens*: suitable for welding and work with lasers, liquid sprays, acids, caustic materials and corrosives.

- *Respirators*: suitable for use in containers or other restricted areas where gas or insufficient oxygen exists, also for use in spray painting and in areas where dust, fumes or asbestos are present.
- *Ear protectors*: must be used where the daily noise level exceeds eighty-five decibels, for example for ground staff at airports and users of pneumatic drills and metal presses.
- *Special protective clothing*: this may be needed to cover arms, body and hands from such processes as shot blasting, use of acids and deep-freeze rooms. It may be necessary to issue fire-resistant equipment in certain circumstances like welding in restricted areas. Other examples include: pierce-proof aprons for boning meat, special gloves for welding and for slaughtering in the meat trade, weatherproof clothing to protect from inclement weather, reflective clothing to ensure visibility on or near public roads, safety harnesses and ropes for working either above or below ground level, and, in certain situations, barrier creams may be required.

See Sixth Schedule, Regulation 21.

VISUAL DISPLAY UNITS

The use of visual display units should not pose a threat to users (see Part VII of the Regulations). Characters on the display screen should be legible with adequate spacing between them. It is recommended that users be at least 600 millimetres from the display screen. The height range of characters displayed should be between 3.1 and 4.2 millimetres. The image displayed must be stable and there should be no flickering; in order to achieve this stability the screen must be constantly refreshed (rewritten) and the recommended refresh rate is fifty hertz. Brightness and contrast must be easily adjustable by the user, this will assist the operator in two ways: it will reduce eyestrain and it will produce better quality work.

The display screen should be non-reflective. Its work surroundings should have a low-reflective finish. The keyboard should have a matt finish to avoid a reflective glare and it should be designed to allow the operator to work in reasonable comfort. It is important that sufficient space is provided in the vicinity of the keyboard to allow the operator to rest his/her hands and wrists; the keyboard itself should be detachable to allow the operator maximum wrist and arm comfort and to avoid injury from strain. The worker should be able to see the most frequently used parts of the keyboard without having to bend his/her head. Two matters are of importance in relation to the keyboard: the keys themselves should be non-reflective and concave to fit fingertips and the symbols must be adequately contrasted with the keys; British Standard 71/79 meets these requirements.

SPACE

Sufficient space is required for the operator to change position and vary movements. Adequate lighting, both spot and work lighting, should be provided.

GLARE AND REFLECTION

Glare and reflection should be prevented by coordinating workstations with the lighting system within the place of work. Correct lighting is essential to prevent both eyestrain and glare on the screen. A visual display unit should not be placed under overhead lights. Where fluorescent lights are in use, these should be parallel to the sides of the unit and not its screen. The workplace windows should be fitted with suitable blinds to reduce the glare effect of the natural light.

RADIATION

With regard to the threat of radiation emissions from the screen of the unit, the World Health Organization has stated that no special protection is needed to protect workers from the effects of the radiation from the screen as it is well below the internationally recognised danger limit.

DISPLAY SCREEN

The display screen should be able to swivel and/or tilt easily. It should be possible to use a separate base for the screen unit. See Tenth Schedule, Regulation 31.

WORKSTATION

The workstation area must be sufficiently large to allow flexibility of movement. The desktop must allow for knee clearance, be adjustable, have adequate storage space, be easily accessible and be of a matt finish to avoid reflective glare.

WORK CHAIRS

A work chair must be stable, adjustable and have a back rest. Instruction in the correct use of the chair should be given to the operator to avoid both back and thigh strain.

NOISE

Noise must be taken into account. For example, if printers cause noise and distract operators the rehousing of those printers in a separate area must be considered.

HEAT AND HUMIDITY

Visual display units generate heat so these areas must be properly ventilated. Where a number of units are in use, the heat will dry the air causing a lack of humidity which in turn may cause both eye fatigue and irritation of the eyes; trays of water strategically placed in the work area will combat this problem.

SOFTWARE

This must be suitable to use, facilitate feedback to operators and display information in an easily read format. The employer is not permitted to carry out any tests on the operator without his/her knowledge. Software must be adaptable to the worker's ability to use it.

FIRST AID

Part IX, Regulation 54 of the General Application Regulations deals with first aid. First aid means attention to a person awaiting treatment by a doctor or nurse or, in the case of minor injury, attention to that injury.

OCCUPATIONAL FIRST-AIDERS

An occupational first-aider is a person who holds a certificate in first aid issued within the previous three years by a person recognised as a first-aid instructor. In order to be certified a period of training of at least three days must be undertaken, including a two-hour examination. At the minimum, the training must be based on the approved syllabus of the Health and Safety Authority in first aid and the assessment of students must be conducted by another competent instructor. To maintain a qualification as an occupational first-aider, a refresher course must be undertaken every three years. The Health and Safety Authority has put in place a system for training and approval of first-aid instructors and for training and certifying occupational first-aiders.

When selecting employees for first-aid training, account must be taken of gender balance in the workplace. In the absence of the occupational first-aider, the employer may nominate another person to take charge of the injured worker until medical help arrives. This person's function is confined to summoning medical assistance and attempting to ensure that the worker's condition does not worsen. All first-aid details, including the names of occupational first-aiders, must be included in the safety statement and in addition a written record of all persons treated must be kept adjacent to the first-aid box and be available if required for inspection by a health and safety inspector.

FIRST-AID EQUIPMENT

It is the duty of every employer to provide and maintain suitable first-aid equipment, suitably marked, easily accessible and appropriate for the particular place of work. Different work activities involve different hazards and as a result different first-aid equipment is necessary. Some work activities such as those that are office-based can be said to pose a low level of risk from hazards, others such as construction have a high risk level, requirements can be said to depend on the:

- size of the undertaking
- numbers employed
- hazards arising
- access to medical services
- dispersal of employees
- extent of employees working away from the employer's place of work
- extent of workers in isolated areas.

First-aid equipment supplied must be conveniently located and kept up to date. A first-aid box should, depending on the number of employees served, have the following contents: adhesives plasters, sterile eye patches, triangular bandages, sterile dressings both large and small, sterile wipes, latex gloves and a paramedic shears. In the absence of a supply of clean running water, sterile eye wash must be supplied. Where workers are exposed to special hazards such as risk of poisoning, burns or exposure to toxic chemicals, one first-aid box with specialised items such as poison antidotes must be provided at a place adjacent to the area of special hazard.

Where workers work away from their place of employment and there are no special risks attaching to that employment no first-aid kit need be supplied, but where special hazards exist a first-aid travel kit must be provided. Workers employed in places more than one hour distant from medical attention must be provided with a first-aid travel kit.

Employers jointly operating at the same location should arrange for one of them to provide the first-aid equipment. First-aid boxes must be kept under the control of the occupational first-aider or other person named in the safety statement.

First-Aid Rooms

All places of work are required to have one or more first-aid rooms if the risk assessment undertaken for the safety statement requires it. The need for first-aid rooms will be based on the following criteria:

- size of premises
- type of business activity carried on therein
- frequency of accidents arising
- existence of special hazards
- distance from nearest appropriate medical facility.

Any workplace which presents a high risk from hazards should have a suitably equipped first-aid room. Where occupational health services exist on the premises the surgery suffices as the first-aid room.

The entrance to the room must be large enough to take a stretcher, trolley or wheelchair and must be fitted with a suitable communications system. This room must be adequately signposted, easily accessible to the workforce and equipped with all essential first-aid equipment. An occupational first-aider should be made responsible for the upkeep and stocking of the first-aid room.

There is no requirement for a first-aid room in means of transport, fishing vessels and outlying agricultural land.

Electricity

Part VIII, Regulation 33 of the General Application Regulations concerns the use of electricity in the workplace. Employees are entitled to be consulted by the employer when protective measures against risk from electrical hazards are being taken. Under this part of the Regulations the carrying out of certain defined tasks is left to an authorised person. The authorised person will be engaged in electrical installation work and must be adequately trained and have the necessary level of expertise to carry out the task. Danger under these Regulations means risk of death or serious injury to health from electric shock, burns or explosion. Such risks may also be presented by the movement of electrically driven vehicles.

OVERHEAD LINES

As electricity can flash from overhead power lines, do not work under them or allow any part of a machine, crane, lorry or ladder within ten metres of such a line without seeking advice.

UNDERGROUND CABLES

Assume there are live electricity cables buried before digging the pavement, street or in the vicinity of buildings. Consult in advance with the Electricity Supply Board (ESB) before working under or digging where power lines or cables are likely to be located. A sufficient number of persons in each employment should be trained to deal with victims of electric shock.

OUTDOORS

Pneumatic tools should be preferred to electric ones when working outdoors. If the latter are used outdoors, a current circuit breaker should be used to enable a power switch-off if an employee receives a shock. Each machine in use must be capable of being switched off either by a switch or circuit breaker situated close to the machine. Power cables to machines must be covered in thick, flexible rubber or PVC or installed in conduits. When in use, light bulbs must be protected from damage; sockets must not be overloaded. It is recommended that a multi-plug socket should be used if needed, not an adaptor. Outdoor sockets need specialist installation and must be protected from weather elements. Plugs must be undamaged and the flex must be firmly clamped to avoid being pulled out from the terminals. It is absolutely necessary that all worn or frayed cables and damaged plugs be taken out of use and replaced; no attempt should be made to repair them. Cables should only be joined with proper cable couplers. All electric fittings should be obtained from a reputable supplier and bear the European Conformity safety logo. Items must be sufficiently robust for business use. Fuses and circuit breakers must be correctly rated for the circuit they protect. The main switches of the system must be readily identified and accessible to all. All employees should know how to switch off the mains in the event of an emergency.

INSTALLATIONS

Installations must be regularly checked and repairs carried out only by competent staff (see Part VIII, Regulation 36). All portable equipment must be listed and checked on a regular basis for faults. Remember to include certain equipment, for example floor polishers, that is used after business hours. Bear in mind also that hired equipment may be used by cleaning contractors and others operating after the premises are closed for business. All suspect or faulty equipment must be taken out of service, properly labelled and kept secure until competently repaired. Where equipment requires special maintenance, a proper record needs to be maintained concerning servicing of that equipment, a person should be made responsible for this and the record should be readily available.

All appliances must be unplugged before even routine maintenance commences. Appliances must be switched off before plugging into sockets. An employee should be responsible for checking the test button on circuit breakers before use.

Persons installing electrical installations must be competent to do so and have adequate experience of similar installations. The installer must have full training in safety procedures and the ability to recognise when it is safe to work. All new installations must be fully tested before use and a certificate of test completed; these tests must be carried out in accordance with national rules for electrical installation.

OUTDOOR PLACES OF WORK

Outdoor places of work (see Part VIII, Regulation 37) should be organised so as to allow both vehicles and pedestrians to move freely and without danger to each other. They require adequate lighting, artificial where necessary, and need to be protected from inclement weather, excessive noise levels, gas, vapours and dust. Slip, trip and fall hazards must also be addressed. Adequate provision must be made in the organisation's emergency evacuation plan for the evacuation of workers employed in outdoor places of work.

SANITARY FACILITIES

Sanitary facilities must be separate, clearly marked and ventilated and must not open directly into places of work (see Fourth Schedule, Regulation 17). Unless the building is fitted with passenger lifts, such facilities must be located on the same floor as the workplace or on a floor level immediately above or below that area.

The Regulations provide for a minimum number of both urinals and water closets. In the case of water closets, this ranges from one facility for up to five employees to five facilities for up to one hundred employees, with one additional water closet per twenty-five extra employees. In the case of urinals, the range is from one facility for up to fifteen employees to four facilities for up to one hundred employees, an extra urinal is required for each additional fifty males. Employers are obliged to provide sanitary facilities for disabled employees and advice in this regard can be sought from the National Disability Authority, Comhairle or Rehab.

WASHING FACILITIES

Washing facilities should be provided near both the place of work and the sanitary facilities. They should contain drying facilities and have a supply of soap and warm water. They should be kept clean at all times. The wash hand basins should be sufficiently large for a person to wash his/her face, hands and lower arms. Adequate ventilation and lighting are essential.

Facilities of this nature may be shared as, for example, in a shopping centre. For office employment the recommended minimum is one wash basin per twenty employees, up to one hundred, and one per forty employees after that. The requirement for industrial work is one wash basin per fifteen employees or 600 millimetres of washing trough for up to one hundred employees, with one extra per twenty-five additional employees. Where heavy spoiling of hands is a feature of the employment, one wash basin for every five employees should be provided.

REST ROOMS

These should be provided where the work is arduous, the noise, fume or dust level is high or there is either excessive heat or cold. The rest room should be situated away from the work area. Workers wearing contaminated clothing need to be accommodated in separate rest facilities, which would apply for example where the canteen serves as the rest room.

PREGNANT WOMEN AND NURSING MOTHERS

Facilities should be provided to allow pregnant women and nursing mothers to rest or lie down; these facilities should be adjacent to the sanitary facilities.

CHANGING FACILITIES

Where employees have to wear special work clothes, separate changing facilities should be provided with lockers to store ordinary clothing. If changing facilities are not required, storage facilities for the use of employees should be provided.

MANUAL HANDLING

Manual handling means any transporting or supporting of a load by one or more employees and includes lifting, putting down, pulling, carrying or moving a load which, by reason of its characteristics or the unfavourable nature of working conditions, involves risk of injury. Load refers to any object requiring lifting or moving and includes humans and animals. The Regulations (Part VI, Regulations 27 and 28) only apply to manual handling involving a risk of injury to employees.

Regulation 28 places a legal onus on the employer to take appropriate measures in the organisation, particularly the use of mechanical aids, to obviate the necessity for manual handling. Organisational work methods can include all or any of the following: introducing automation into the work system, wrapping items when processed, bringing treatment to a patient, or purchasing raw materials in bulk. Employers must ensure that, in the design of work systems, manual handling be either eliminated or reduced by the use of appropriate mechanical aids.

Where manual handling cannot be avoided, employers must take the following factors into account in order to reduce risk to employees:

- the weight, shape and stability of the load to be carried
- the physical effort required
- the working environment
- the requirements of the activity.

The emphasis to be accorded to each factor depends on the nature of the activity and where it is to be performed. Any risk of injury should be assessed bearing in mind the physical capacity of the worker concerned. A well-organised work system should eliminate most of the need for manual handling, for example the use of fork-lift trucks, lifts or tables to raise loads to a comfortable level or the use of trolleys to move heavy loads. Particular problems may be encountered in changing work situations such as hospitals, superstores, building sites, mines, quarries and fishing vessels.

Employers must consult with their employees before purchasing equipment, containers and packaging to be used in the workplace.

ASSESSING RISK AT PLACE OF WORK

Where manual handling cannot be avoided, employers are required to organise places of work to reduce the risk of injury from manual handling as far as possible by:

- identifying areas where manual handling is taking place
- assessing the risks there
- putting in place all necessary control measures, in this regard special account must be taken of the physical effort involved, the work surroundings and the type of work activity.

The identification of hazards arising from manual handling can be achieved by direct observation of work practices and by an analysis of accidents that take place in the workplace.

In assessing risk at the place of work, account must be taken of the following issues:

- nature of load handled
- range of weights handled
- duration and frequency of the task
- actions and movements involved
- training and experience of the employee
- age and physical capability of the employee
- availability of lifting and moving equipment
- force to be applied
- length of time and distance load is carried
- working posture of the employee
- working environment
- workplace layout and level of housekeeping
- protective clothing and equipment required for the task
- analysis of relevant injury statistics
- any other factor found to be relevant by the employer/employee and safety representative.

The principal focus of any risk assessment must be the activity of the person at the place of work. Consultation between employer and representatives of affected employees is vital in this regard.

Where the necessary expertise is not available within the organisation, the assistance of a competent person from outside the organisation is required to assess the degree of risk from manual handling and to put in place necessary control measures; this does not release the employer from his/her legal obligation to protect the health and safety of his/her workforce.

Where possible, employees should be informed of the precise weight of loads to be handled. This information is usually available from weight markings on the load itself. In the absence of this information employers must give a general indication as to weight through instruction, information or the use of warning signs. As a general rule, heavy weight should carry a warning sign. Where goods are loaded in a manner that the centre of gravity is off-centre, such as a box of glasses or bottles, the centre of gravity should be indicated on the load; manual handling training is essential in this regard.

It should be noted that team handling may be required when dealing with either humans or live animals.

A risk of back injury is present when the load is:

- too heavy or too large
- unwieldy or difficult to grasp
- unstable or its contents are likely to shift
- positioned where the object must be held at a distance from the trunk of the body or where bending or twisting of the body is necessary
- likely to result in injury to employees especially if one collides with another.

Where a risk of back injury may arise from hazards identified, necessary control measures may suggest themselves from answers to the following questions:

- Can the load be made lighter?
- Can the load be made less bulky?
- Can either the shape or the texture of the surface be changed to make the object easier to grip?
- Could the surface be cleaner, cooler or have fewer sharp edges so as to enable the employee to hold the object against the body?
- Could handles or a sling be provided?
- Does the design and packaging of the load protect against unexpected movement when handled?

Physical effort can be said to pose a risk of back injury where it is:

- too strenuous
- only achieved by a twisting movement of the truck
- likely to result in a sudden movement of the load
- made with the body in an unstable position.

REDUCING RISK

Lifting and lowering forces can be reduced by:

- using suitable lifting appliances
- raising the work level
- lowering the position of the employee using gravity dumps and chutes
- reducing size by specifying to suppliers that they reduce the amount of packaging thereby reducing the weight of containers
- reducing the number of objects lifted or lowered at any one time
- changing the shape of the object
- providing suitable grips or handles thereby making the load easier to access
- improving the layout of the workplace
- pushing and pulling instead of lifting.

Pushing and pulling forces can be reduced by:

- using powered conveyors, trucks, rollers and chutes
- use of non-powered conveyors such as tables on castors and monorails
- changing the workplace layout to reduce push and pull distances.

Carrying forces can be reduced by:

- converting to pushing and pulling by using conveyors, fork-lifts or hand-wheel trucks
- reducing the capacity and weight of containers
- reducing distance by relocating storage or production areas.

Holding forces can be reduced by:

- reducing the size and weight of loads
- reducing the time the weight is held
- eliminating holding by using either jigs or fixtures to hold objects
- using mechanical aids where possible when loading and unloading.

When applying force, the following principles will minimise risk:

- pushing and/or pulling is more efficient if applied at waist height
- pushing in and pulling out is stronger than pulling left to right across the body
- in manual handling, significantly higher push and pull force is achievable standing rather than seated; use of body weight is preferred in pushing and pulling motions.

Twisting movements can be reduced by:

- positioning tools and equipment in front of the employee
- using conveyors and turntables to change the flow of material
- the provision of an adjustable swivel chair
- providing sufficient work space for the employee's whole body to turn
- improving the layout of the working area.

Reaching motions may be reduced by:

- close positioning of tools and machine controls to the employee
- positioning all materials in use as near as possible to the employee, thus enabling the employee to handle loads close to the body
- reducing the load or container size, thus allowing the employee to either walk around the load or rotate it.

Reduction in bending movements can be achieved by:

- using lift tables or work dispensers
- raising the level of the work
- positioning all materials in use at work level
- avoiding the lowering of objects that must at a later stage be lifted
- eliminating large horizontal reaches.

GUIDANCE ON THE MANUAL HANDLING TRAINING SYSTEM

The Health and Safety Authority, in conjunction with the Further Education and Training Awards Council, has issued this guideline, which came into effect on 31 March 2010 and aims to have all existing manual handling instructors attain a Level 6, Manual Handling and People Handling Award by 30 April 2012. All new Manual Handling and People Handling Instructors should complete and be familiar with both direction and guidance on key components that should be included in a manual handling training programme for employees.

KEY AIMS OF MANUAL HANDLING TRAINING

- to gain the skills necessary to carry out manual handling activities in a way that either eliminates or reduces risk of injury
- to become familiar with the legislation governing manual handling
- to acquire the basic knowledge necessary to maintain a healthy back
- to become aware of the necessity of risk assessment in deciding on load suitability
- to learn to use mechanical aids or work reorganisation
- to learn the principles of safer handling of loads
- to demonstrate safe manual handling techniques and understand the need to further develop these skills

KEY LEARNING OUTCOMES OF MANUAL HANDLING TRAINING

- basic knowledge of legislation relevant to manual handling
- basic knowledge of the back and its functions and how to keep it healthy. (Flexibility exercises should not be engaged in by the participants without the opinion of a health professional being sought)
- ability to carry out a personal risk assessment to determine if a load can be handled safely
- awareness of specific manual handling problems in the workplace and the measures necessary to combat those risks including mechanical aids
- ability to demonstrate practical applications of the main principles of manual handling to relevant tasks
- consciousness of the need to further develop manual handling skills at work

ADDITIONAL LEARNING OUTCOMES FOR PATIENT/CLIENT HANDLING

Those involved in patient/client handling need to achieve the following additional outcomes:

- awareness of local policies and procedures relating to handling patients that are relevant to their work; for example, infection control, falls strategies, hoist management, etc.
- ability to identify the additional risk factors involved in handling people
- awareness of written documentation in relation to patient manual handling
- awareness of all handling aids available and the safe use of same
- participation in a range of core manual handling techniques relevant to their area of work

HOUSEKEEPING ISSUES IN MANUAL HANDLING TRAINING

While there are specific requirements as to how a manual handling programme should be conducted there are some points that need to be borne in mind in planning and implementing a training programme:

- class sizes should not be too large – no more than ten or twelve – to allow for individual demonstrations and practice
- enough time should be allowed to ensure that all the aims of the training programme are achieved
- training should include classroom instruction and practical demonstrations, ideally conducted in the workplace

REFRESHER TRAINING

Refresher training should be conducted at intervals of not more than three years.

THE ROLE OF SUPERVISION IN MANUAL HANDLING

Line managers need to set standards of good work-related behaviour, which is especially important in the area of manual handling. A culture of safety must be in place that enables employees to carry out personal risk assessment and to use the skills learned at training. It should be a matter of company policy that when employees return having completed a course in manual handling that there be follow-up supervision to ensure that the techniques acquired are put to their proper use. On returning to the workplace, training course participants have a responsibility to put into practice skills learned at the course.

REPETITIVE STRAIN INJURY

Four factors when combined can lead to repetitive strain injury:

- force
- high levels of repetition
- awkward positioning of the body or poor posture
- insufficient rest.

When the recovery time between work-related motions is insufficient and when high levels of repetition are combined with high levels of force and poor posture, the worker concerned is in danger of developing repetitive strain injury. This form of injury is preventable through the appropriate training of employees and the practice of safe manual-handling techniques.

The remedy available is the provision of a properly adjusted chair combined with sufficient work space in a properly organised place of work.

FIRE SAFETY

The Fire Services Act 1981 places a legal onus on persons in charge of premises to which the public have access to do all that is reasonable to prevent the outbreak of fire. The Code of Practice for the management of fire safety in places of assembly, issued by the Minister for the Environment in 1989, covers the following main elements:

- *fire prevention*: to be included under this heading is good housekeeping practice that, for example, would provide for regular cleaning and disposal of waste materials, periodic inspection of the premises, identification and elimination of potential fire hazards
- *management duties*: the most important management duty is to undertake a fire safety programme and appoint a responsible staff member to manage it, in this regard fire evacuation drills should be practised on a regular basis. Informing members of the public using the premises of the fire safety precautions in place is essential
- *escape routes*: Fire Safety Regulations that came into force in 1985 provide for precautions to be taken in relation to ease of escape through escape routes. In this regard an escape route means a route by which a person may reach a place of safety and means in relation to any point in the building the nearest and safest route from that point. Every person having control over any place where the public assemble shall take the following precautions:

  a   all escape routes are to be kept free from obstruction and available for immediate use

  b   all chains, padlocks and removable fastenings for securing doors and barriers are to be kept where they may be readily inspected by a fire safety officer

  c   hangings or drapes should not obstruct the escape route

  d   do not position mirrors in a way that may confuse the direction of escape

  e   all escape routes and exit doors (inside and outside) must be kept free at all times of obstruction and must be clearly indicated and illuminated

f all doors and the devices for closing them should be inspected before the public are admitted and exit doors must be capable of being readily opened at all times

g roller shutter doors, if deemed acceptable by the fire authority, should be kept locked in the open position before and while the public are on the premises

h all floor coverings should be secured and not pose a slip or trip hazard. In this regard where exit doors open over mat wells the mat must be secured in the well

i external areas adjacent to exits must be kept free of vehicles and other obstructions, and doors, gates or barriers must not impede escape from a yard area to a place of safety

- *record-keeping*: written records should be maintained of all efforts to both implement and maintain a fire safety programme
- *place of safety*: a place of safety under this enactment is defined as any open-air place on level ground where persons who assemble there are in no danger from fire
- *management*: for the purposes of this legislation management can include any person(s) who either leases or hires the premises to which the Code applies and can include management personnel with responsibility for fire and emergency safety
- *training*: staff to whom specific duties are assigned should receive training, particulars of which should be entered in the fire safety register. In addition all staff should receive training in good housekeeping, emergency evacuation, keeping exits clear and assisting the fire and other emergency services. All members of staff should be aware of the position of all fire alarm points, the location of fire-fighting equipment and the location and safest routes to assembly points.

CONTENTS OF FIRE SAFETY NOTICE

On discovering the fire:

- activate the nearest alarm point
- inform staff of the location of the fire
- leave the premises immediately using the nearest safe available exit
- do not rush or use the lift
- do not re-enter the building until told that it safe to do so
- obey the instructions of staff organising the evacuation.

On hearing the alarm:

- leave the premises immediately by the nearest available exit
- do not rush or use the lift
- obey the instructions of staff
- if there is no alarm, verbally warn staff of the danger.

AMENDING REGULATIONS

On 2 May 2001 amending General Application Regulations came into force. These Regulations reinforced the existing requirement on all employers to provide information in a format that is easily understood by all. This information is to include notice of any changes in the use of work equipment likely to affect employees.

These Regulations require periodic and if necessary special inspection of equipment to ensure its safety, and the results of those inspections must be recorded and retained for five years for inspection by inspectors of the Health and Safety Authority. Any inspection is to be carried out only by a person competent to do so. These Regulations also impose more stringent duties on employers with regard to the safety of equipment during its installation and use and also during necessary maintenance. New provisions are introduced concerning the safe use of fork-lift trucks and other equipment used to lift loads.

A further amendment to the 1993 Regulations came into operation on 30 January 2003 which strengthens the existing rules governing the duties of employers, provides a definition of the competent person required to deal with preventive and protective measures and strengthens existing provisions to deal with workplace emergencies.

SAFETY, HEALTH AND WELFARE AT WORK (GENERAL APPLICATION) REGULATIONS 2007

The purpose of these Regulations, which came into force on 1 November 2007, is to encourage an improvement in the health, safety and welfare of workers. Their immediate objective is to bring all current Regulations in line with the 2005 Act and to make existing legislation clearer and accessible to those affected by it. Ultimately the objective is to reduce the number of occupational injuries and to increase general safety awareness.

Figures available from the database of the Heath and Safety Authority for the year ending 2006 indicate that 35 per cent of all reported injuries in 2006 were triggered by manual handling. The most common type of injury was physical strain or stress to the body (41 per cent) and the most frequently injured part of the body was the back (24 per cent). A total of fifty-one work-related fatalities were reported to the Authority in 2006, of these forty-five were worker fatalities. This leaves Ireland with an unacceptably high rate of 2.2 fatalities per 100,000 workers.

The most common accident triggers for 2006 were manual handling (35 per cent), other (29 per cent), slips, trips and falls (17 per cent), other movement by injured person (6 per cent), fall, collapse or breakage of material (5 per cent), violence of others (4 per cent) and fall from height (4 per cent).

The 2007 Regulations continue the general thrust of the first set of Regulations introduced in 1993. Their introduction is not expected to increase employer safety costs significantly, especially where there is already a reasonable effort being made to implement existing Regulations. The enforcement of the new Regulations, as with other health, safety and welfare legislation, will be a matter for the Health and Safety Authority.

OUTLINE OF MAIN PROVISIONS

The 2007 Regulations set out provisions for the safe use of buildings, emergency evacuation, the safe use of equipment, duties of employers in relation to instruction and training, personal protective equipment, manual handling of loads, the use of visual display equipment, safety issues relating to electricity, control of noise and vibration, and working at heights. Requirements relating to sensitive risk groups, such as children and young persons, and pregnant and breastfeeding workers, are also addressed. In addition, the general duties of employers are outlined in relation to night and shift workers. A regulatory impact analysis on the 2007 Regulations was published by the Health and Safety Authority in June 2007.

CONTROL OF ARTIFICIAL RADIATION IN THE WORKPLACE

In May 2009 the Health and Safety Authority published a regulatory impact analysis of the Safety, Health and Welfare at Work (Amendment) Regulations 2009, which came into force on 27 April 2010. These regulations deal with the control of artificial optical radiation in the workplace and cover all aspects of artificial radiation including lasers, ultraviolet radiation sources and some furnaces. The sun is not included here as a source of radiation.

The following definitions are key to a better understanding of radiation and the threat it poses:

- *optical radiation*: a wavelength between 100 nanometres and one millimetre, including ultraviolet, visible and infrared light.
- *laser radiation*: optical radiation from a laser.
- *non-coherent radiation*: optical radiation other than laser radiation.
- *laser*: light amplified by stimulated emission of radiation.
- *radiance*: light that passes through or is emitted from an area and falls within a given solid angle in a specified direction.

Artificial optical radiation is used in a wide range of processes including surgery, dentistry, industrial applications and research. The development of technology such as laser printers, barcode scanners and treatment for acne and cellulite all involve artificial optical radiation. Areas of the body most at risk from artificial optical radiation are the skin and eyes. Effects on the skin include redness, burning, blistering and an increased risk of skin cancer.

The Irish Safety Standard Code for the use of laser equipment is EN 60825, and all such equipment in use in Ireland must comply with that standard. The primary objective of these Regulations is to set down minimum safety standards for the protection of employees from optical radiation exposure and to provide appropriate training, health surveillance and suitable medical treatment for staff members who suffer the effects of exposure.

Any costs involved in compliance with regulations should be minimal, and any employer who is already health and safety compliant will simply be required to carry out a specific risk assessment for artificial optical radiation. No further action will be necessary unless that risk assessment shows a significant risk to the health of employees. If such a risk exists, then some expense will be involved in introducing safety measures to either eliminate the risk of optical radiation or at least minimise its effects.

Because of the absence of specific data on the number of Irish employers using artificial optical radiation, the Health and Safety Authority has used the estimate obtained from the Health Service Executive that approximately 16 per cent of workers are employed in workplaces using artificial optical radiation. Based on those figures there are approximately 22,000 employers who need to familiarise themselves with these regulations. The maximum average financial outlay in total for specific risk assessments would be between €500,000 and €1 million. Only in high-risk working environments would additional staff training be required.

Additional training and action plans (mainly to upgrade existing equipment in order to reduce exposure) would only be required if a serious risk of exposure were shown to exist.

REVISION QUESTIONS

1   Define the term 'temporary employee'.
2   List the factors necessary in deciding on the suitability of a ventilation system for a place of work.
3   As a general rule, what is the preferred option for lighting in the workplace?
4   In what circumstances will the use of warning signs be necessary in a place of work?
5   What is a danger zone in the context of a place of work?
6   List the rules essential to the use of control devices on machinery.
7   What are the essential safety features of a machine guard?
8   Outline the principal causes of work-related accidents.
9   List the five principles essential to the elimination of workplace hazards.
10   What is first aid?
11   What are the principal dangers associated with overhead power lines?
12   List the circumstances in which there exists a risk of back injury in the manual handling of loads.
13   What information should a fire safety notice contain?

REFERENCES

Fire Services Act 1981

Health and Safety Authority (2007), *Regulatory Impact Analysis, Safety, Health and Welfare at Work General Application Regulations 2007*, Dublin: Health and Safety Authority

Health and Safety Authority (2009), *Regulatory Impact Analysis on Health Safety and Welfare at Work (General Application Regulations) (Amendment) Regulations 2009, Control of Artificial Optical Radiation at Work*, Dublin: Health and Safety Authority

Safety, Health and Welfare at Work (General Application) Regulations 1993 (as amended in 2001 and 2003)

Safety, Health and Welfare at Work (General Application) Regulations 2007

3
Health Issues in the Workplace

This chapter addresses workplace health issues. These include the duty owed by the employer to protect his/her employees from the threat of infection posed by airborne contaminants; legal issues concerning the safe use, storage and disposal of chemicals; legal duties imposed on employers to protect their employees from contact with asbestos and other carcinogens; measures to protect the workforce from dermatitis and asthma; the potential for injury to health caused by noise and vibration; the relatively modern hazard of stress in the workplace; issues for pregnant and breastfeeding women; issues arising from legislation on environmental protection and the disposal of hazardous and non-hazardous waste.

AIRBORNE CONTAMINANTS

Threshold limits or occupational exposure values on levels of airborne contaminants have been set to protect workers' health. Airborne contaminants – dust, fumes, gases and vapours – may be inhaled, ingested or absorbed through the skin. The most significant route of infection is inhalation and for that reason occupational safety values have been set. An occupational safety value is defined as the concentration of a substance in the air below which it is believed the majority of workers may be exposed over a daily period of eight hours and a weekly period of forty hours. Some of these levels are based on sound medical practice, others are based simply on comparisons with chemical exposure of animals. Measurement is based on milligrams of contaminant per cubic metre of air for dusts; for gases, vapours and mists the measurement is parts per million by volume.

Airborne dust and fumes are forms of what are called particulates and differ in size; the size range for dust is from one micron to one hundred microns, and for fumes, from one-tenth of a micron to one micron. For the purposes of scale it should be noted that one hundred microns is equal to one millimetre. It also should be noted that any airborne particle up to ten microns in size is likely to be inhaled, particles more than five microns in size will only get as far as the nose or mouth; the real threat is posed by particles smaller than five microns as they have the ability to penetrate the human body as far as the extremities of the lungs. The larger particles will simply be swept back up by mucous in the respiratory tract.

A problem can arise in recognising some potential dust hazards as they may be present in the atmosphere in concentrations above occupational safety limits without any indication of their presence. Examples of such dusts are asbestos, lead and cadmium, and for that reason it is imperative to know and identify in detail materials being processed at work.

NUISANCE DUSTS

The occupational safety value for nuisance dust is the highest allowable, ten milligrams of contaminant per cubic metre of air. Controls, however, are still necessary as high concentrations of nuisance dusts in the workplace will result in respiratory problems. Examples of nuisance dusts are calcium carbonate, soft woods and aluminium oxide.

TOXIC DUSTS

Lead has an occupational safety value of 0.15 milligrams per cubic metre of air. Cadmium has an occupational safety value of 0.05 milligrams per cubic metre of air.

Fibrogenic dusts can cause fibrosis of the lungs and have an extremely low occupational safety value, and from a health standpoint the preferred value is zero. Examples are asbestos and silica quartz.

Frequently and wrongly described as fumes, any airborne contaminant (and in particular solvent, paint and alcohol vapours) are in fact relatively small particles of airborne dust. The most common fume is created by smelting and welding processes.

MISTS

Mists are airborne droplets in a certain particle size, examples of which are oil mist in a machine shop and mists from the use of acids in industry. Mists are usually formed by condensation from liquids.

GASES AND VAPOURS

A vapour is best described as the gaseous form of a substance that is sometimes liquid and sometimes solid at room temperature. The level of release of a vapour is a function of its temperature. Examples of vapours encountered in industry are monostyrene formed from glass-reinforced plastic moulding, xylene from paint processing, and acetone and alcohol from chemical processing. Examples of gases found in industry are carbon monoxide from engine exhausts, nitrogen oxides and ozone from welding, and hydrogen sulphide from chemicals.

RECOGNISING POTENTIAL HEALTH HAZARDS

To identify potential health hazards in the workplace, begin by listing all raw materials used in the workplace. In this regard it is important that a hazards material safety data sheet be available in respect of every proprietary chemical substance on the premises. By law suppliers of chemicals for commercial use must supply information on all hazardous ingredients, state the occupational exposure value of those ingredients and list protective measures required to be taken for the safe use of the chemical. This information will be supplied in the safety data sheets.

Use the list to assess the potential exposure of workers to any of these substances. Consider the answers to the following questions:

- Do workers handle substances in a manner that may cause gases, vapours and dusts to be inhaled?
- Is exposure to the substance infrequent or continuous?
- Are new and potentially hazardous substances being formed by a particular work process?
- Are chemical odours detectable?
- Is dust escaping from a work process?
- Are members of staff complaining of headaches or are they suffering from respiratory problems?
- Is absenteeism a problem from particular areas of the workplace?

MEASURING EXPOSURE TO HEALTH HAZARDS

Only measurements taken from the breathing zone of an individual worker will give accurate information on personal exposure to dust and fumes. A personal sample is taken by drawing air at a known rate of flow (the recommended rate is two litres per minute) through a filter attached to the lapel of the worker. This filter is connected by tube to a small pump at the waist of the worker.

Where nuisance dust is suspected, a fibreglass filter is used and is merely weighed after use, and the increase in weight and volume of the filter can then be converted to an airborne concentration. In dealing with suspected asbestos dust, the filter is mounted on a slide after use and dissolved in an organic solvent which sets into a transparent mass. The slide is then viewed at high magnification under a microscope and the fibres counted. Asbestos dust is always measured in fibres per cubic centimetre.

Exposure can also be measured using stain detector tubes and personal sorption tubes. There are approximately two hundred stain detector tubes, each one designed for a particular gas or vapour. Each tube is gradated in concentration units, usually parts per million. The tube will contain a chemical in solid form which changes colour when the contaminant is drawn into it, and the depth of stain or change of colour will be read off directly in parts per million. The problem that arises with the use of stain detector tubes is that they can be as much as 30 per cent inaccurate and other substances in the atmosphere can interfere with the accurate development of the stain. They only serve as spot samples and do not accurately gauge exposure over an eight-hour period. Their shelf life is also limited.

Instruments to measure contamination will not give a completely accurate picture of personal exposure but can be valuable as a back-up to the use of sorption tubes. It is possible to sample with an instrument close to the breathing zone of the worker, at intervals over a period of time. This will give an approximate picture of personal exposure. The advantage of the use of an instrument is that it can be connected to a recorder that in turn gives a continuous picture of personal exposure, unlike the sorption tube, which will establish an average concentration with no indication of peaks and lows in exposure. Another advantage from a cost perspective is that the use of this system does not involve laboratory testing. It should be noted that some instruments have a specific use and others may be used generally.

THE IMPORTANCE OF LABELS ON CHEMICALS

All containers of chemical products are required to have a label which will tell you what you need to know about the safe use of that chemical. Common terms found on labels are:

- *sensitiser*: such chemicals may cause an allergic reaction in its users and may trigger either dermatitis or asthma
- *carcinogen*: this product may cause cancer in humans
- *harmful or toxic for reproduction*: such chemicals may either cause fertility problems or injure a developing foetus.

The following Labelling of Hazardous Chemicals Regulations are in force: Statutory Instruments 77 of 1994; 272 of 1995; 317, 354 and 513 of 1998; 363 of 1999.

Chemicals, if not correctly used, may catch fire, cause burns, injure your health or cause damage to the environment. Suppliers of chemicals are under a legal obligation to supply sufficient information about the safe use of that product and where any doubt exists as to the safe use of a particular product further information should be obtained from the supplier before using that product. Both the Health and Safety Authority and the National Poisons Information Centre are in a position to give appropriate advice where requested.

BIOLOGICAL HAZARDS

Biological hazards are micro-organisms that can be categorised as fungi, bacteria or viruses. Unlike other workplace contaminants, micro-organisms can increase and multiply. In order for this to happen fungi and bacteria need warmth, moisture and food. A single cell of bacteria has the capacity to increase to 250 cells within a three-hour period. Most fungi are capable of rapid expansion and can produce millions of tiny spores. A virus however requires a host, that is another micro-organism, animal or plant, on which to multiply. In a suitable host the virus is capable of expanding extremely rapidly. Only a small number of micro-organisms are known to cause disease in humans or animals, as the vast majority are harmless and even necessary. Some such micro-organisms however, whilst not affecting the healthy, may cause infections in vulnerable people such as the aged, the sick or children.

Very few fungi are considered to be seriously injurious to humans and animals. Superficial infections such as athlete's foot and ringworm may occur, and spores of fungi are known to cause serious allergic reactions such as farmer's lung, an illness contracted by members of the farming community from the spores of mouldy hay.

Bacteria cause many serious diseases, for example tuberculosis, diphtheria and brucellosis, and are believed to be mainly responsible for such diseases as salmonella, listeriosis and botulism.

Viruses cause some of the most serious diseases in humans and animals, the HIV virus and hepatitis being examples. Less serious ailments such as influenza, colds and enteritis are also virus-based. Some viruses are suspected of causing BSE in cattle and scrapie in sheep but the viral agent as yet has not been identified.

HEALTH MEASURES TO PROTECT AGAINST MICRO-ORGANISMS

Micro-organisms in the main are to be found in hospitals, laboratories, abattoirs, sewers, toilets and garbage areas. The human system has developed complex defence mechanisms against infection, the first line of defence being our skin: most bacteria and viral infections do not have the capacity to penetrate the human skin. Our second line of defence can be said to be our immune system: many infections are acquired only once because, in the case of non-fatal infections, the human body learns to recognise the invading infection and rapidly destroys it the next time it comes across it.

In many cases it is now possible to immunise people likely to be exposed to infection. Treatment with a vaccine disarms forms of bacteria or viruses and enables the human body to develop immunity to a particular disease. Vaccines, however, may be expensive, may carry risks of reactions to them and are not available for all diseases.

ROUTES OF INFECTION

Infection may occur as a result of:

- *ingestion*: in high-risk areas eating and drinking should be confined to a designated area such as a canteen, protective gloves and/or clothing should be worn and there should be a strict regime of hand-washing
- *injection*: there exists an obvious risk in the use of hypodermic needles, for example there is a danger of self-injection where animals are injected by farmers or others who lack the requisite training in the use of hypodermics. It is possible that fragments of contaminated glass could penetrate the skin, and as far as possible all containers in use should be of the highest quality glass or plastic
- *skin abrasions*: even minute abrasions are routes of infection because they cause the continuity of the skin to be broken, so all abrasions and minor cuts should be covered and appropriate gloves worn
- *eye*: there is a risk of infection from splashes and airborne particles. A particular danger arises where a worker rubs his/her eye with a contaminated hand or glove
- *inhalation*: airborne organisms are a common source of infection; regular cleaning of workplaces and safe work practices reduce the danger from airborne contamination
- *zoonosis*: diseases of animals that are transmitted to humans, for example brucellosis and tuberculosis from cattle, anthrax from sheep, leptospirosis from the urine of rats. Brucellosis is a common infection in veterinary

surgeons, farmers and those employed in the meat industry. The most effective method for dealing with brucellosis would be to eliminate the disease from the national cattle herd. Food processing factories require very high standards of hygiene to combat infection, meat is an ideal medium for the proliferation of bacteria, decomposing meat and contaminated water are two likely sources of infection.

Industrial organisms used in breweries are generally recognised as safe to use, however procedures should be in place to protect those organisms from contamination. Some workers may suffer an allergic reaction to some process organisms. Genetically manipulated organisms may be used in some industries, but European Union directives in this matter require that the use of these organisms pose only minimal risk to the health of workers and that they in addition pose no environmental threat; high standards of hygiene and safe disposal methods are essential to their safe use. The state science agency Eolas monitors the use of generically manipulated organisms; abattoirs and the food processing industry are regulated by the Department of Agriculture.

FOOD POISONING

The three common causes of food poisoning are:

- contamination of cooked meat by raw meat. In order to avoid contamination, keep cooked and raw meat in separate areas and do not use the same work surfaces for both meats; cooked meat should be refrigerated separately
- pre-cooking food and keeping it warm increases the risk of salmonella poisoning
- incomplete cooking of frozen food.

OCCUPATIONAL ASTHMA

Occupational asthma is caused by breathing in substances such as dust or chemicals. These substances are known as respiratory sensitisers and are to be found in a wide range of workplaces. They can arise as a result of vehicle spray painting, handling grain and/or flour in the milling industry, soldering in electronic assembly, sawmilling or other woodwork and working with glues or resins. When inhaled, a respiratory sensitiser can trigger an allergic reaction in a worker that cannot be reversed. Once this reaction occurs, further exposure, regardless of how little, will produce symptoms. Sensitisation could take months or even years to develop.

The symptoms of respiratory sensitisation are runny/stuffy nose, watery/prickly eyes, attacks of coughing/wheezing and chest tightness. When sensitisation occurs, the exposed worker can immediately develop these symptoms once he/she has to work with the sensitiser again. Permanent damage can be caused to the health of the worker once sensitisation occurs and can result in asthmatic attacks triggered by such things as cold air or tobacco smoke. These attacks will continue long after exposure to the sensitiser ceases.

Under the 2005 Act, an employer is obliged to:

- provide a safe working environment
- include in the safety statement a written risk assessment of respiratory sensitisers found in the workplace
- ensure that all employees are trained in the use of necessary safeguards
- ensure adequate supervision of the workplace
- provide health checks for exposed workers.

GUIDELINES ON OCCUPATIONAL ASTHMA

In July 2008 the Health and Safety Authority issued the above guidelines to provide both employers and employees with useful information in the management and prevention of work-related asthma. Under these guidelines, asthma is described as an inflammatory disorder of the airways. When an asthma attack occurs, the muscles surrounding the airways swell, thus reducing the flow of air, which in turn can lead to wheezing, which in most sufferers is intermittent. Shortness of breath, coughing and chest tightness are also symptoms of this disorder.

WORK-RELATED ASTHMA

Work-related asthma accounts for approximately 10 per cent of irritant-induced and allergic asthma, which may also be known as either work-aggravated asthma or occupational asthma. In extreme cases, this disease may prevent workers from continuing in employment. The disease also has financial implications, such as medical expenses and loss of earnings, and may also result in litigation.

WORK-AGGRAVATED ASTHMA

Those who suffer with work-aggravated asthma usually have a history of asthma, having either received treatment for the disorder or in some cases have grown out of childhood asthma. Such workers may tell of recurring asthmatic episodes caused by the cold, excessive exercise or exposure to irritants such as dust, fumes or vapours. This category of worker may get wheezy or display other symptoms such as coughing or chest tightness. Either improving the work environment or avoiding the irritant can often eliminate this health problem.

OCCUPATIONAL ASTHMA

Occupational asthma is a direct result of work-related exposure. There are two types of occupational asthma: irritant-induced and allergic.

- *irritant-induced occupational asthma*: develops usually after a single very high exposure to an irritant chemical, burning the airways on contact. Examples of chemical agents likely to cause this disorder include ammonia acids and smoke. Such exposure is usually triggered by an accident or a major failure of the control system in an enclosed space. Symptoms usually manifest within twenty-four hours and the symptoms will improve over time and may go away entirely. However, if symptoms persist beyond a period of six months an ongoing condition is possible. It is a matter of debate whether recurrent exposure to lower levels of an irritant can lead to irritant-induced asthma, though the majority of experts in this field finds that it does not do so.
- *allergic occupational asthma*: caused by a worker developing an allergy to a specific chemical agent over a period of time; this is the mechanism by which approximately 90 per cent of workers with allergic occupational asthma are affected. Sensitisation can occurs over a period of time ranging from several weeks to as much as thirty years. If a worker is subject to continuous exposure, the period of greatest risk is the first two years of exposure, after which point the risk of exposure does not disappear, but rather may decrease to some extent.

HISTORY OF OCCUPATIONAL ASTHMA

If exposure to a sensitising agent ceases completely, in most cases, the condition will improve. If exposure ceases within two years of the condition developing, then it is usual for the worker to recover completely. Although a cessation of exposure is always beneficial, the longer a worker is exposed, the less likely it is that full recovery will occur. It is therefore essential to identify the disorder at an early stage, hence the importance of health surveillance.

RESPIRATORY SENSITIZERS

These are substances which when inhaled can trigger an allergic reaction in the respiratory system. Sensitization only occurs after a period of weeks or months of inhaling the sensitizing substance. Such substances have the following risk phrase and number on chemical safety data sheets: 'May cause sensitization by inhalation (R42)'. The risk of developing occupational asthma is usually related to the dose of the substance inhaled; the higher the level of exposure, the more likely it is that sensitization will occur. This is true even where exposure time is relatively short. Smokers are in greater danger of contracting asthma as the smoke acts as a sensitizer on the respiratory system. For the majority of substances, the chances of becoming sensitized are much lower when exposure to the substance falls below the recommended occupational exposure level. Once sensitization has occurred, further exposure to even the smallest amount of the substance will produce symptoms. It is important to note than a recommended occupational exposure level will not protect those already sensitized. Symptoms can occur immediately or some hours after work has finished. Hundreds of substances found in the workplace have been found to be respiratory sensitizers. The following non-exhaustive list of examples of substances known to be sensitizers includes: isocyanates found in vehicle spray-painting and foam manufacture, flour/grain/hay risk arises when handling, loading or unloading baking and milling materials, using electronic soldering flux in electronic assembly, wearing latex gloves in laboratories and healthcare, contact with laboratory animals, wood dusts arising in saw milling and furniture manufacturing, hair dyes used in hairdressing and nickel sulphate used in electroplating. It should be noted that the above list of sensitizers is not exhaustive; it is necessary to consult chemical safety datasheets and contact the suppliers of any product used in the workplace where any doubts exist as to its safe use.

DUTIES OF EMPLOYER

Employers must by law provide a safe working environment where exposure to substances that can cause asthma is controlled. In particular, employers must have an up-to-date safety statement based on a current risk assessment and have adequate hazard control measures in place. They must keep employees informed as to control measures taken or about to be taken in the workplace, and where appropriate, provide health surveillance mechanisms.

RISK ASSESSMENT

All employers are required by law to have a written safety statement, the contents of which must be brought to the attention of all employees. It is a further legal requirement to implement all health and safety measures identified in the safety statement. The safety statement will include and be based on a risk assessment of workplace hazards, which will identify if respiratory sensitizers are in use. Issues addressed by the risk assessment should include information on who is likely to be exposed and for how long, whether the sensitizer can become airborne, and whether the level of exposure exceeds the daily occupational exposure level specified in the Chemical Agents Regulations. An employer may be required to have the air in the workplace either measured or monitored in order to detect the level of the airborne sensitizer and whether the exposure of the workers is above or below that set out in the Chemical Agents Regulations. Monitoring must be conducted by a competent occupational hygienist using the correct equipment.

PREVENTION AND CONTROL OF EXPOSURE

Should the risk assessment confirm that workers are being exposed to respiratory sensitizers, the following control measures must be taken:

- stop using the sensitizer and replace with a safer alternative
- minimise worker exposure
- consider total enclosure of the process in question
- if total enclosure is impossible, partially enclose the process and use local exhaust ventilation
- if exposure still exists, supply suitable personal protective equipment to workers

It is important that where personal protective equipment is relied upon that it be fit for purpose. It may be necessary to test the equipment before issue for general use. Where despite the use of all control methods there is still a danger of exposure, health surveillance must be put into effect.

WHAT EMPLOYEES NEED TO KNOW

Not only are employees legally entitled to know about hazards in their places of work, they are also entitled to information about any protective or preventive measures that the employer intends to implement. Employees likely to be exposed to respiratory sensitizers need information and training on the use of chemical safety data sheets, respiratory sensitizers, the proper implementation of control methods, results of relevant risk assessments, and the importance of knowing the risks to health, the symptoms of sensitization and finally, recognising the importance of health surveillance and reporting symptoms early.

ROLE OF HEALTH SURVEILLANCE

This type of surveillance is used to detect the early onset of asthma symptoms. Health surveillance is not as effective as primary prevention, as it simply detects early symptoms of the disease rather than preventing the disease. As a result, health surveillance should be used in conjunction with primary prevention measures and may take the form of a pre-employment medical assessment, an annual respiratory questionnaire or lung function tests.

PRE-EMPLOYMENT MEDICAL

A pre-employment health questionnaire should be completed by all candidates for work involving known respiratory sensitizers. Unless the likelihood of exposure is slight, the pre-employment medical should include a lung function test and a medical examination. There may be employment limitations on workers with a previous history of asthma, although a balance must be struck between the risks a prospective employee might encounter in the workplace and their employment rights under equality legislation, in this instance with regard to asthma. It is advisable to seek the opinion of a respiratory physician before allowing a person with asthmatic tendencies to work with significant quantities of a known respiratory sensitizer.

ROUTINE HEALTH SURVEILLANCE

Any decision to carry out routine health surveillance should be based on the risk assessment where that assessment shows the potential for an employee to develop asthma due to workplace exposure. A competent health professional should carry out this surveillance at intervals of three months and twelve months after commencement of employment and annually thereafter. A respiratory questionnaire should be completed and compared to the pre-employment questionnaire. Any abnormal results should be assessed by a competent medical practitioner. Where health surveillance indicates that an employee has become sensitized, the employer should remove that employee from working with the sensitizer and advise him/her to seek medical help. Such an instance will also indicate that existing control measures are inadequate and will necessitate a review of the risk assessment. Occupational asthma can only be diagnosed after suitable tests and physical examination for symptoms have taken place. At the end of the day, a medical professional may have to decide whether the employee is fit for work.

GUIDELINES ON OCCUPATIONAL DERMATITIS

In February 2009 the Health and Safety Authority issued new guidelines for the management of work-related dermatitis. Dermatitis is described as an inflammation of the skin that is akin to eczema where the skin becomes red, itchy and can blister. The skin then hardens, thickens and cracks. If dermatitis is work-related it would appear mainly on hands and other exposed skin areas. If the condition improves away from work and relapses on return to work, and if more than one person is affected in the same work area, then the dermatitis is work-related.

Occupational Dermatitis is caused by the skin coming in contact with certain substances in the workplace. This is known as contact dermatitis and is the most common work-related disease in Ireland. In extreme cases, this disease may prevent workers from continuing in employment. The disease also has financial implications, such as medical expenses and loss of earnings, and may also result in litigation. The irony of this disease is that in most cases it is totally preventable by adopting simple inexpensive measures.

SKIN STRUCTURE

The skin is a protective body layer best described as an elastic-type envelope that secretes a slightly oily substance that covers the skin area to provide it with an additional protective barrier. Human skin has three layers. The outer layer, known as the epidermis, is as thin as 0.1mm in most parts of the body but increases to 1mm on the palms of the hands and the soles of the feet. Over a period of one to two months new skin cells form and migrate to the skin surface where they harden and die, forming another protective layer called the horny layer, which is constantly worn away by friction. The first inner skin layer is known as the dermis, and is approximately four times thicker than the epidermis. The dermis contains blood vessels and nerve endings responsible for sensitivity and the sense of touch. The innermost skin layer is called the hypodermis and contains the hair follicles, sweat glands, nerve fibres and a capillary network responsible for skin temperature. Two types of protein, namely collagen and elastin, add strength to the dermis. Older workers are more prone to skin diseases, as a reduction in protein levels caused either by the aging process or by certain medications weakens the skin, causing it to thin in the longer term, and giving it an increased tendency to bruise. Skin problems arise when the rate at which skin is being damaged exceeds its rate of repair.

CONTACT DERMATITIS

There are two forms of contact dermatitis: contact irritant dermatitis and allergic contact dermatitis. In contact irritant dermatitis, the substance that damages the skin is known as the irritant. A highly irritant substance is known as a corrosive. Irritant contact dermatitis makes up 80 per cent of all contact dermatitis cases, the other 20 per cent being allergic contact dermatitis cases. Damage to skin from contact dermatitis can occur in any of the following ways:

- use of detergents, soaps and frequent hand-washing
- use of solvents, which can remove the oily barrier on the skin
- physical damage by friction
- minor cuts and grazes, which can break down the protective layers of the skin
- chemicals such as strong alkalis and acids, which can burn the skin.

Hand creams can and should be used to replace the loss of the naturally occurring oily substances that the skin secretes during frequent hand washing or solvent use. Cuts and grazes should be covered immediately to avoid infection. Irritation is akin to a chemical burn because it erodes or burns the outer protective skin layers.

Several factors control the rate at which irritation occurs:

- the corrosiveness of the substance; a strong acid will take much less time to have an effect than a weaker acid
- the concentration of the substance; the higher the concentration of the irritant, the greater the effect
- the length of contact time; the longer the period of contact, the greater the effect.
- the vulnerability of the individual worker; for example, those with childhood allergic dermatitis, dry skin or very fair complexions are more susceptible.

Repeated exposure to an irritant can have a cumulative effect. Irritant contact dermatitis usually occurs in the parts of the body in direct contact with the substance, namely hands, arms and face. Examples of common irritants are wet work, oils used in cutting materials, solvents and degreasing agents. Contact with any of these irritants will remove the outer protective skin layers and allow easier penetration of the skin by acids and alkalis. An example of a common irritant is wet cement coming in contact with exposed hands or feet.

ALLERGIC CONTACT DERMATITIS

In the case of allergic contact dermatitis, the worker becomes sensitised or develops an allergic reaction some time after contact is made, known as delayed hypersensitivity. The period of sensitization can vary from days to years, and the risk of developing an allergy will depend on a number of factors such as the nature of the substance; a substance with a high likelihood of sensitising a worker is called a sensitizer, but substances that are not considered to be sensitizers may also cause an allergic reaction in a worker. The nature of the contact with the substance is also crucial; the more a worker is exposed, the more likely sensitization will occur. If for example the exposed worker has a history of non-allergic dermatitis, the substance may enter the bloodstream of the worker more easily. Once the worker becomes sensitized, every time he/she comes in contact with the irritant even for short periods of time, further sensitization will occur. This is different to irritant dermatitis, which is related directly to the dose of the sensitizer received. With allergic contact dermatitis, there can be long-term health consequences and the ability to remain in employment can be at risk. With allergic contact dermatitis, the rash can occur in skin areas not in direct contact with the irritant substance. Common sensitizers are chromates (found in cement), nickel (found in cheap jewellery), epoxy resins, formaldehyde, wood dust, flour, printing-plate chemicals and adhesives. It must be noted that both types of dermatitis can occur together.

CONTACT URTICARIA

This is a hive-like response to the application of certain substances to healthy skin. Like allergic contact dermatitis, the disease depends on previous exposure to the substance. Sensitization is usually caused by histamine release and this is known as type 1 or immediate hypersensitivity response. Latex is the commonest cause of occupational immunological contact urticaria. Amongst the substances likely to cause non-immunological contact urticaria are cobalt and platinum salts.

SAFETY PHRASES

The following safety phrases indicate substances that are harmful to the skin:

- avoid contact with skin (S24)
- wear suitable gloves (S37)
- irritant to skin (R38)
- may cause sensitization by skin contact (R43)
- toxic in contact with skin (R24)
- very toxic in contact with skin (R27)
- causes burns (R34)
- causes severe burns (R35)

LEGAL REQUIREMENTS OF EMPLOYERS

Employers are legally obliged to provide a safe working environment within which exposure to substances that can cause dermatitis is controlled. The employer should have in place a safety statement based on a risk assessment of all work-related hazards in addition to sufficient control measures to avoid exposure of workers to the hazards that cause dermatitis. Information on the dangers of work-related dermatitis should be made available to all potentially affected employees, and where necessary, health surveillance should be put in place. The safety statement must include a written risk assessment, which will identify the existence or otherwise of substances in the workplace that may cause work-related dermatitis.

PREVENTION OF EXPOSURE

Both contact irritant and allergic contact dermatitis can be prevented by avoiding or at least minimising skin contact with irritants. Should the risk assessment confirm that workers are being exposed to potential irritants or sensitizers, the following control measures should be considered:

- remove the substance
- substitute a less hazardous substance
- introduce closed systems of work that either eliminate or minimise worker contact with the substance
- remove excess materials by drainage, vacuuming or local exhaust ventilation.

WASHING AND DRYING HANDS AND APPLYING HAND CREAMS

The easiest way to avoid dermatitis is to wash hands thoroughly after contact with a hazardous substance. Adequate washing facilities including hot and cold or warm water, suitable hand cleaners, drying facilities and hand creams are essential. Any hand cleanser used should not contain abrasives or organic solvents. In general, workers should be advised to wet hands before applying soap as many soaps are irritants in their concentrated state. Clean dry towels, disposable paper towels or hot air dryers may be used to dry hands. It is helpful to use hand creams or emollients after hand-washing as these will assist in replacing the natural oily layer of the skin.

BARRIER CREAMS

Barrier creams must be used with caution because, as a general rule, they do not form an effective barrier against hazards and they are not a substitute for appropriate gloves. Even when they are effective, the effect of the cream wears off quickly after first application, and unlike when gloves are worn, the wearer will not be aware of when protection begins to fail. Barrier creams may sometimes be used with gloves, and can facilitate hand-cleaning after work is completed.

THE USE OF PERSONAL PROTECTIVE EQUIPMENT

The objective of wearing gloves as personal protective equipment is to prevent skin contact with a hazardous substance. Special care is needed in the selection of appropriate gloves, as no glove will provide protection against all chemicals. Advice should be sought from glove suppliers as to the appropriateness of particular gloves for particular functions. In order to avoid latex allergy, the use of latex gloves should be avoided if possible. In some instances however, the latex glove may be the best option. Gloves should be changed regularly or cotton under-gloves worn where sweat is a problem. It is essential that the skin be protected and that no gap exist between the glove and the sleeve of the protective overall. If gloves are torn or damaged they must be replaced immediately. Training should be provided to the work force in the correct use and removal of gloves to ensure that skin contact with the hazardous substance on the outside gloves is minimised when they are being removed. Depending on the nature of the hazardous substance, aprons and face masks may be required in addition to gloves and protective overalls.

WHAT EMPLOYEES NEED TO KNOW

Employees are entitled to information about potential hazards in their places of work. They are also entitled to information about the steps that the employer proposes to take concerning both protective and preventative measures. Employees who are likely to work with substances known to cause dermatitis need to know and fully understand the following:

- the labels and safety data sheets for workplace chemicals
- substances in the workplace that are known to cause dermatitis
- details of the risk assessment of those substances
- correct use of controls
- the need to report control systems failures
- risks to health posed by particular substances should be assessed by a medical doctor, preferably one qualified in occupational medicine
- symptoms of sensitization
- the role of health surveillance
- the importance of reporting results of self-examination.

ROLE OF HEALTH SURVEILLANCE

Health surveillance is used to detect the early onset of dermatitis, the earlier a skin condition is detected the better the chance of successful treatment. This method however is not as effective as primary control measures designed to prevent dermatitis from occurring. Health surveillance where used must be implemented in conjunction with the primary control measures, as health surveillance can help to show that control measures in the workplace are working.

PRE-EMPLOYMENT MEDICAL

A pre-employment questionnaire should be completed by all those likely to be working with substances that cause dermatitis. The objective of a health assessment is to evaluate the effect of work on health, in this case with regard to the skin. Those with a previous known sensitivity to a particular irritant or sensitizer may be required to undergo a medical assessment before commencing employment where potentially hazardous substances are used that may cause health-related issues to arise. The health professional conducting the assessment must be familiar with both substances and processes used. Whilst the initial assessment may be carried out by any healthcare professional, the decision regarding suitability for employment should be made by a medical doctor, preferably a doctor qualified in occupational medicine. The issue of equality of opportunity may arise because dermatitis when diagnosed is considered to be a disability. Another issue is the effect of the dermatitis on the workplace; some industries, such as those manufacturing medical devices have what are called 'clean areas'. Working in these areas may cause several health-related issues to arise, two examples of which will suffice:

- the need for repeated hand-washing
- skin conditions that can shed skin or act as a focus for infection may not be consistent with product safety for the item being manufactured in the workplace.

ROUTINE HEALTH SURVEILLANCE

The decision to carry out health surveillance is based on the risk assessment where the risk assessment suggests that a potential risk of dermatitis exists because of workplace exposure. In such cases, health surveillance is usually required. Education and training of employees is crucial and must include the principles of prevention, skin care and the detection of the early signs of dermatitis. Because dermatitis is firstly evident to the individual, self-examination and reporting of problems detected is vital. Self-examination can be supplemented by a health questionnaire, which should be completed and the results obtained compared to any pre-employment records available. Ideally, any abnormal results should lead to the affected worker being assessed by a suitably qualified doctor. If health surveillance identifies a suspect cause of dermatitis and the disease goes away either by avoiding the substance or by changing work practices, no further action is usually required. Should the condition persist, however, the opinion of a specialist physician should be sought, and Guidelines on Occupational Dermatitis published by the Health and Safety Authority in February 2009 referred to. Any assessment made may include a workplace inspection, and if allergic dermatitis is diagnosed, patch-testing may be performed. This involves the application of various test substances to the skin, which are left in place for forty-eight hours. On removal of the patches, the skin is examined and re-examined forty-eight hours later for any response. This testing is usually performed by a dermatologist and can assist in establishing what allergens could be aggravating the worker's skin condition. Any new case of dermatitis in the workplace will indicate that existing control methods are inadequate and will require a review of the risk assessment and necessary changes to be made.

CARCINOGENS

Carcinogens are any substance to which the risk phrase 'may cause cancer' applies. They are regulated by Carcinogen Regulations in force since 1993. These Regulations impose a legal responsibility on all employers in whose premises a carcinogen or a carcinogenic process is or is likely to be used, to eliminate the risk of adverse health and safety effects due to exposure of those workers to that carcinogen or process. A risk assessment must be conducted by the employer to identify both carcinogens and carcinogenic processes and to eliminate them.

Where elimination is not practicable, the employer must substitute a safer process, consider the introduction of engineering controls such as an enclosed system, monitor the workplace continuously and, where collective measures are not adequate, consider supplying suitable personal protective equipment. Employees potentially exposed must be provided with information and training on both the nature and risks pertaining to carcinogens and must be consulted about the nature of proposed preventive measures. Facilities need to be provided for health surveillance.

Employers are required to maintain written records of risk assessments they have undertaken to identify carcinogens in the workplace. In addition written records must be maintained of the measurement of levels of exposure and health surveillance, these records must be kept available for inspection by the Health and Safety Authority. Where an assessment reveals a risk to any employee, the employer shall, on request, provide the

Health and Safety Authority with information relating to activities, including reasons for using carcinogens, quantities of substances and preparations manufactured or used that contain carcinogens, the number of employees exposed, details of prevention measures including the issue of suitable personal protective equipment, nature and degree of exposure, and replacement substances used to reduce exposure.

All containers, packaging and installations that contain carcinogens must be clearly labelled with visible warning hazard signs.

Where an accidental discharge or a spillage of a carcinogenic substance occurs, the employer must inform his/her employees of any abnormal exposure resulting from that spillage or discharge. An emergency response plan, agreed with the workforce, should be in place to deal with such an eventuality. Until those abnormal conditions cease to exist, only workers properly equipped and trained to do so should be allowed in the area where abnormal conditions pertain and then only to carry out essential maintenance and repair. Such workers must be issued with suitable personal protective equipment and individual respiratory protection. The exposure of workers issued with suitable equipment should still be kept to a minimum because individual respirators may not give 100 per cent protection against the contaminant; the level of protection provided depends on the nature and quality of the respirators used. The employer must ensure that the cause of abnormal exposure is eliminated as soon as possible by, for example, cleaning up spillages promptly under carefully controlled conditions and ensuring that levels of exposure return to normal as soon as possible.

GENERAL CONTROL MEASURES

It is the duty of the employer to ensure that:

- employees do not eat or drink in contaminated areas
- appropriate protective clothing be provided
- separate storage be provided for that clothing
- personal protective equipment be properly stored, cleaned and inspected before use
- defective items be either replaced or competently repaired
- relevant information and training be provided
- programmes to combat work-related incidents be updated on a regular basis
- there be continuing assessment and consultation to monitor the ongoing effects of carcinogens

- control measures be introduced only after consultation with the workforce.

A legal duty is imposed on the employer to take, in consultation with employees, the following measures that may affect the health and safety of employees:

- the appointment of an employee to carry out specified activities in relation to the carcinogen
- the engagement of an occupational hygienist to carry out either preventive or protective measures in the workplace
- the appointment of a person to implement emergency evacuation measures
- the keeping of appropriate written records of accidents and dangerous occurrences
- health surveillance, if necessary
- health and safety training following changes to work processes or technology.

Any health surveillance here must be conducted by a designated medical practitioner and should be conducted prior to exposure and at regular intervals thereafter; written records should be maintained of all health surveillance. The medical practitioner is required to keep a separate confidential record of each individual worker surveyed and must also propose any measures necessary in respect of the safety of that worker. If a case of occupational cancer is diagnosed it must be notified to the Health and Safety Authority. It should be noted that health surveillance does not necessarily include a medical examination; it can include record-keeping, self-examination, questionnaires, biological monitoring and medical examinations.

EXPOSURE TO ASBESTOS

Asbestos is the name given to a group of fibres which are strong and are resistant to chemicals and heat sources. Breathing air that contains asbestos fibres can lead to asbestos-related illnesses, such as chest and lung cancer. There is usually a lengthy incubation period between first exposure and eventual diagnosis; this period can vary from fifteen to sixty years.

A safe level of asbestos exposure does not exist. The greater the level of exposure, the higher the risk of disease. It is absolutely essential that any worker who is exposed to asbestos in the workplace takes the strictest precautions.

The use of most types of asbestos is now banned, but the substance is still to be found in a sizeable proportion of older buildings. Asbestos is not easy to identify and its presence can only be positively established by a skilled analyst using a microscope. In the past the most common use of the substance was as a fire protection coating and in insulation of pipe work, boilers and ducts.

Where the asbestos products are in good condition, specialist contractors may not always be needed. Stringent safety precautions are necessary, however, including damping the material, using only hand tools in removal and suitable respiratory equipment and dedicated clothing which must either be cleaned by a specialist laundry or disposed of safely as hazardous waste. Each sheet of asbestos removed must be wrapped in heavy-gauge plastic and clearly labelled as asbestos.

GENERAL DUTIES ON EMPLOYERS

Regulations that became law in 2006 impose stringent duties on employers with regard to asbestos. Employers are required to:

- assess the degree of risk to employees from either asbestos or materials that contain asbestos
- determine the degree of that exposure
- lay down adequate preventive measures.

Employers shall take all steps necessary to identify materials on the premises that are presumed to contain asbestos before commencing either demolition or maintenance of a place of work. Employers should seek from the owners of work premises information relating to identification of materials presumed to contain asbestos. If any doubt exists as to the identification of materials, asbestos should be presumed present and all necessary precautions taken.

An employer shall not undertake any work which would expose any employee to asbestos fibres unless that employer has:

- carried out a risk assessment to establish the presence or absence of asbestos. If having carried out that assessment any doubt exists as to the presence of asbestos, it shall be assumed that asbestos materials are present and appropriate action taken
- fully complied with Regulations.

Employers are prohibited from allowing any employee to carry on any work activity that would expose that employee to asbestos, unless that employer has first made an assessment of that risk. In carrying out that risk assessment the employer must:

- identify the asbestos-based material
- determine the condition of the material
- make a suitable assessment of the risk
- record significant findings
- record each assessment in a permanent form
- take steps to minimise exposure
- determine the nature and degree of exposure
- consider the effects of control measures which have or will be taken
- consider the results of monitoring exposure
- set out steps to limit exposure as far as possible
- consider the results of any relevant medical surveillance
- include all necessary additional information.

The assessment must be reviewed on a regular basis, and immediately where there is reason to believe the current assessment is incorrect or is no longer valid, there have been material changes in the workplace or monitoring results shows it to be necessary. A review must take place only after full consultation with employees in respect of the risk assessment.

GENERAL CONTROL MEASURES

An employer shall:

- limit to the lowest possible number employees likely to be exposed to asbestos fibres
- design work systems to achieve zero release of asbestos fibres into the atmosphere
- ensure that all premises and equipment involved in the treatment of asbestos be effectively maintained and thoroughly cleaned
- ensure that all asbestos material be stored and transported in properly sealed packaging
- ensure that asbestos waste be disposed of in suitably labelled packaging.

Where employees work in areas where there is a likelihood of exposure to asbestos materials, employers shall implement the following provisions:

- clearly mark and indicate by signs areas of exposure to asbestos
- ensure that suitable protective clothing be worn

- deny access to non-essential workers
- prohibit smoking
- provide appropriate respiratory equipment and ensure that it be worn.

MEASUREMENT OF ASBESTOS IN THE AIR

Measurement of asbestos levels in the atmosphere must be conducted on a regular basis where the level of asbestos fibres in the air is either equal to or exceeds the exposure limit value. The exposure limit value is 0.1 fibres per cubic centimetre as a time-weighted average over an eight-hour period. Sampling shall represent the personal exposure of an employee to asbestos, this sampling shall be carried out by a competent person, after consultation with the employees, over an eight-hour working period. These samples shall be analysed by a person competent to do so, using where possible a phase contrast microscope. Only fibres five micrometres or more in length and a width not less than three micrometres are taken into account in assessing contamination levels.

NOTIFICATION REQUIREMENTS

Employers are required to give fourteen days' notice or such shorter period as agreed with the Health and Safety Authority of any work activity that would expose employees to asbestos fibres. Any material changes of activity including the ending of that activity must also be notified to the Authority. Copies of all such notifications must be kept by employers, and employees must be afforded reasonable access to them.

MEASURES REQUIRED WHEN EXPOSURE LIMITS ARE EXCEEDED

When exposure to asbestos limits are exceeded due to unforeseen circumstances, the following measures are required. The employer must:

- identify the reasons for the limit being exceeded
- discontinue work in the affected area until suitable protective measures are taken
- carry out a further determination of the concentration of asbestos in the air immediately
- ensure that individual protective breathing apparatus is only used as a last resort and never as a permanent response to the problem
- provide for suitable rest breaks.

Where exceeding the exposure limit is foreseeable, the employer must issue suitable respiratory and other protective equipment, erect and maintain suitable warning signs adjacent to the affected area and ensure that the spread of asbestos fibres is prevented. Employees are obliged to comply with all preventive measures. Examples of foreseeable circumstances would arise in demolition, removal, repair and maintenance of buildings. Here an employer must, in advance of the commencement of activity, determine and implement necessary protective measures.

Plan of Work for Removal of Asbestos

Work involving the removal of either asbestos or asbestos-based products from any place cannot commence before a suitable plan of work is prepared in writing. This plan of work will specify that asbestos products are to be removed and that personal protective equipment will be supplied to all affected workers. The information in the plan will include the location of the place of work and the nature and probable duration of the work. Details of protective measures will be included and will cover the protection of those adjacent to the site.

A copy of the plan of work shall be supplied to the Health and Safety Authority not less than fourteen days before the work commences; copies of this notice must be available for production to inspectors from the Health and Safety Authority and the Environmental Protection Authority.

A site clearance certificate must be obtained from a competent person, stating that the site is now free of asbestos and is safe to occupy; this certificate when issued must be kept available for inspection by an inspector of the Health and Safety Authority.

Safe Use of Chemicals

Chemicals are in widespread use commercially and in the domestic context. If not handled correctly, chemicals can catch fire, cause burns to the skin and cause damage to people's health and the environment.

By law every chemical container must be labelled. This label will tell you all you need to know about the safe use of that chemical. Chemicals in use in the domestic context must have a child-resistant cap and are required to have a roughened area which when touched by a visually-impaired person will alert that person to the danger.

Some common terms in use on chemical labels are:

- *sensitiser*: this product can cause an allergy in humans, the most common illnesses being asthma and dermatitis
- *carcinogen*: this product can cause cancer to develop in humans
- *harmful or toxic for reproduction*: this product may affect human fertility and could damage a developing foetus.

ESSENTIAL SAFETY RULES

- Always study the label on chemical containers carefully.
- Read and follow safety instructions before use.
- Use any protective clothing recommended.
- Ensure that all chemicals are safely out of reach of children.
- Never transfer chemicals into an unmarked container.
- Never use flammable chemicals near a source of ignition.
- Never throw an aerosol container into a fire.
- Never mix chemicals unless you are certain that they do not react to each other.

DANGERS FROM CHEMICALS

Chemicals present a range of dangers. A splash from caustic soda can cause loss of eyesight. Vapours from solvents found in adhesives, paint strippers and aerosols can affect both the brain and nervous system. If you breathe in air contaminated by harmful chemicals your health can be impaired. Chemicals may also enter your system by ingestion, for example where a worker touches his/her mouth with a hand contaminated by chemicals. Some chemicals may enter your body through skin contact, even where no cut or abrasion exists.

Having entered the human body, by whatever means, the chemicals then pass into the bloodstream, which in turn can carry them to the liver, kidneys, brain and nervous system. Health problems may not manifest themselves immediately, and sometimes it takes years as is the case with cancer.

Substances that carry harmful, toxic or very toxic symbols act as poisons and either immediately or gradually cause nausea, vomiting, dizziness, breathing discomfort and, in serious cases, loss of consciousness and death. The corrosive symbol indicates that the substance can burn skin, eyes and lining of the throat, nose and lungs if breathed in. Substances that carry the irritant symbol can irritate the eyes, throat and nose, cause reddening and burning of the skin and may also trigger an allergy.

The highly flammable symbol indicates that vapours from the substance will catch fire at room temperature, especially if a spark or flame is present, examples of highly flammable substances are alcohol and acetone. Any substance that carries the extremely flammable sign will catch fire at low temperatures, for example ether. Substances carrying the oxidising symbol, when in contact with flammable substances, can either start a fire or worsen an existing one. The explosive symbol indicates that the substance will explode when exposed to heat, shocks or friction, for example TNT.

Substances carrying the 'dangerous to the environment' symbol can cause damage to animal, fish or plant life and can also damage the ozone layer.

Some chemicals are so dangerous that they affect human fertility, safety phrases such as 'inheritable genetic damage' or 'toxic for reproduction' are indicators of this danger.

SAFE STORAGE OF CHEMICALS

When storing chemicals:

- keep them out of direct sunlight and in their own clearly labelled containers
- care must be taken to separate flammable, oxidising and explosive chemicals
- keep them in a locked storage area, the key to this store being the responsibility of a senior staff member
- only remove them from storage for use
- any spillages should be collected on a metal tray, mopped up and disposed of as hazardous waste
- never transfer them to an unlabelled container.

Chemicals must always be returned to storage, in their own containers, after use.

GUIDE TO THE CHEMICALS ACT 2008

The Guide to the Chemicals Act 2008 was issued by the Health and Safety Authority to explain the terms of the Chemical Act 2008, which came into force on 15 July 2008. The main purpose of the Act is to facilitate the registration, evaluation, authorisation and restriction of chemicals. Section 6 of the 2008 Act provides for the Health and Safety Authority to review relevant statutory provisions for chemicals. In carrying out this review the

Authority is obliged to consult with bodies it considers appropriate for this purpose. Section 7 enables the Authority to draw up and publish codes of practice or to approve the codes of other bodies setting out practical guidance on compliance with the Health and Safety and Welfare at Work Act 2005.

NOISE

The sensation of sound is produced when pressure variations reach a responsive ear and any object that vibrates may produce noise. Amplitude is the term used to describe the intensity of sound. Sound waves vibrate through the air at different high and low frequencies. The unit of frequency is known as a cycle or hertz, and young ears have a range of 20 to 20,000 hertz. Loudness is an observer's impression of the intensity of sound and will depend on the hearing capacity of the observer. The range of sound is almost infinite from the quietest sound, perhaps that of a sheet of paper falling to the ground, to the loudest, such as the engine of a jet-propelled aircraft revving before take-off; the latter sound is ten million times louder than the former.

Loud noise causes irreversible damage to the cochlea or inner part of the ear, the part of your ear that carries out the final complex stage of the hearing process. From here, sound messages are transmitted to the brain.

Noise-induced hearing loss is one of the most common work-related diseases in Ireland, and for this reason the European Union has issued directives to member states to introduce legislation establishing maximum permissible noise levels in the workplace. The most recent noise directive was implemented in Ireland in 2006 (Health, Safety and Welfare at Work Control of Noise Regulations 2006) and provides that the daily exposure value shall not exceed eighty-five decibels but, where daily exposure limits vary greatly in the workplace, employers may use the average exposure limit of workers over a five-day week with eight-hour days, although the limit must not exceed eighty-seven decibels. Under these Regulations noise is defined as any audible sound.

NOISE CONTROL

As with any other work-related hazard, noise has a hierarchy of protection measures:

- stop buying new noise problems
- use quieter machines and processes

- reduce force on vibrating surfaces and reduce speed of rotation
- reduce the response of the vibrating surface by damping
- either reduce or perforate the surface area
- reduce the velocity of the fluid flow
- confine the sound wave and absorb it through soundproofing
- use suitable hearing protection.

A screening test can be used as an early warning system in occupational health, and eudiometry is an example of this type of screening. An audiogram is used to measure a worker's hearing ability at different pitches of sound. Workers developing noise-induced hearing loss show a particular pattern at high and low noise frequencies. All workers exposed to a daily noise level of eighty-five decibels or more are entitled to hearing tests at the expense of the employer. This test must include eudiometry and be conducted in suitably quiet conditions, and the person carrying out the test must be suitably qualified to do so.

Research has established that forty out of every one hundred workers at normal retirement age who have been subjected to noise levels above eighty-five decibels will have difficulty hearing others speak. This loss of hearing cannot be reversed but it can be prevented. Employers are legally required to protect their employees from the hazard posed by loud noise. This includes supplying those employees with suitable hearing protectors where collective measures have proven unsatisfactory.

A simple test to establish excessive noise levels would be for two people to stand apart at a distance of two metres or less and attempt to converse; if it is necessary to shout to be heard, the noise level may well be in excess of that permitted. If doubt exists about the level of noise to which a worker may be exposed, a specially trained person should be employed to measure the noise level. Employers are legally required to provide employees with adequate information about the level of noise to which they are subjected and to take all steps that are reasonably practicable to reduce that noise level, including the provision where necessary of hearing protectors.

The provision of hearing protectors is an individual protection measure and only provides protection to the wearer. The level of protection afforded depends on the quality of protectors provided and the continuous use of the ear protectors whilst exposed to the noise hazard, as their removal, even for a short period, will considerably reduce the effectiveness of the protection supplied. Practice has shown that waxed ear plugs provide the same protection as the most expensive ear protectors and on balance are more comfortable to wear. Where noise levels are high, a refuge or quiet area should be provided by the employer.

The risk to which employees are subjected will depend on the intensity of the sound and the length of time exposed to that sound. Damage to hearing caused by noise is cumulative so it is imperative that employees be protected from the time of first contact with the noise source.

DETERMINATION AND ASSESSMENT OF RISKS

Where employees are liable to exposure in excess of the daily maximum value of eighty decibels, the employer, having consulted his/her employees, shall make an appropriate assessment of the risk from such exposure. As part of this assessment the employer shall if necessary measure noise levels to which employees are exposed. The employer has full responsibility for both planning and carrying out this assessment and any sampling should be representative of the daily personal exposure of an employee to noise. Particular attention should be paid to:

- the level, type and duration of noise, including any exposure to impulsive noise
- daily and weekly exposure limits
- the effects of exposure on employees most at risk
- the effects on employees' health from interaction between noise and vibration
- the interaction between noise and warning signals needed to prevent workplace accidents
- information on noise emissions provided by manufacturers
- the availability of quieter equipment
- noise exposure outside normal working, for example during overtime
- information obtained from health surveillance.

Employers shall review a risk assessment where the results of health surveillance show this course to be necessary. The employer shall record in his/her safety statement the findings of the risk assessment and steps taken to combat noise at source. Any assessment conducted must be reviewed at suitable intervals.

PROVISIONS FOR NOISE REDUCTION

The general principles of prevention, as set out in the Third Schedule to the 2005 Act, provide that an employer shall ensure as far as is reasonably practicable that the risk of exposure to noise by his/her employees be either eliminated at source or reduced to a minimum. For this purpose, an employer must:

- avail of work methods that reduce exposure to noise
- use work equipment that emits the lowest level of noise
- design places of work having in mind noise reduction
- train employees to use all equipment both correctly and safely
- reduce levels of airborne noise by using shields, enclosures or sound-absorbent materials
- reduce structural noise by either damping surfaces or isolating the process
- maintain and service machinery efficiently
- limit the duration and/or intensity of the sound
- operate work schedules that provide for adequate rest periods.

Where the risk assessment indicates that workplace noise levels assessed on a daily basis exceed eighty-five decibels, the following provisions apply:

- warning signs must be erected that clearly convey the information that the permitted noise level has been exceeded and that hearing protectors must be worn
- barriers must be erected to prevent unauthorised access to that place
- where rest facilities are provided, care must be taken to reduce noise to an absolute minimum in that facility.

In circumstances where risk from exposure to noise cannot be prevented by using collective protection measures, appropriate ear protectors must be provided by the employer and worn at all times by the employee in work areas where the noise level exceeds that permitted by law.

EMPLOYER'S CHECKLIST

Employers are advised to utilise a checklist to establish sources of workplace noise. For example:

- Are all noise sources identified by warning signs?
- Are all persons present in the noise area essential to that area?
- Have employees been adequately warned about noise dangers?
- Has the manufacturer's information about noise levels been checked at the source of noise?
- How will changes in work practices affect noise levels?

- Would better or more regular maintenance reduce the problem?
- Has everything reasonably practicable been done to reduce noise levels?

CONTROL OF VIBRATION

The Safety, Health and Welfare at Work Control of Vibration Regulations 2006 set out exposure limits to vibration for employees above which the employer is legally obliged to take action to reduce the level of that vibration. The exposure action value is the level of daily exposure to vibration which if exceeded requires the employer to take specific action to reduce that risk.

The exposure limit value is the level of daily exposure to noise for any employee that must not be exceeded except where an exemption certificate has been issued in writing by the Health and Safety Authority. Such an exemption certificate may only be issued where exposure to mechanical vibration is usually below the exposure action value, but because of the nature of the work this value may vary from time to time and occasionally exceed that value. However, exposure averaged over a forty-hour period must be below the exposure limit value and evidence must show that the actual pattern of exposure is less than the risk of constant exposure at the exposure limit value. The Health and Safety Authority shall not grant an exemption here unless it consults with the employer and employee representatives, and conditions are attached to any exemption granted to ensure risk from exposure is minimised and employees are subject to appropriate health surveillance. Exemptions granted are subject to a review at four-yearly intervals and shall be revoked as soon as the circumstances justifying that exemption no longer exist.

Three types of vibration to which the body may be subject are defined under the Regulations:

- *hand/arm vibration*: mechanical vibration that when transmitted to the human arm and hand entails risks of vascular, bone/joint, neurological or muscular disorders
- *mechanical vibration*: vibration in a machine part, equipment or a vehicle when driven
- *whole-body vibration*: mechanical vibration which when transmitted to the entire human body can cause lower back morbidity and/or spinal trauma.

The daily exposure limit value averaged over an eight-hour day shall be a maximum acceleration rate of five metres per second squared and the daily exposure action value, again with reference to an eight-hour period, is a maximum of 2.5 metres per second squared. With regard to whole body vibration, the daily exposure limit value averaged over an eight-hour period is 1.15 metres per second squared, the daily exposure action value over the same reference period is 0.5 metres per second squared.

An assessment of exposure levels may be carried out based on information supplied by manufacturers concerning levels of emission from the equipment used, observation of specific work practices and measurements made including sampling. This however must be representative of the worker's personal exposure. Where devices are held in both hands, measurement shall be made on each hand, the level of exposure being determined by reference to the higher value of the two hands measured. When employers are carrying out a risk assessment, particular attention must be paid to:

- the level, type and duration of exposure, including exposure to intermittent vibration or repeated shocks
- exposure limit and exposure action values
- employees at particular risk from vibration exposure
- any indirect effects to health and safety resulting from interaction between mechanical vibration, other equipment and the place of work
- information required to be supplied by manufacturers on work equipment
- the existence of replacement equipment designed to reduce workplace vibration
- the extension of exposure to whole-body vibration beyond normal working hours
- abnormal conditions such as low temperatures
- appropriate information gleaned from health surveillance.

The legislation imposes a duty on employers to record their assessment findings as soon as possible, together with details of prevention action in their safety statement.

STRESS IN ORGANISATIONS

Sometimes described as the stress experience, stress can be seen as either a demand on mind and/or body referred to as a stressor or what is referred to as a stress response, that is the body's reaction to an experience that we find stressful. Stress is simply the arousal of the human mind and body to demands made on it, though in general stress will connote something unpleasant in our minds: an unpleasant situation that leads to an uncomfortable state of mind that in turn leads to an unpleasant mixture of physical sensations. This is a useful model of what constitutes stress but it is not the entire picture. Technically speaking, a pleasant as well as an unpleasant event may lead to stress-related illness, and positive in addition to negative emotions can be part of a stress-related incident.

Stress may be viewed as a trigger for a response, or it may be considered a cause and called a stressor, which is any demand on mind and body. Stress may also be seen as a response, this stress response is made up of psychological and biological patterns, which do not operate in isolation but feed on each other to create the stress experience.

DIFFERENT APPROACHES TO STRESS

A study by Hans Selyne focused on the physiological aspect of stress and defined stress as the non-specific response of the body to any demand made on it. Selyne believed that there were three stages to stress: the first, alarm reaction; the second, adaptation to the situation; and the third, exhaustion when the responses, if severe and prolonged, result in the possibility of life-threatening illness.

An alternative approach, focusing on the psychological, was taken by Folkman and Lazarus, who provide us with the best definition of stress to date. Here stress is described as a particular relationship between the person and his/her environment that is appraised by that person as taxing or exceeding his/her resources to cope and is seen as endangering general well-being. When a person is unable to deal with this relationship, he/she will experience a reduction in general well-being. The psychological approach views the person's appraisal of the particular situation as crucial, from this appraisal will come the response or lack of it as the case may be.

STRESSORS

Anything that makes demands on a person that requires adaptation or adjustment can properly be described as a stressor. Stressors can be external or internal to the person. External factors include, for example, heat, cold, noise, toxic chemicals, relationships with supervisors, crowding, job demands and family conflicts. Internal stressors include, for example, anger, fearful beliefs, sorrow and attitudes to individuals. It should be noted that not all stressors have negative outcomes. Eustress or good stress is examined from the perspective of what makes a person healthy as against sickness in the individual, and examples of positive stressors are fitness training or positive examination results. Distress is used to describe the negative effects that can result from exposure to stress. What is important to note is that many stressors we meet every day have no effect one way or the other on us.

Holmes and Rahe identify life events that range from the very stressful to the less stressful. Those mentioned as very stressful include the death of a spouse and loss of work, and less stressful events include Christmas and a change in social activities. Holmes and Rahe consider any change, desirable or otherwise, as being potentially stressful; some changes in life are positive such as marriage or outstanding achievement, while others such as business or career re-adjustment could be positive or negative depending on the circumstances.

SOURCES OF ORGANISATIONAL STRESS

Stress at work can be defined as the imbalance between work-related demands and the capacity of the individual to cope with those demands. Stress is generally produced by inappropriate work demands, no sense of control by the individual over his/her output and inadequate support socially. Research has identified seven major sources of organisational stress:

- work overload, time pressures, pressures of mistakes
- lack of proper job description, conflicting demands of the job and responsibility for others
- workplace relationships
- career factors such as promotion, redundancy and skill factors
- poor organisational structures, level of or lack of participation, trust and mistrust
- lack of training and learning opportunities
- workplace discrimination on gender and other bases.

The sources identified here have in the past led to job dissatisfaction, workplace tensions, poor industrial relations and poor health.

Background stressors at work include daily problems such as noise, unreasonable management and an inconsiderate colleague. If help is not obtained in solving these daily issues, a major health problem could arise in the future from their accumulation.

Research in Scandinavia has isolated the following core characteristics that have a high inbuilt stress factor:

- work overload, too much to do in too little time
- work is too simple and uninteresting
- no control over work done
- poor communications and workplace isolation
- lack of personal and professional development.

Where these characteristics exist, they can give rise to chronic stress. Improvements in the work environment and better-designed work programmes can enhance the quality of working life.

Information technology has links with the following physical stressors:

- fatigue following close monitoring of displays and being tied to terminals for long periods of time
- noise from printers
- social isolation from work colleagues at the terminal.

It is a generally accepted fact that some occupations are more likely to cause stress than others, for example air traffic control, police work, nursing and teaching.

PSYCHOLOGICAL PERSPECTIVE ON STRESS

The psychological view of stress focuses on the person's perception of the situation being faced. This appraisal includes the recognition of potential harm and threats, as well as the ability to deal with those harms and threats. Lazarus believes that more attention should be paid to a person's appraisal of stress factors than to any other aspect of stress. Research in this area now focuses on the meaning that a particular event has for a person based on the person's feelings of threat, vulnerability and ability to cope. Such an approach relates to the person and his/her relationship with his/her environment. Central to this is the person's ability to perceive or appraise a particular situation; further, the event appraised must be seen as threatening, challenging or harmful.

There are three types of recognised appraisal: primary, secondary and re-appraisal. Primary appraisal occurs when the person first encounters an event. The person will appraise the situation, deeming it positive or harmful, in accordance with its significance for his/her well-being. An event may be appraised as potentially harmful as it may lead to injury or illness or perhaps as challenging with a potential for growth or gain. Harm, threat and challenge will all produce separate emotions. With an appraisal of harm will come anger and/or disappointment, with an appraisal of threat will come worry or fear, with an appraisal of a challenge will come excitement or anticipation. All of these emotions are generated by the person's appraisal of a particular situation, they do not of themselves produce stress.

Secondary appraisal refers to a person's ability to control or cope with a threat or challenge. Three questions are pertinent to secondary appraisal: What are the available options open to me? How likely is it that I will produce the correct coping strategy? Will this procedure work and will it alleviate my stress? Secondary appraisal of a situation depends on the extent to which people believe they can manage stressful situations successfully.

New information may require reappraisal of a stressful situation; this may not result in less stress but could increase it.

Stress is most likely in persons who for some reason are more vulnerable than others, not only because they lack the resources to handle stress, but also because of their perception that they are less able to handle particular situations.

Guidelines on Stress Management

In 2009 the Health and Safety Authority issued a guide for employers on work-related stress. This guide defines stress as the negative reaction that people have to aspects of their environment. Two matters need to be kept in mind regarding the nature of stress. Firstly, stress is a state, and therefore it passes. Secondly, a stressed person is not rational, and is therefore less likely to behave in the rational way one does when calm. Work-related stress is most likely to occur when employees are performing difficult tasks, doing things under difficult circumstances or whilst under emotional strain, which comes mainly from our personal lives. Each person will have different coping strategies, some healthy, like exercise, and others unhealthy, like excessive alcohol consumption. Work-related stress is either caused or worsened by work and relates to reactions to pressures and deadlines in the working environment.

Role of the Employer

Each employer is under a legal obligation to ensure that employees are not in any danger in their place of work, and that all work-related demands made on employees must be reasonable. This requirement of reasonableness applies from the time the worker enters the work place until s/he leaves.

It is not sufficient here that the employer be simply well intentioned, both risk assessments and control methods must reflect reasonableness in the employer's approach to his/her employees.

DUTIES OF EMPLOYEES

Some work-related demands may make some workers feel stressed, but workers for their part must learn to cope with reasonable pressures at work and develop methods of adapting to the demands of the task in hand. Each task to be performed will require specific skills and it is important that the worker match the demands made by the task in hand. Work-related stress should not be an issue where the worker has the required skills for the task to be performed as s/he will learn to cope with any short-term stress. However, constant stress that is not relieved can lead to physical illness.

EMPLOYER OBLIGATIONS

There are no set rules that address all places of work, so each employer is legally obliged to do what is reasonable in the circumstances to combat work-related stress. Work-related stress has the potential to incur high financial costs; it is estimated that the total financial cost of stress-related illness across the European Union to date is thirteen billion euro.

PRINCIPAL CAUSES OF WORK-RELATED STRESS

There are different causes of work-related stress for everyone; some work-related factors such as badly organised shift work, poor communication, bullying and harassment are more likely to cause work-related stress than others. The context within which work is performed and the content of the work are both stress-related factors. One issue that frequently arises is role clarity: is the role of the worker clear or is it in potential conflict with others? Other issues such as workplace relationships, leadership and degree of control exercised by the worker over the task are equally crucial. Training in how the task is to be performed both efficiently and safely and demands made on the worker by the task at hand are all factors in any place of work, but when issues arise from some or all of these factors there is a high risk of work-related stress arising in one or more workers. The experience of stress can radically alter behaviour patterns, the most notable changes being a tendency to anger, lower resilience, tearfulness and being prone to becoming upset. In extreme cases phobic-type behaviour necessitating professional intervention manifests itself.

Stressed workers will be less likely to eat or sleep well, take exercise or relax. Attention span and even memory can be impaired. Stress may be categorised as follows:

- mental (how the mind works)
- physical (how the body works)
- behavioural (the things we do)
- cognitive (the way that we think and concentrate).

Experience has shown that prolonged stress can lead to blood pressure problems and cardiovascular disorders.

PREVENTION OF WORK-RELATED STRESS

By law, an employer must assess the workplace for risks to health and safety including stress and put in place adequate preventative measures. Employment policies that benefit employee health can improve productivity levels. Low levels of work-related stress are associated with the following positive outcomes:

- low staff turnover
- low level of staff absence
- low rates of injury.

Organisations that are seen as health-conscious tend to have clearly defined health policies and active methods of addressing problems, including:

- respect for employee dignity
- recognition of performance based on regular feedback
- clear employee goals in line with the goals of the organisation
- career progression for staff and input into decision-making
- consistent and fair management.

HOW TO MANAGE WORK-RELATED STRESS

Three main types of stress management exist:

- *primary intervention*: concentrates on the prevention of stress by looking at the sources of stress. A change in work systems is usually required as a result of primary intervention.
- *secondary intervention*: focuses on the employee during his or her time with the organisation. This includes training and support in the form of adequate management systems.
- *tertiary intervention*: focuses on counselling and providing support services.

It is advisable to have a combination of all three types of intervention in place rather than focusing on any one type. A structured risk assessment is essential to managing employee stress in the workplace, which involves an examination of the organisation as it is and an assessment of how the organisation needs to improve in terms of achieving health and safety consciousness. A structured risk assessment for stress will include the following:

- identification of causes of stress
- assessment of the likelihood and severity of risk factors for stress
- elimination of the risk by changing the stressful elements of the task
- containing the risks by limiting the impact and/or reducing the causes of stress
- protection from the risk by reducing the degree of exposure to the causes of stress
- monitoring the risks with an ongoing review of stress levels in the workplace through audits, absenteeism rates and exit interviews.

CONTROL STRATEGIES

Control strategies are methods use to reduce levels of work-related stress and these include:

- changing aspects of the working environment
- changing aspects of the task itself
- providing support for workers through training programmes
- providing feedback to workers on their performance.

Because our levels of satisfaction at work are closely related to how the work makes us feel, addressing work-related stress is in the interests of all concerned.

PREGNANCY

Even though pregnancy is not an illness, the Health, Safety and Welfare at Work Pregnant Employees Regulations 2000 provide specific legal protection to prevent damage to the human foetus and it is essential therefore that potential risks to pregnant workers are part of the routine health risk assessment at each place of work and that this assessment is not left until a pregnancy is notified.

The Regulations provide specific protection during pregnancy and whilst breastfeeding. They identify a list of conditions known to affect either pregnant or breastfeeding women and they outline the ways in which health, safety and welfare issues may be managed during pregnancy and breastfeeding.

A pregnant employee is defined as one who has given her employer a medical certificate stating that she is pregnant, or an employee in the period of fourteen weeks after giving birth, even if this was either a stillbirth or a miscarriage. A breastfeeding employee is one who is breastfeeding during the twenty-six weeks immediately after giving birth.

These Regulations come into force when an employee informs her employer that she is either pregnant, has recently given birth or is breastfeeding, and supplies an appropriate medical certificate. An employee may choose to inform her employer through her supervisor or through direct contact by her doctor with her employer. On receiving notification of pregnancy, the employer must assess the specific risks to the worker. This involves determining what the pregnant worker is exposed to, how often this exposure occurs and for how long. Should this risk assessment reveal a work-related threat to the employee, the employer must inform the worker of that risk and the steps to be taken to ensure that neither she nor the developing foetus is injured.

The employer must assess if there are any practical ways that such a risk can be avoided. The first step in such a process could involve an adjustment of either working conditions or hours, if this is not practicable, suitable alternative work must be provided. If a worker during pregnancy and for fourteen weeks thereafter is working regularly for at least three hours between 11 p.m. and 6 a.m. or for 25 per cent of her monthly working time and has a medical certificate stating that night work will damage her health, she must be found alternative work. If the above steps are not feasible, safety and health leave under the Maternity Protection Act 1994 must be given to the employee.

Hazards to Pregnant Workers

General hazards include physical shocks, vibration, manual handling of loads, noise, excessive heat and cold, abrupt or severe movement, incorrect posture, radiation, biological agents, chemicals including cancer-bearing drugs, mercury and carbon monoxide. Additional hazards specific to pregnancy include work with pressurisation chambers, rubella, toxoplasmosis and lead/lead substances and underground mine work. Regular exposure to shock, low-frequency vibration or excessive movement may increase the risk of miscarriage. Heavy physical work may result in premature birth or low weight at birth. After twenty-eight weeks the pregnant worker is at greatest risk from manual handling injuries, this is due to hormonal relaxation of ligaments and posture problems due to the advanced state of the pregnancy. The risks to pregnant workers from excessive noise include high blood pressure and increased levels of tiredness. Specific risks to breastfeeding mothers include exposure to lead/lead substances and underground mine work.

If a pregnant woman or a nursing mother is working with radioactive liquids or dusts, these can expose the foetus to harm through either ingestion or skin contact; a breastfeeding mother and child may also suffer contamination. Workplace procedures should ensure the lowest possible exposure of workers in this category to this type of radiation. Advice on this topic is available from the Radiological Protection Institute of Ireland. Electromagnetic radiation (radio frequency) is not known to cause harm to pregnant workers, exposure to extreme levels however might cause harm by raising the body temperature. According to the World Health Organization, the level of radiation emanating from the screens of visual display units is below the level that can cause harm to humans.

Pregnant workers tolerate heat less well than others and may faint or suffer from heat stress; breastfeeding may be impaired by heat dehydration. No specific problems arise from working in cold conditions, warm clothing would however be necessary for general health reasons.

Antimitotic drugs are used for treating cancer in humans and in the long term these drugs can cause damage to both sperm and eggs, some can cause cancer; exposure occurs through inhalation or the skin. Chemicals marked with the letters 'SK' can penetrate intact skin and become absorbed in the body causing ill health. Contamination can occur from a splash on the skin or clothing or from exposure to high concentrations of atmospheric vapours; pesticides and organic solvents are examples of substances easily absorbed. Special precautions are needed including the provision of appropriate personal protective equipment and engineering controls.

A particular risk arises from the discharge of carbon monoxide in enclosed areas, this can result in the unborn foetus being starved of oxygen; no evidence exists of harm to breastfed babies as a result of the mother's exposure to carbon monoxide. Under the Dangerous Substances Labelling Regulations 1994, carbon monoxide is defined as a substance toxic for reproduction and carries the hazard warning label R61 'may cause harm to unborn child'.

When exposure to lead and lead derivatives was poorly controlled these substances were associated with spontaneous abortions and stillbirths. Recent studies draw attention to an association between low-level lead exposure before birth and mild decreases in intellectual performance in childhood. Because lead can enter breast milk, the exposure of breast-feeding mothers to lead and its derivatives should be viewed with concern. Lead and lead substances carry the same hazard warning as carbon monoxide (R61). It is advised that the level of lead in the blood of female workers should not exceed 25 micrograms per 100 millilitres of blood. The objective here must be to protect the foetus from injury in the weeks before a pregnancy is confirmed.

Various chemical agents can endanger the health of pregnant women and the unborn child. There are about 800 such chemical agents listed with the following risk phrases:

- R40: possible risk of irreversible effects
- A45: may cause cancer
- R46: may cause heritable genetic damage
- R61: may cause harm to the unborn child
- R63: possible risk of harm to the unborn child
- R64: may cause harm to breastfed babies.

The only effective way of determining a risk to health from a particular substance is by risk assessment of that substance at a particular place of work. There may be no risk in practice if, for example, the exposure is at a level below that that may cause harm.

ENVIRONMENTAL PROTECTION

Legislation passed in 1992 established the Environmental Protection Agency, this legislation had a twofold purpose:

- the creation of specialist expertise to deal with complex environmental problems

- recognition of the fact that local authorities did not adequately control activities with an impact on the environment.

The functions of the Agency are set out as follows in the legislation:

- licensing, controlling and regulating activities that have an impact on the environment
- monitoring environmental quality, including the provision of information on the environment
- provision of an advisory service to local authorities on environment-related issues
- promoting research on environmental matters and providing advice and assistance on environmental remedies
- liaising with the European Environmental Agency
- carrying out any additional function assigned to the Agency by the Minister for the Environment
- compiling reports on the environment and maintaining environmental records including a database
- preparing and publishing codes of best practice
- promoting audits of the environment
- promoting quality objectives
- investigating incidents of pollution
- control of noise.

The Environmental Protection Agency has control over the environment-related activities of local authorities, which must now take account of any advice given by the Agency concerning the protection of the environment. Scannell suggests that the Agency would be most likely to tender advice in the following circumstances:

- guidelines and codes of practice
- preparation of legal proceedings to enforce controls
- monitoring of emissions and environmental management
- the management and preparation of local authority landfill sites.

The Agency has a number of specific powers under the legislation; for example, it may require a sanitary authority to supply it with specific information about monitoring drinking water for human consumption. It is empowered to both specify and publish criteria for the selection, operation and termination of landfill sites. In addition it may seek a report from a local authority that, in the opinion of the Agency, has failed to discharge an environmental function or has done so in an unsatisfactory manner.

INTEGRATED POLLUTION CONTROL

The 1992 Act confers on the Environmental Protection Agency power to establish a system of control for polluting industries. Integrated Pollution Control Licensing Regulations made in 1994 apply to the following industries: minerals and other materials, energy, mineral filters and glass, chemicals, food and drink, and cement. Certain categories of manufacturer need an Integrated Pollution Control Licence; those in the pesticide, pharmaceutical and veterinary products industries employing two hundred or more workers fall into this category. Application for this licence must be made to the Agency and notice of application must be published in a national newspaper at least fourteen days prior to the submission of the application, the planning authority must also be notified of any such application.

In considering any licence application the Agency must have regard to:

- any relevant air quality management plan
- noise regulation
- any special control area orders in the local authority area concerned
- any environmental impact statement submitted with the application plus any observations on same
- any matter related to the prevention, elimination, limitation or reduction of environmental pollution.

The Agency will not provide a licence for any activity unless satisfied that any emissions from that activity will not contravene standards for air and water, that any noise from the activity will not breach noise regulations and that the best available technology is used to prevent, abate or reduce emissions. Conditions may be attached to licences if appropriate, such conditions would include those considered proper by the planning authority. Where conditions are likely to be attached to licences the Agency must consult with the planning authority. Objections may be made to the issue of licences and objectors are allowed a period of twenty-one days to lodge an objection, any such objection must be in writing and state clearly the grounds of objection. The Agency is obliged to investigate all reasoned objections and must give a response to each objection within a maximum period of four months.

Under the terms of the Integrated Pollution Prevention and Control Directive a high level of control is required in order to protect the environment, the object being as far as possible to prevent harmful emissions. This directive covers installations rather than processes and includes intensive livestock units and food and drink plants. It requires the adoption of emission limit values and the use of best available technology in order to minimise pollutant discharges. Environmental quality standards must be taken into account in setting release limits in permits. If best technology is not sufficient to control pollution, anti-pollutant measures such as lowering the output of firms or reducing the number of polluting firms in a region must be considered. Integrated pollution prevention controls require the following activities to be licensed: minerals, energy, metals, mineral fibres, glass, chemicals, intensive agriculture, food and drink, cement, waste and fossil fuels. Under this directive, Irish industry must prevent pollution, avoid the production of waste where possible, recover waste efficiently and safely and use energy efficiently.

ENVIRONMENTAL IMPACT ASSESSMENT

European Community Directive 85/337, in force in Ireland since 1989, requires that member states of the European Community should adopt measures to ensure that projects likely to have a significant impact on the environment are assessed in order to ascertain their impact on the environment. An environmental impact study is required to contain:

- a detailed description of the project
- a description of the measures to be taken to avoid, reduce or eliminate adverse environmental conditions
- data identifying the main effects the project is likely to have on the environment
- a non-technical summary of all information supplied.

The information in the study must be supplied by the developer of the project. In assessing this study regard must be had to the direct and indirect effects of the project on humans, flora and fauna, its impact on water, air and landscape must also be considered. Guidelines issued in 1994 must be taken into account when preparing and assessing an environmental impact study.

Some projects are automatically subject to assessment, such as projects in the mining, petroleum extraction, chemicals, pharmaceuticals, fish meal and oil product industries. For other projects the crucial issue is the location of that project in, for example, an environmentally sensitive area or a place of historical or cultural interest. Any new project that is subject to integrated pollution control also requires an environmental impact study. Alterations and reconstructions may also require this study.

MANAGEMENT OF WASTE

The Waste Management Act 1996 provides for the development of waste management plans by local authorities and addresses all aspects of the prevention, minimisation, collection, recovery and disposal of non-hazardous waste within the functional area of that authority. Waste management plans must be reviewed every five years.

The Environmental Protection Agency is required under this legislation to formulate a national hazardous waste management plan, dealing with the prevention, minimisation, recovery, collection and safe disposal of such hazardous waste that cannot be prevented or recovered. This plan will describe the type, quantity and origins of hazardous waste arising in the state, including details of the movement of that waste and its safe disposal; specify prevention and minimisation targets; identify hazardous waste sites; recommend cost-effective remedial measures; and give effect to the principle that the polluter pays. The Agency is required to review this plan from time to time.

The Minister for the Environment is entitled under this legislation to make regulations incorporating measures to carry out audits of waste and waste reduction programmes. Regulations may also be introduced that are designed to either prohibit or limit the manufacture of specified materials. A general duty is imposed by this Act on the holder of waste to hold, recover and/or dispose of that waste in a manner that does not pollute the environment. Each local authority must provide disposal facilities in its area.

Waste licences issued by the Environmental Protection Agency are required in respect of waste disposal and recovery at public and private facilities. Certain activities do not require a waste licence, such as those activities already licensed under the 1992 Act, household waste disposal, litter disposal in a litter facility, water treatment sludge, some agricultural waste and animal by-products. The Agency will only issue a waste licence where it will replace any relevant licences issued under the Air and Water Pollution Acts. The licence shall cease to have effect if the activity licensed has not commenced within three years of the granting of that licence.

ACTION TO LIMIT OR PREVENT POLLUTION

A local authority may serve a notice requiring specified action to prevent or limit environmental pollution. If the notice is not complied with, the local authority may itself remedy the problem and recover the financial cost from the defaulter. The courts are also empowered by Part VI of the Waste Management Act 1996 to take measures to prevent or limit pollution, such powers would usually be invoked on application by local authorities who are charged under the Act with the responsibility for legal enforcement within their own administrative area.

REVISION QUESTIONS

1 List four airborne contaminants.
2 What are the occupational safety values of lead and cadmium?
3 What does the term 'sensitiser', often found on chemical labels, mean?
4 List the routes of infection to the human body.
5 In what sector of business activity is zoonosis likely to occur?
6 What are the causes of occupational asthma?
7 In the context of occupational health, what is the function of health surveillance?
8 What is workplace dermatitis?
9 List five control measures that an employer must put in place to protect employees from either carcinogens or carcinogenic substances.
10 What is asbestos?
11 List the essential safety rules for the correct handling of chemicals at work.
12 Define noise as set out in the Noise Regulations 2006.
13 In the context of the control of vibration, what does exposure action value mean?
14 Define stress.
15 List the four ways that stress can be categorised.
16 List the three methods of management intervention in stress.
17 Briefly outline the role and function of the Environmental Protection Agency.

REFERENCES

Chemical Agents Regulations 1994
Environmental Protection Agency Act 1992

Folkman, S. and Lazarus, R.S. (1986), *Journal of Personality and Social Psychology*, p. 131

Health and Safety Authority (1990), *Is Your Work Making you Deaf?* Dublin: Health and Safety Authority

Health and Safety Authority (2000), *Chemwise*, Dublin: Health and Safety Authority

Health and Safety Authority (2002), *Use Chemicals Safely*, Dublin: Health and Safety Authority

Health and Safety Authority (2003), 'Medical Guidance Notes on Occupational Asthma', Dublin: Health and Safety Authority

Health and Safety Authority (2004), *Guide to Exposure to Noise in the Entertainment Industry*, Dublin: Health and Safety Authority

Health and Safety Authority (2005), Safety with Asbestos, Dublin: Health and Safety Authority

Health and Safety Authority (2008), *Guidelines on Occupational Asthma*, Dublin: Health and Safety Authority

Health and Safety Authority (2009), *Guidelines on Occupational Dermatitis*, Dublin: Health and Safety Authority

Health and Safety Authority (2009), *Work-related Stress: a Guide for Employers*, Dublin: Health and Safety Authority

Health, Safety and Welfare at Work Act 1989

Health, Safety and Welfare at Work Control of Noise Regulations 2006

Health, Safety and Welfare at Work Pregnant Employees Regulations 2000

Holmes, T.H. and Rahe, R.H. (1967), 'The Stress Inventory', *Journal of Psychosomatic Research*, vol. 3, p. 140

Integrated Pollution Control Licensing Regulations 1994

Labelling of Hazardous Chemicals Regulations (SI Nos. 77 of 1994; 272 of 1995; 317, 354 and 513 of 1998; and 363 of 1999)

Lazarus, R.S. (1966), *Psychological Stress and the Coping Process*, New York: McGraw-Hill

Maternity Protection Act 1994

Safety, Health and Welfare at Work Act 2005

Safety, Health and Welfare at Work Asbestos Regulations 2006

Safety, Health and Welfare at Work Carcinogen Regulations 1993

Safety, Health and Welfare at Work Control of Vibration Regulations 2006

Scannell, Y. (1995) *Environmental and Planning Law in Ireland*, Dublin: Round Hall Press

Selyne, H. (1936), *The Stress of Life*, New York: McGraw-Hill

Waste Management Act 1996

4
Safety in the Workplace

This chapter deals with the important issues of safety management, safety representation and consultation, the responsibility of the employer to prepare and review annually a safety statement, the role of the employee in cooperating with the employer's safety plan and the role of both employer and employee in carrying out safety inspections and audits in the workplace.

MANAGING WORKPLACE SAFETY

The Safety, Health and Welfare at Work Act 2005 imposes a duty on employers to take all steps that are reasonably practicable to protect the health, safety and welfare of their employees. Employers are required to identify hazards in the place of work and to put in place necessary control measures to combat those hazards. Section 19 of the 2005 Act imposes a legal duty on employers to carry out a risk assessment and Section 20 imposes a duty on employers to prepare a safety statement based on the findings of that risk assessment. It is crucial that employers consult with their workforce at all stages of this process. Employers must prepare a safety statement setting out the health, safety and welfare measures that they are implementing to protect their employees. The duty of the employer is to the workforce as a whole, individual protective measures will only come into play when the collective measures have failed or are found to be unsatisfactory.

The safety statement is prepared based on the findings of a risk assessment of the hazards in the place of work. Some workplaces, such as those in the chemical industry, carriage of dangerous goods and the transport and classification of dangerous substances, require more extensive risk assessment than others. Any assessment conducted requires full consultation with the affected workers. All risk assessments are concerned with the identification of hazards, which are defined as anything in the workplace that causes or is likely to cause injury to employees. Equally important is the assessment of the level or degree of risk emanating from that hazard.

Accident prevention is an essential of both good management and workmanship. Full cooperation from the workforce is essential in achieving freedom from accidents. Top management must lead in the provisions of safety in the organisation and a definite and known policy on safety must exist. The organisation must provide the necessary resources and use best knowledge and practice to deal with hazards.

Managing safety in the workplace is no different from any other management function, it is simply a matter of recognising a problem, making an assessment of that problem and then ranking suitable preventive measures. Loss control is a management system designed to reduce or eliminate all aspects of accidental loss that may lead to a wastage of the organisation's resources. This is synonymous with the reduction of risk at work and the practical techniques associated with each stage of loss control are closely related to risk management. Loss control management can be said to involve:

- identification of risk exposure
- measurement and analysis of exposure
- determining exposures that will respond to treatment by existing or available loss control measures
- selection of appropriate loss control action based on its effectiveness and economic feasibility
- managing the loss control effectively subject to economic constraints.

SAFETY STATEMENTS

A safety statement can be said to be a management programme to manage health, safety and welfare at work. It represents the employer's commitment to implementing the goals set out in health, safety and welfare legislation. Preparing a safety statement will not of itself prevent accidents, but it will demonstrate the employer's commitment to promoting health, safety and welfare. Managers and supervisors must ensure compliance with the terms of the safety statement by all employees, where necessary measures must be taken to ensure best practice.

Employers are legally obliged to have a current safety statement: under the 2005 Act all employers having three or more employees must maintain a safety statement and self-employed persons and those employing fewer than three employees are bound by codes of practice issued by the Health and Safety Authority for their industry. Employers must review their safety statement every year. If a safety statement is found to be inadequate by a health and safety inspector, the employer will be required to revise that statement.

Areas covered by a safety statement include details of health and safety management, risk assessments undertaken in the place of work, cooperation required from employees, those responsible for the implementation of safety plans, arrangements for consultation with employees and information available on health, safety and welfare. Responsibility for the preparation, review and updating where necessary of the safety statement rests with the employer.

The following categories of persons should have access to and be aware of the contents of the safety statement:

- all employees, including full-time, part-time, casual and seasonal contract workers
- outside contractors operating on the premises
- delivery persons
- self-employed persons who provide services from time to time on the premises.

Responsibility for ensuring that the contents of the safety statement and any necessary revision is communicated to the workforce rests with the employer. Employers may avail of verbal and written communication to achieve this goal. The safety statement's contents could, for example, be included in the worker's handbook and be communicated through ongoing training. The question of translating the safety statement into other languages may also arise given the diversity of the Irish workforce, current legislation requires the employer to do so where necessary. (See *Guide to Health, Safety and Welfare at Work Act 2005*, step 4.)

A safety statement should begin with a declaration of commitment by a senior manager to the effect that all reasonable steps will be taken to protect the health, safety and welfare of all employees including periodic evaluation of all workplace hazards. As already stated, current legislation requires an annual review of the safety statement.

The principal provisions of the safety statement must cover the following points:

- provision of a safe place of work
- a safe means of access and egress
- provision of adequate training and supervision
- provision of suitable personal protective equipment
- emergency planning with built-in revision
- appointment of staff to emergency evacuation duties
- prevention of risk to health from any article or substance

- provision of adequate welfare facilities
- provision, where appropriate, of suitably trained persons to provide training for staff.

The senior manager with overall responsibility for health, safety and welfare should sign the safety statement when completed.

A safety statement rests on the principles that health, safety and welfare can be managed and that accidents are foreseeable and may be prevented. For that reason it is essential that hazards be properly identified, the risk from that hazard fully assessed and effective preventive measures put in place. Any risk assessment made (see below) must be reviewed on a regular basis and any changes in work practice taken into account.

The safety statement is the place to record the significant findings of your risk assessment and your conclusions based on that assessment. Your employees should be informed of the result of any risk assessment conducted. Safety statements can make reference to other documents that may contain safety instructions, such as operating instructions for machinery, manufacturers' guidelines or company rules. Whether all safety documentation is kept together or separately is a matter of choice, but all concerned should be aware of the whereabouts of such documents.

A safety statement must specify how the organisation's assignment of responsibilities for health, safety and welfare operates on a day-to-day basis, the following must be addressed:

- resources available
- cooperation required from employees
- names of persons with responsibilities
- consultation and participation
- commitment to employee training and the budget for this.

Cooperation from employees is an essential feature of any health, safety and welfare strategy, and the need for this cooperation must be clearly set out in the safety statement. Under Section 13 of the 2005 Act, employees have an increased number of legally enforceable duties and therefore the method of reporting defects in plant and machinery by employees must be clearly spelt out.

The law requires employers to put in place and maintain a consultation process on health, safety and welfare issues with their employees, and the method of doing so is a matter for discussion and agreement with the workforce.

DIRECTORS' RESPONSIBILITIES

Directors of a company are obliged under health, safety and welfare legislation to assess the extent to which the policies set out in the safety statement have been evaluated. In assessing that statement the directors should consider the following questions:

- Are the aims of the statement appropriate?
- Are significant hazards identified, assessed and has appropriate preventive action been taken?
- Have the safety measures identified actually been implemented?
- What new measures were introduced following a reportable incident?
- Is management, consultation and training sufficient to comply with legal requirements?
- Is there anything more that reasonably could be done?
- Are adequate resources committed?
- What future improvements are needed?

As part of this evaluation, reference to existing records such as health surveillance, accident reports, training schedules and maintenance logs will prove useful; consultation with safety representatives may also form part of this review process.

The safety statement must by law be reviewed on an annual basis. Where hazardous activities are concerned more frequent evaluation will be necessary, and also where the work or its extent are constantly changing more frequent examination of existing work practices are advised. On completion of evaluation, details of any proposed changes should be brought to the attention of safety representatives and any person affected by those changes.

RISK ASSESSMENTS

The assessment of risk in the workplace depends on many and varied factors but as a general rule the following questions should be taken into consideration:

- Is anyone exposed to the hazard identified?
- Is the hazard likely to cause injury?
- How serious is the risk of injury?
- Is the hazard controlled?
- Is the level of supervision in the workplace adequate?
- What is the length and degree of exposure of workers?

Two matters are crucial when assessing risk: how likely is the risk of harm and how serious is that risk? Both issues are essential in the search for preventive measures.

Employers should adopt the method that best suits their organisation, but a tabular format is the one most often used. Some of the assessment may already be carried out, as in the case of chemicals supplied for commercial use, for which a materials safety data sheet is obtainable from the supplier of the product containing the precautions to be taken in both the use and storage of that product. A risk assessment based on an estimation of the probability of an undesired event occurring can be used. Probabilities can be established mathematically based upon the probable failure rates of individual components in the work system. Data on individual components may be obtained from manufacturers, reliability statistics or quality assurance information. The Institute of Industrial Research and Standards may also be in a position to provide advice and assistance.

Whatever methodology is adopted, employers should ensure that as many employees as possible are involved in the preparation of the risk assessment. If expertise from outside the company is availed of, employers should ensure that the person is familiar with the industry. Employers must decide who may be harmed by the activity and include members of the public and others with whom they share either space or activities. All new plant and work practices must be the subject of further assessment and be included in an updated statement. The result of the risk assessment and any subsequent revision of the safety statement must be brought to the attention of all concerned.

See Section 19 of the 2005 Act and step 1 of the *Guide to the Safety, Health and Welfare at Work Act 2005*.

SAFETY PRECAUTIONS

Most companies will have in place some safety precautions and the risk assessment will indicate whether those precautions are adequate in all circumstances. It need not be very expensive for employers to meet their legal obligations; sometimes all that is required is the provision of a non-slip surface or a mirror on a blind corner. If something needs to be done, employers should determine whether they can eliminate the hazard or change the way a job is done. If they cannot do either, they must determine what they can do to control the risk.

The law requires employers to do all that is reasonable to prevent accidents, but no workplace activity is risk-free and accidents sometimes happen despite our best efforts to prevent them.

Some methods of risk control in common use are:

- extraction or containment of the hazard
- adequate ventilation, natural air is best but forced ventilation may be required
- isolation of particular work processes
- adequate guarding of machinery
- efficient housekeeping
- adequate training and supervision
- emergency planning
- as a last resort, the use of personal protective equipment
- health surveillance
- accident reporting and recording
- the use of permits to work
- adequate welfare facilities.

The need for risk control will vary with the type of workplace activity being conducted, but risk control must provide adequate protection for all affected workers. A 'permit to work' system may be necessary, especially where repair, maintenance or cleaning work is being carried out in areas of potential danger. The permit will set out in a systematic way the work to be done, the hazards involved and the precautions to be taken, for example where an employee is required to work near machinery that could restart or in a confined space or where there exists a risk of contamination.

EXAMPLES OF SPECIFIC RISK ASSESSMENTS

The Health and Safety Authority's 2009 annual report states that slips, trips and falls are the most common type of workplace accident and account for a majority of accidents reported annually to the Authority. The degree of risk will depend on a number of factors, including how clean and tidy the premises are, the state of repair of flooring and stairs, control of trip hazards such as trailing cables from machinery and prompt cleaning of spillages.

Assessing the risk of being struck by a fork-lift truck involves determining the likelihood that someone will be struck and the severity of injury that may be received. Any assessment would take account of whether separate paths are used by pedestrians, the number of pedestrians likely to use the area where the machine is operating, degree of ongoing training, supervision of the area and the mechanical condition of the fork-lift truck.

The risks of using isocyanine paint will be indicated in the safety data sheet supplied with the product, which will contain details of the iso-cyanides contained and the necessary precautions when using it as its fumes can induce asthma in humans. Any risk assessment must look at the need for the paint, if needed how often is it used, how many use it, any area where use should be isolated and the proper personal protective equipment to be issued and used. Provision must be made for mechanical ventilation, spillages and accidental discharge into the atmosphere. The potential for harm to the health of affected workers is severe and every necessary precaution must be taken where the substance is in use.

GUIDANCE ON CARRYING OUT RISK ASSESSMENTS

Look for hazards that could cause significant harm in the workplace, for example poorly maintained floors or stairwells, flammable materials, chemicals, machine parts such as rotary blades, working at heights, ejection of materials as in moulding, steam boilers, vehicle condition and use, poor quality electrical wiring, dust, fumes, manual handling, poor lighting and cold conditions.

There is no necessity to list by name the persons actually exposed to risk in the workplace, but particular categories of workers must be borne in mind, for example maintenance personnel, hygiene operatives, independent contractors and members of the public. Particular attention should be paid to inexperienced workers, physically challenged workers, visitors and those working alone.

Having identified the hazards and those exposed to them, the next issue is control of the risk arising from those hazards. Some control measures may already be in place and it must be determined whether those precautions are adequate and, if not, what additional measures are needed. Do they meet existing legal requirements? Do they comply with the code of best practice for the industry? Has risk of injury been reduced as far as possible?

Any risk assessment must be carried out in the manner best suited to the business concerned, the form of assessment will depend on the complexity of the task involved. Hazards are classified as biological, chemical, human, and physical environment; and risks are usually classified as high, medium or low, but in some instances a numerical classification of risk may be adopted. Each category of person at risk must be clearly identified in the organisation's safety statement as well as the precautions necessary to combat risk and the identity of those responsible for implementing those precautions. The person responsible for risk control should be clearly identified in the safety statement.

HEALTH AND SAFETY CONSULTATION

Consultation on health, safety and welfare matters between employers and employees or their safety representatives must include consultation on any measure proposed that substantially affects health, safety and welfare in the workplace, including any measures required to be undertaken by legislation. Employees must be consulted where persons are named to carry out emergency duties and where it is proposed to employ competent persons from outside the organisation to advise on health, safety and welfare issues. Consultation should cover the content of the safety statement, its annual review and protective measures found necessary to introduce following risk assessments. All employees, but in particular experienced workers, will have a great deal to contribute to the safety process, effective consultation can with certainty be said to be the key to effective participation by employees in the safety process.

See Part IV of the 2005 Act, Sections 25 to 31, and the *Guidelines on Safety Representation and Safety Consultation* published by the Health and Safety Authority in January 2006.

CONSULTATION MECHANISMS

A number of key issues can be said to influence the type and size of safety consultation mechanism that an organisation may require. All of the principal activities need to be represented and members of management, particularly those with the power to effect change in the organisation, need to be part of the consultation structure. While it is important that the safety representative be a member of any consultation process, it will also be important to respect the role and function of the safety representative who continues to be the principal representative of the employees in health, safety and welfare matters.

JOINT SAFETY COMMITTEES

Should they so wish, employees employed in a place of work to which the 2005 Act applies may select and appoint from amongst their number members of a safety committee to perform the functions assigned by law to safety committees. In terms of the composition of a safety committee:

- the number of members appointed may not be less than three or more than ten

- where the committee has four or fewer members the employer may appoint one member and the employees the remainder
- if the committee consists of at least five and not more than eight members, the employer may appoint two and the employees select and appoint the remaining members
- if the committee has more than eight members, the employer may appoint three and the remainder are appointed by the employees
- where an employee ceases to be employed at that place of work, he/she ceases to be a member of the committee
- where a safety representative has been selected by the employees, he/she shall be selected by the employees to be a member of the committee.

Those involved in the safety consultation process have the same rights to time off and training in the carrying out of their functions as the safety representative. The Regulations provide that employees involved in consultation shall not suffer disadvantage in their employment because of their participation in safety consultation.

With regard to the operation of a safety committee:

- the committee shall assist the employer and employees in relation to the implementation of relevant statutory provisions
- the quorum for a meeting of the committee shall not be less than three
- the employer or a person nominated by him/her shall be entitled to attend every meeting of the committee
- the employer or nominee shall attend the first meeting of the committee and shall as soon as it is available present the safety statement to the committee
- the committee shall consider any matter brought to its attention by the employer that affects the health, safety and welfare of employees
- on request, the employer will consult with the committee concerning facilities for the holding of meetings and the frequency and duration of those meetings
- except in the case of emergency, meetings will be held during normal working hours and be held not more than four times annually
- the duration of meetings should not exceed one hour and should not interfere with the efficient running of the organisation.

These meetings should have a specific agenda and where necessary address the following issues:

- progress being made on implementing the safety statement
- examination of workplace accidents since the last meeting

- consideration of any special issue arising from recent serious accidents and dangerous occurrences
- suggestions on proposed solutions for work-related hazards
- use of protective clothing
- training needs and training courses attended by management or staff.

Meetings need to be varied and to make progress on issues addressed. Committee members must look at problems with an open mind and be prepared to consider new methods of problem-solving.

The employer is obliged to provide reasonable meeting facilities and assistance in the preparation of minutes and reports. The success of the process will depend on such matters as financial commitment by management to health, safety and welfare, encouragement of staff to communicate their views and complaints and to participate in decision-making, and a commitment by line managers to implement safety recommendations.

Safety Representatives

Employees at a place of work are entitled to select and appoint one of their fellow employees to act as a safety representative. The function of a safety representative can be said to be to represent the views of his/her colleagues on health, safety and welfare matters and to consult with and bring those views to the attention of the employer. The employer is obliged to consider those representations and to act on them where appropriate. Consultation between the safety representative and the employer is vital, especially when safety plans are being drawn up or when new technology is being introduced. The purpose of these consultations is to prevent workplace accidents and ill health and to highlight safety-related problems.

Conducting Inspections

A safety representative is entitled to carry out safety inspections of his/her place of work, provided the employer is notified in advance of that inspection. The frequency of such inspections will depend on factors such as:

- the size of the place of work
- the extent and nature of work-related activity
- range of hazards likely to be encountered
- changing hazards and risks.

Employers may not without good reason withhold permission for inspections, although the frequency of those inspections must be agreed with the employer. There is no standard timeframe for the completion of inspections, however a place of work with relatively few hazards could be inspected in one session. Any place of work with a relatively high hazard level will generally take longer. Also, different risk factors may exist in different parts of the workplace and for that reason more frequent or longer inspections may be required.

Guidelines for safety representatives issued by the Health and Safety Authority in 2006 recommend that the frequency and duration of inspections should be agreed with the employer after consulting the joint safety committee, where appointed. The recommendations cover organisations from low-risk employments with fewer than ten employees (inspection duration of one hour at least every four weeks) to large, high-risk construction sites (weekly inspections taking approximately two hours, here the entire site would be inspected). Inspection frequency and duration will be determined by the level of risk, the changing nature of the work and the proximity of the safety representative to the place to be inspected. It is important that a safety representative only be responsible for inspecting the unit that he/she represents. The guidelines recommend that a safety representative should not be required to travel more than twenty kilometres to the place that he/she is to inspect. This situation would arise where the employer's organisation is multi-located and only one safety representative has been selected to represent the workforce.

There are various forms of inspection, for example, a safety tour that involves a general inspection of the entire workplace, safety sampling that involves sampling in a systematic way of dangerous processes, or a safety survey that involves a general inspection of dangerous activities or processes. The types of inspection outlined can be used separately or in any combination. In this regard the safety representative may wish to consult the employer on the most suitable method of inspection.

On occasion it could be useful for the safety representative to be accompanied on a safety inspection by either the employer or his/her representative. In given circumstances it might be appropriate for the safety officer/advisor to be present to advise on technical health and safety issues. An opportunity should be afforded the safety representative to discuss privately, if necessary, health, safety and welfare matters with his/her fellow employees.

OTHER RIGHTS OF SAFETY REPRESENTATIVES

A safety representative may investigate situations in the workplace where there exists a reasonable fear of risk of personal injury to employees; the employer must be notified of any such investigation.

A safety representative may investigate both work-related accidents and dangerous occurrences in order to ascertain the causes and suggest suitable remedies to prevent the incidents from occurring in the future. The safety representative, however, cannot interfere with the scene of an accident which is being investigated by either a Health and Safety Authority inspector or any other statutory authority.

The employer is obliged to inform the safety representative when a health and safety inspector arrives at the premises to carry out an inspection. If the safety representative makes a request to that effect, he/she may accompany the inspector on the tour of inspection but not when the inspector is investigating a workplace accident; the employer or his/her representative may also accompany the inspector.

A safety representative needs reasonable office facilities, time off from his/her regular work and clerical assistance where necessary to discharge his/her functions satisfactorily. In normal circumstances two to three hours per week will be sufficient time off to discharge his/her functions; in industries with high-risk factors a longer period will be required. The safety representative should keep written records of all health, safety and welfare matters found to be unsatisfactory; records of any inspection made regardless of whether a problem was unearthed; and a note of all information received from the employer.

INFORMATION FOR SAFETY REPRESENTATIVES

Safety representatives are entitled to two types of information. The first arises from the employer's general duty to provide information, training and supervision where necessary to ensure the health and safety of his/her employees as far as is reasonably possible. Second, the safety representative will be entitled to information over and above what is required to be given to employees in general. Such information would include all that is necessary to allow the safety representative to discharge his/her functions effectively and to play a full part in preventing both accidents and illnesses in the workplace.

All safety representatives should be issued with a copy of the safety statement of their organisation and be fully informed on all arrangements for implementing the statement. In addition, details of any necessary technical information concerning workplace hazards should be supplied, including copies of materials' safety data sheets supplied by manufacturers. Adequate information should be supplied to the safety representative concerning both the place and the system of work that are likely to have adverse effects on health and safety of employees. Information about permit to work systems, emergency measures and any data collected on health assessments, or any other measures currently in place and that are designed to minimise risk to health and safety, should be supplied.

A fully informed safety representative can play an important role in preventing accidents and workplace illness, but limited exceptions exist to what information an employer may legally supply:

- any information whose disclosure would be in breach of the law
- information about individual employees without their consent
- information which for reasons other than health, safety or welfare could damage the business of the employer
- any information concerning the legal position of the employer in legal proceedings.

Safety representatives are entitled to consult either orally or in writing with a health and safety inspector concerning any health, safety or welfare issue that arises at his/her place of work. The safety representative is entitled to receive advice on such matters from the inspector.

Inspectors may provide factual information about health and safety in the place of work inspected and any information about any action that the inspector proposes to take in connection with that workplace, this information must also be given to the employer. The type of information supplied could include any matter relevant to health, safety and welfare at that workplace and also details of any legal action that the inspector proposes to take. An inspector will be in a position to supply information to the safety representative that the employer cannot, such as results of measurements and samples taken during inspection or investigation by the inspector.

TRAINING FOR SAFETY REPRESENTATIVES

It is essential that safety representatives have the requisite skills and training to discharge their functions effectively. Courses for training safety representatives are provided by a number of bodies and there is an agreed syllabus for this course. Participation in a course designed for safety representatives will provide general training on the role of the safety representative.

An individual employer has the specific responsibility of training his/her safety representative in the specific risks from hazards at his/her workplace. Current legislation places a legal onus on employers to pay for any necessary health, safety and welfare training required. The employer is obliged to ensure that safety representatives or members of joint safety committees have adequate time in which to perform their duties, paid time off must be provided to allow those involved in safety representation to acquire adequate knowledge to discharge their functions. Legislation specifically provides that safety representatives cannot suffer any disadvantage in their place of work by virtue of discharging their functions.

Guidelines issued by the Heath and Safety Authority recommend that the course content of a training course for those involved in safety representation should include:

- details of the safety and health legal system
- role of the safety representative in the safety consultation process
- communication skills required by representatives to properly discharge their function
- hazard identification and assessment of risks
- preparing and implementing safety policy and statements
- carrying out safety and health inspections
- accident investigation, recording and analysis
- sources of health, safety and welfare information
- risk control and safety and health management at work.

The course should include an evaluation of the progress of the course's participants and a written evaluation should be prepared for each participant. The need for follow up and retraining should also be addressed.

NUMBER OF SAFETY REPRESENTATIVES

In most organisations a single safety representative will be sufficient to meet health, safety and welfare requirements, but if the workplace has more than one location it may be necessary to have a safety representative at each location. This is a matter for the employees concerned and they are free to choose to have only one safety representative to cover more than one workplace location.

In some instances a single safety representative may be unable to discharge all the required health, safety and welfare functions, in this case a consultation mechanism such as a joint safety committee could usefully assist the consultation process. A decision on the necessity or otherwise of more than one safety representative should be agreed between employer and employees. The following factors may increase the number of safety representatives appointed:

- work is at more than one location
- work is performed in shifts
- places where work conditions change rapidly such as on construction sites
- places where either a risk or a wide variety of work activities exist
- work is at locations that are constantly changing or at premises outside the control of the employer
- transport or other workers from a central location work at different places of work
- any current or planned safety consultation mechanisms.

SELECTION OF SAFETY REPRESENTATIVES AND PERIOD OF OFFICE

The actual details of selection are left to the workers in each organisation. The normal process within that organisation for the selection of employee representatives will be used, or workers may simply be balloted on the selection and appointment of a safety representative. If no selection mechanism is in place, one should be adopted.

What is important is that the representative selected is available to represent all employees in that organisation. As a general rule the person selected should be an experienced worker, that is a person with at least two years' work experience with the employer or in a similar employment.

The 2005 Act does not lay down a specific term of office, but, in order to gain sufficient experience from knowledge and training received, a period of three years is recommended. A review of the appointment should take place perhaps on an annual basis or sooner if the safety representative is not found to be satisfactory.

WORKPLACE BEHAVIOUR AND SAFETY MANAGEMENT

Behavioural science can be said to have three main aims: to describe, explain and predict human behaviour. In order to achieve this, it has developed models of particular aspects of human behaviour. These models cannot be considered perfect as they do not explain all patterns of work-related behaviour. They can however serve as a basis on which safety management proposals may be made and effective causes of action established.

No health and safety programme is effective unless it addresses the needs of employees. Psychological factors influencing health and safety must be understood before an organisation can take effective steps to improve health, safety and welfare practice. The interaction of the individual with the physical dimensions of his/her workplace is commonly described as a 'human factor' (see below).

Ridley suggests that behavioural science allows the safety specialist to address the following issues:

- the types of hazard that the individual can spot and those he/she cannot
- the extent to which accidents can be predicted and by whom
- the time of day and the types of job where people are least likely to create hazards
- why people ignore safety rules or fail to use personal protective equipment
- what changes an organisation can make in either rules or equipment to make compliance with safety rules more likely
- knowledge required by employees to cope with emergencies
- the influence of workplace incentives such as payment
- the role of training in developing safety consciousness
- the participatory role of employees in developing a culture of safety in the organisation.

HUMAN FACTORS IN SAFETY MANAGEMENT

Human factors focus on interaction with products, equipment, facilities, procedures and the environment, the emphasis being on human beings and how characteristics of the organisation influence employee behaviour. It has been argued that a human-factors approach identifies and applies information about human behaviour, activities and limitations to the design of the workplace and uses it to explain safety behaviour. Sanders and McCormick have summarised some of the features that distinguish a human-factors perspective on health and safety from other perspectives as:

- commitment to the concept that all systems or machines are designed to serve humans and are designed with the user in mind
- belief that machine procedure and system design influence human behaviour
- recognition that people, machine procedure and the work environment do not exist in isolation
- reliance on scientific methods and objective data to test theories and generate basic data about human behaviour.

A fundamental of the human factors approach to safety management is the belief that a human being is a system. In this context a system is defined as an organised entity characterised by distinct boundaries from its own working environment. Sanders and McCormick suggest that systems as they apply to human work interaction have a number of characteristics:

- every system must have a purpose otherwise it is simply a mixture of odds and ends
- each system may be part of a larger system (sub-system)
- systems operate in an environment
- all components serve particular functions, in this regard human beings possess action functions
- all components of the system interact and have inputs and outputs.

Hale and Glendon suggest that human beings are systems capable of absorbing and processing information; accidents and ill health are perceived as damage to the system.

Human factors may be categorised as:

- *personal factors*: including attitude, motivation, perception, memory and mental ability
- *job factors*: including equipment, design, machine systems and tasks to be performed
- *organisational factors*: including formalisation, specialisation, standardisation, hierarchy of structure, complexity of organisation and professionalism
- *contextual factors*: including the size of the undertaking, technology, working environment, goals, strategies and cultural climate.

Focus on Behaviour/Attitude

The behaviour-based approach to workplace safety focuses on behaviour in the place of work. It has been suggested that approximately 96 per cent of all accidents, dangerous occurrences and near misses in the workplace are attributable either directly or indirectly to human error or behaviour. The behavioural approach to safety at work represents an alternative way of understanding why people in given situations behave as they do and how influences could be brought to bear to persuade them to behave more safely. It concentrates on the behaviour of individuals rather than their attitudes, which many safety campaigns concentrate on, the assumption being that behaviour is based on attitude. Under the behavioural approach to safety, this assumption is considered to be inaccurate; attitudes do have a tenuous link with behaviour and show how we like to see ourselves behaving rather than how we actually behave. Attempting to improve safety via attitude change is therefore extremely difficult.

Getting people to behave safely and not attempting to change attitudes assists in improving workplace attitudes to safety. The behavioural approach to safety encourages good behaviour rather than penalising poor behaviour. It is necessary to be specific in regard to the behaviour encouraged, for example defining the wearing of personal protective equipment in specific work areas. Behavioural safety programmes focus on people-oriented techniques, for example team-building, goal-setting, skills training and feedback.

Factors influencing work-related behaviour include:

- *perception*: to do something about the presence of danger, the danger must be perceived either directly through human senses or by measurement
- *evaluation/decision*: a number of factors are assessed here such as level of danger, responsibility to take action, what is appropriate action and practical considerations about that course of action
- *decisions on action*: action will involve a person's reflexes, abilities, experience and dexterity, it is recognised that age and experience reduce the level of risk-taking behaviour. Environmental factors such as work area design and layout are also important.

The attitude-based approach to workplace safety starts from the proposition that attitude influences behaviour. An attitude will be based on a predisposition to react either in a positive or negative fashion, it is not however a guarantee of particular behaviour. For example an employee may be convinced of the need to use personal protective equipment, which represents a positive attitude, but is unable to use it because it is not available. Attitudes have objectives; a worker may be favourably inclined towards accident prevention in general but may not favour a machine guard as it slows his/her rate of production. Such practical considerations may take precedence over relatively strong attitudes that lean in the opposite direction. Sometimes a worker may have no real choice, and in this instance negative attitudes of frustration and resentment will manifest themselves. Attitude has three components: a tendency to like/dislike something or someone, a predisposition to evaluate something in a positive or negative fashion and a tendency to act in a certain way (this is difficult to distinguish from stereotyping).

In our attitude to risk-taking the first aspect evaluated is perceived control, when the situation is under control the process stops there, but if control is insufficient the result is a state of general unease, which in turn produces an urge to do something. Severity of risk is only evaluated where control is seen as insufficient. Potential severity is measured in terms of magnitude of loss involving personal injury and damage; hazards with the highest rating are natural disasters since they are totally out of human control and have extremely severe consequences. The final stage in this process is the evaluation of the likelihood of mishap, and given that most people believe that being cautious is enough to be in control, this part of the evaluation is frequently not carried out.

Assessing the likelihood of an accident/incident is usually subjective and generally speaking people are not good at this. The likelihood of an accident is perceived as much lower when a worker feels he/she is in control. Amongst the most potent factors of influence are the attitudes of reference groups to which the worker wants to belong. If a worker feels the need to be accepted by a particular work group and if the view prevalent in that group is bravado, then this worker will adopt a risk-taking attitude. The closer this group comes to the worker, the more potent the influence that it exercises.

ATTRIBUTION THEORY IN SAFETY MANAGEMENT

Behaviour is influenced by both internal and external factors and attribution theory is concerned with an understanding of what causes the behaviour of others. Anecdotal evidence suggests that when an accident happens in the workplace there is often too much concentration on internal attributes and not enough on external factors. If individual weaknesses can be blamed then this means that the organisation is 'off the hook' and need not examine too closely weaknesses in organisational structure. An explanation based solely on internal factors will also pose problems for workplace risk management because internal factors such as being accident-prone or having a poor attitude to work-related safety are extremely difficult to change.

SAFETY INSPECTIONS

Safety inspections are a means of observing and evaluating unsafe work conditions and practices in the workplace, such inspections are an essential part of any safety programme because conditions of work and work practices are in a state of constant change due to stock depletion, disposal of waste materials, wear and tear of machinery, changes in the layout of workplaces, etc. A safety inspection should provide for:

- *detection*: seek out unsafe conditions and methods of work
- *analysis*: establish why these unsafe conditions exist
- *correction*: eliminate these unsafe conditions and methods.

Examples of what to check in a safety inspection include:

- *building conditions*: the state of repair of flooring, walls, stairs, ceilings, ramps, platforms and driveways
- *housekeeping*: waste disposal, proper storage of tools and materials, spillages and leakages, cleanliness of windows and floors and tidiness of work areas
- *electricity*: all electrical installations including cables, switches and plugs, in particular check for damage to cable extensions
- *lighting*: type and intensity of lighting used, issues of glare and shadow must be addressed
- *heating and ventilation*: type and efficiency of systems used, and where local exhaust ventilation is used it should be checked both for cleanliness and efficiency
- *machinery*: all machinery should be checked for its safe use including maintenance and adjusting of machinery
- *storage and shipping areas*: safety in layout, loading procedures, loading equipment, height of loading and floor loads.

PREPARING FOR A SAFETY INSPECTION

Preparation requires the following steps:

- planning in advance of the procedures that are to be followed
- review available records on the past history of the area to be inspected
- obtain and study all relevant information on the hazards likely to be encountered in the inspection
- prepare a list of specific items required to be checked
- procure safety information, including posters, for distribution on the inspection.

When carrying out an inspection one should be in possession of the following equipment: pencil and notebook, hard hat, goggles, flashlight and measuring tape.

Plan the route of your inspection and have specific objectives in mind such as machine-guarding and/or housekeeping. It is important to observe operations in sequence by following the material from first process through to shipping. The inspection should take account of general hazards such as lighting and ventilation and specific hazards such as tools, machines and other equipment, work practices also need to be observed to establish how the work is actually done.

Inspection Tips

A person carrying out a safety inspection should:

- make notes of the inspection but avoid being obvious in doing so
- not disturb or disrupt operations
- adopt a constructive approach, seeking answers to problems observed but only for the purpose of taking appropriate corrective action
- seek the assistance of supervisors
- not interview an employee without first seeking the permission of his/her supervisor
- discuss particular problems with supervisors without getting involved in arguments about those issues
- having completed the inspection, be in a position to discuss recommendations with both line supervisors and top management
- make sensible and well-argued recommendations.

Workplace Audits

A workplace audit will involve interviewing key people in the organisation, asking questions, reviewing documentation and observing conditions in the place of work. It is crucial that the person carrying out a workplace audit has an understanding of the organisation to be audited. The auditor must be sure to interview the right people, be prepared and spend a short time initially explaining the audit process to those being interviewed. Any information required should be quickly obtained to allow that person to return to work as soon as possible. A more formal approach is required when interviewing senior management and it may be necessary to make an appointment to meet senior managers. The auditor should only ask questions that require feedback: open questions that begin with who, why, where or how require informative answers and generally speaking such questions cannot be answered with a simple yes or no. Combining such questions with a request to show the auditor what happens enables what has been said to be verified. Whilst interviews may be recorded on tape, many persons are uneasy at this approach and it can therefore distort the answers given. Auditors recording interviews by hand should only write down key points because this will keep the interview moving.

The range of documents required to be reviewed depends on the scope and the focus of the audit. An examination of documents before interviewing persons who carry out the activities specified in the documents is useful because a gap often exists between what management thinks is happening and the actual practice in the workplace.

OBJECTIVES OF THE AUDIT

An audit may have several objectives and it is important to understand the exact nature of the particular audit undertaken. An audit could, for example, look at the entire facility, at a single operation at work, at a single issue such as personal protective equipment or at technical aspects of work such as compliance with best practice standards for that type of work.

Auditing can be classified into three categories:

- *horizontal auditing*: in this type of audit each working area must be examined for compliance with relevant heath, safety and welfare requirements
- *vertical auditing*: this involves auditing across different areas of the organisation in a specific safety area, for example training in the correct use of personal protective equipment. Such audits should adopt a logical sequence from purchase through correct use and level of protection afforded
- *random auditing*: this involves particular aspects of the operation, in which the auditor simply determines what is to be examined, for example a need may be felt to probe part of the work system or to examine a particular process after a serious incident/accident has occurred.

INTERNAL/EXTERNAL AUDITS

The advantages attached to the employment of an auditor from within the organisation would be the relatively low cost of such an audit and the knowledge of the organisation already gained by that auditor, employers may also feel that a breach of confidence could occur through the employment of an external auditor. Disadvantages of an internal auditor could be summarised as too much familiarity with the problem, lack of objectivity through being too close to the problem and familiarity with the existing workforce.

External auditors would be expected to bring an independent viewpoint and are frequently selected by employers because of their expertise in particular aspects of work and because they are capable of bringing that high level of expertise to the problem. The major disadvantage in external audits is their cost and for that reason internal audits are held more frequently.

A team approach to auditing is considered the best as it improves cooperation between management and employees, including their safety representatives.

AUDIT PLANNING

Audit planning has five functions:

- *description*: parties responsible are identified and their role outlined
- *definition*: the nature and scope of the audit is crucial to establish before commencement
- *designation*: clearly identify the roles of all participants
- *communications*: all reporting procedures must be clear
- *record-keeping*: audit reports should be retained for future reference and review.

REVISION QUESTIONS

1 What is meant by loss control in the context of managing workplace safety?
2 List the categories of persons to whose attention the contents of the safety statement must be brought.
3 List five methods of risk control in common use.
4 What are the particular categories of workers that must be borne in mind when carrying out a risk assessment?
5 Outline in brief the role and function of the safety representative.
6 What are said to be the three aims of behavioural science in the context of the workplace?
7 What are the principal factors that are said to influence work-related behaviour?
8 What are the three matters that a safety inspection should provide for?
9 What are the circumstance in which an external auditor would be preferred in the carrying out of a safety audit?
10 List the five functions of audit planning.

REFERENCES

Hale, A. and Glendon, I. (1987), *Individual Behaviour in the Control of Danger*, cited in T.N. Garavan (2002), *The Irish Health & Safety Handbook*, 2nd edn, Dublin: Oak Tree Press

Health and Safety Authority (2006), *Guide to the Safety, Health and Welfare at Work Act 2005*, Dublin: Health and Safety Authority

Health and Safety Authority (2006), *Guidelines on Safety Representatives and Safety Consultation*, Dublin: Health and Safety Authority

Health and Safety Authority (2007), *Annual Report 2006*, Dublin: Health and Safety Authority

Ridley, J. (1993), *Safety at Work*, cited in T.N. Garavan (2002), *The Irish Health & Safety Handbook*, 2nd edn, Dublin: Oak Tree Press

Safety, Health and Welfare at Work Act 2005

Sanders, M.S. and McCormick, E.J. (1992), *Human Factors Engineering and Design*, cited in T.N. Garavan (2002), *The Irish Health & Safety Handbook*, 2nd edn, Dublin: Oak Tree Press

5
Safety in the Construction Industry

This chapter outlines the legal duties imposed by the Safety, Health and Welfare at Work Construction Regulations 2006 on the client, project supervisor design stage, project supervisor construction stage, contractors on site, the mandatory safety representative, safety officer, safety advisor and employees. Safety issues that arise on construction sites and the introduction of new regulations for working at heights on such sites are discussed. The health, welfare and safety of those employed on construction sites are also addressed, as are legal requirements for site welfare provisions.

The Construction Regulations 2006 came into force on 6 November 2006, however Regulation 1 allows for their limited phasing-in to allow parties to familiarise themselves with new preparation, design and management duties and with the new standard form construction and engineering contracts being developed by the Government Contracts Committee, which operates under the aegis of the Department of Finance. The Safety, Health and Welfare at Work Construction Regulations 2001 will continue to apply to project supervisors design and construction stages appointed before the 2006 Construction Regulations came into force on 6 November 2006. If project supervisors were not appointed before that date, the 2006 Regulations will apply.

CONSTRUCTION SKILLS CERTIFICATION SCHEME

The Construction Skills Certification Scheme, which was initiated by the 2001 Regulations, provides for skills certification by the Irish Training Authority (FÁS) for certain categories of workers in the construction trade. The 2006 Regulations (Regulation 25) provide for five additional categories of certification from 6 May 2008:

- mobile tower scaffold, unless the employee is already a certified scaffolder under the 2001 Regulations
- mini-digger operator, unless the employee is already trained and certified as an excavator operator

- signing and lighting on public roads
- locating underground services
- shot firing.

The 2006 Regulations are wide ranging and cover not only building and engineering projects but also general maintenance of both buildings and equipment.

DUTIES OF THE CLIENT

The client is defined under the 2006 Regulations (Part 2, Regulation 6) as a person for whom a project is carried out in the course or furtherance of a trade, business or undertaking, or who undertakes such a project directly in the course of a trade, business or undertaking.

It is the duty of the client to appoint, in writing, competent persons to fill the roles of project supervisor at design and construction stages. The client shall obtain from such persons written conformance of their acceptance. Nothing in these Regulations prevents the client from appointing him/herself to either position, provided he/she is competent to undertake that role, or from appointing one individual or company to fill both roles. These appointments shall be made in the case of the design stage at or before its commencement, and in the case of the construction stage, also at or before its commencement. Any such appointment can, where necessary, be made, terminated, changed or renewed. The above rules do not apply in relation to a person's domestic dwelling or where the project is not in furtherance of trade or business.

A client shall not under these Regulations appoint a project supervisor for either the design or the construction stage unless satisfied that adequate resources have been or will be allocated to allow that person to satisfactorily discharge his/her functions. No contractor or designer should be appointed under these Regulations unless he/she is a competent person, has the resources to carry out the task allocated and will comply with all relevant legal requirements.

A client is required under these Regulations to keep available any safety file he/she has in relation to the project and to pass that file to the subsequent owner when he/she disposes of his/her interest in the project. The person to whom the file is passed must keep that file available for inspection. The client shall provide a copy of his/her health, safety and welfare plan for the project to any person either being considered for the role of project supervisor construction stage or tendering for that position. If construction work is planned to last longer than thirty working days or the volume of work is scheduled to exceed five hundred person days, the client shall give the Health and Safety Authority such particulars in writing as are known at the time about the appointment of the project supervisors for the design and construction stages.

DUTIES OF THE PROJECT SUPERVISOR DESIGN STAGE

The duties of the project supervisor for the design stage of a construction project are set out in Regulations 11 to 14 of the 2006 Construction Regulations. The project supervisor design stage must take account of the general principles of prevention during the various preparation and design stages of the project and in particular when either technical or organisational aspects of the work are being decided. In order to plan the orderly running of the project, and when estimating the time of stage or final completion, the project supervisor design stage:

- will take account of any available safety plan/file
- will ensure that activities of designers on the same project be coordinated with the aim of protecting the health, safety and welfare of employees
- may appoint a competent person to coordinate health, safety and welfare for the design process.

The project supervisor design stage is required to provide a written safety and health plan for the information of the project supervisor construction stage. The plan must include:

- a general description of the project and the timeframe for its completion
- information on any other work activities on that site
- details of particular risks to the health, safety and welfare of employees that may arise from the proposed activities
- details of how the timeframe for completion is calculated
- conclusions drawn as to the implementation of the general principles of prevention and any relevant safety and health plan or file
- the location of electricity, water and sewage connections to facilitate appropriate welfare facilities.

This safety and health plan must be prepared in good time in order that it may be provided as required to every person tendering for the position of project supervisor construction stage. A copy of the plan must be kept for a period of five years after preparation for inspection by a health and safety inspector.

The project supervisor must also prepare a safety file, containing all relevant health, safety and welfare information pertaining to the construction work to be undertaken and must deliver this file promptly to the client on completion of the design project.

DUTIES OF THE PROJECT SUPERVISOR CONSTRUCTION STAGE

The duties of the project supervisor for the construction stage of a construction project are set out in Part 2, Regulation 16 of the 2006 Construction Regulations. The project supervisor construction stage must:

- further develop the safety and health plan if necessary before commencing construction
- coordinate the implementation by contractors on site of the general principles of prevention
- ensure the implementation of all statutory regulations by contractors on site
- organise cooperation between contractors on site
- provide appropriate information to the site safety representative
- coordinate procedures for checking on work practices
- coordinate measures to prevent unauthorised entry to the site
- coordinate arrangements for the provision of site welfare facilities
- ensure that all required to do so have a valid safety awareness card and, where relevant, construction site skills certification
- coordinate the construction site certification scheme
- keep records of safe pass and construction site certification
- facilitate and coordinate consultation between contractors on site
- facilitate the appointment of a site safety representative
- inform the site safety representative when a health and safety inspector arrives on site
- take account of representations made to him/her by the site safety representative.

DUTIES OF PROJECT SUPERVISOR CONSTRUCTION STAGE NOTIFICATION TO THE HSA

Regulation 22 of The Health, Safety and Welfare at Work (Construction Regulations) 2010 sets out that if construction work on a building site is planned to last longer than 30 working days, or the volume of work scheduled is likely to exceed 500 person days, then the project supervisor for the construction stage before the work commences shall give written notice to the Health and Safety Authority. The minimum particulars to be set out in any such notice are contained in the 7th Schedule of the 2010 Regulations:

- the client's full contact details
- the contact details of the project supervisor design stage and the health and safety coordinator, if appointed
- the contact details of the project supervisor construction stage and the health and safety coordinator, if appointed
- information on construction work to include description of project, address of construction site, planned date for commencement and termination including estimate of construction time, maximum numbers of workers on site and planned numbers of contractors and self-employed persons
- details of contractors chosen
- date notice forwarded to the Authority
- signature and position of sender.

In order to assist in the reporting process the Health and Safety Authority has made available an approved form (Form AF2) that can be completed either electronically or downloaded for manual completion. It is not mandatory to use this form provided that the information set out in Schedule 7 is contained in your notice.

DUTIES OF ON-SITE CONTRACTORS

The duties of on-site contractors on a construction project are set out in Part 3, Regulation 24 of the 2006 Construction Regulations. On-site contractors must:

- cooperate with the project supervisor construction stage to enable that person to discharge his/her legal duties
- provide the project supervisor construction stage with any information likely to affect the health, safety and welfare of employees on site or that might justify a review of the safety and health plan
- provide information in relation to any accident or dangerous occurrence that the contractor is obliged to notify the Health and Safety Authority about
- promptly report in writing all information necessary for the preparation of a safety file

- comply with all lawful directions given by the project supervisor construction stage
- ensure that all relevant workers under their control are currently registered under the safety awareness certification programme
- ensure that all workers required to undergo construction site skills certification have done so and are in possession of a current registration card
- confirm to the project supervisor construction stage that all relevant workers are in possession of current safe pass certification and construction site skills certification where required.

ON-SITE CONTRACTORS–SAFETY PRECAUTIONS

Regulation 51 of the Health Safety and Welfare at Work Construction Regulations 2010 provides that any contractor responsible for a construction site shall ensure that adequate safety precautions be taken in any excavation, shaft, earthwork, underground works or tunnel in order to:

- guard against danger from a fall or dislodgement of any material
- guard against dangers from falls or the inrush of water into any excavation, underground works or tunnel
- secure adequate ventilation and limit any gases, fumes, dust or other impurities to levels that are not dangerous or injurious to health
- guard against fire and flooding
- enable persons to reach safety in the event of an emergency
- avoid risks to persons from possible underground dangers such as cables or pockets of gas
- provide a safe means of access to and egress from each workplace.

Other important aspects of these Regulations include:

- these Regulations do not apply to any excavation that is not likely to either trap or bury a person
- these Regulations do require that anyone in the vicinity of the excavation must be protected from dislodgement of the sides of the excavation
- any person engaged in shoring or other work required must comply with these Regulations and must be similarly protected
- the Health Safety and Welfare at Work Act 2005 requires that a risk assessment be conducted before any excavation work is commenced
- the risk assessment should identify the hazards associated with the work undertaken such as the nature of the ground and ground water, depth

of excavation, nature and location of work within excavation, (For example, is it readily accessible? Is the ground contaminated? Is it in a heavily serviced urban area?)

- all factors likely to increase the risk of excavation collapse must be explored. Non-exhaustive examples include loose soil, the presence of groundwater, proximity to other excavations, weather conditions and undercutting of the road pavement structure.
- the above factors may change from day to day, and for that reason it is essential to keep all risk assessments under review and to introduce additional protective measures if necessary
- poor ground conditions may necessitate the installation of trench supports even in relatively shallow excavations of less than 1.25 metres deep. Supports may also be necessary if the nature of the task requires workers to lie or crouch in a trench.

Contractors engaged on a construction site are required to consult with employees, their safety representatives and the site safety representative in relation to the legal requirements of these Regulations and to take account of the need for cooperation with employees and the different safety representatives.

MANDATORY SITE SAFETY REPRESENTATIVES

The project supervisor construction stage shall, where twenty or more workers are employed on a construction site, in cooperation with other contractors and employees on site, facilitate the appointment of a site safety representative. For the purpose of the effective performance of his/her duties, the project supervisor construction stage shall ensure that the site safety representative has access to:

- the risk assessment required to be carried out by virtue of Section 19 of the Safety, Health and Welfare at Work Act 2005
- information relating to accidents and dangerous occurrences that are required to be reported to the Health and Safety Authority
- any information arising from protective or preventive measures required by law to be taken or any information supplied by the Health and Safety Authority or any person prescribed by the Authority to perform specified duties under the 2005 Act or to enforce it.

The project supervisor construction stage shall inform the site safety representative:

- when a health and safety inspector enters a construction site for the purpose of carrying out an inspection
- the time and place of all site safety meetings and facilitate the attendance of that representative.

A site safety representative for a construction site may inspect the whole or part of a construction site:

- after giving reasonable notice to both the project supervisor construction stage and the contractor employing him/her
- immediately in the event of an accident, dangerous occurrence or imminent danger or risk to the health, safety and welfare of employees.

The frequency of inspections will be agreed between the project supervisor construction stage, the contractor and the site safety representative, however agreement to such inspections may not be unreasonably withheld.

A site safety representative may:

- investigate accidents and dangerous occurrences on site. However, he/she is not permitted to interfere with or obstruct the performance of any statutory duty by a person authorised to do so
- investigate health, safety and welfare complaints made by any employee he/she represents, having given reasonable notice of this intention to the project supervisor construction stage and to his/her employer
- accompany an inspector carrying out an inspection other than where an investigation of an accident or dangerous occurrence is taking place
- at the discretion of the inspector, accompany an inspector who is investigating an accident or dangerous occurrence
- where an employee is being interviewed in connection with an accident or dangerous occurrence, attend that interview at the invitation of the person interviewed and at the discretion of the inspector
- make representations to both the contractor and project supervisor construction stage on any health, safety and welfare matter, these representations should not be limited to the investigation of accidents and dangerous occurrences
- receive advice and information from health and safety inspectors on matters relating to health, safety and welfare
- consult and liaise with any other safety representatives that may be appointed at that construction site.

The project supervisor construction stage and, where appropriate, any contractor engaged on the construction site are obliged to take account of any health, safety and welfare issue raised by the site safety representative. The 2006 Regulations (Part 2, Regulation 23) require contractors who employ site safety representatives to allow that representative adequate time off from his/her duties without loss of income to:

- acquire sufficient knowledge to discharge his/her duties effectively as a site safety representative
- discharge his/her functions as a site safety representative.

SAFETY OFFICER AND SAFETY ADVISOR

The Construction Regulations 2006 require the appointment of a safety officer and a safety advisor in the following circumstances.

SAFETY OFFICER

Every contractor who normally has at any one time twenty employees on a construction site or thirty persons engaged in construction work shall appoint one or more competent persons to act a safety officer. The safety officer's role is:

- to advise the contractor on his/her statutory duties in relation to the health, safety and welfare of his/her employees
- to supervise health, safety and welfare practice on site
- where necessary, to cooperate with the safety advisor where appointed.

Nothing in these Regulations prevents a safety officer from being appointed to a number of sites, or a number of contractors appointing the same safety officer. A person appointed as a safety advisor may also be appointed a safety officer.

When appointing a safety officer the contractor should ensure that the person appointed is competent to discharge the function, has experience of the work being undertaken and knowledge of how to control hazards associated with the work and has completed sufficient training such as the Institution of Occupational Safety and Health's (IOSH) Managing Safety in Construction Programme or another safety management programme. The safety officer appointed must be given adequate time and resources to discharge the functions specified in the 2006 Regulations (Part 3, Regulation 26).

SAFETY ADVISOR

Part 2, Regulation 18 requires the project supervisor construction stage to appoint a full-time competent safety advisor where more than one hundred persons are employed on site. The role of the safety advisor is to advise both the project supervisor construction stage and contractors on site of their duties under relevant statutory enactments and to exercise general supervision of safe work practices.

The project supervisor construction stage must make reasonable enquiries to check the competence of the person selected as safety advisor. The advisor should preferably have management experience in construction and possess the appropriate health and safety training, for example a recognised certificate in health and safety management of construction and a higher certificate or degree in safety, health and welfare at work. It is also desirable that the person chosen have experience of the type of work to be undertaken.

It should be noted that the presence on site of a safety advisor does not relieve any employer or contractor of their own statutory duties to plan, manage, monitor and take corrective action in the place of work.

DUTIES OF EMPLOYEES

The duties of employees on a construction project are set out in Part 3, Regulation 29 of the 2006 Construction Regulations. Employees must:

- fully comply with health, safety and welfare legislation
- cooperate fully with their employer and fellow employees in discharging legal responsibilities
- report to their employer any defect in equipment that might endanger health, safety or welfare
- make proper use of all personal protective equipment
- comply with all health, safety and welfare rules that apply to employees
- make proper use of all work equipment
- show the relevant registration card when requested to do so by the project supervisor construction stage or by their employer.

Employees must not:

- make a false statement when applying for a registration card
- forge or alter either a registration card or a certificate
- make or supply with intent to deceive any registration card or certificate.

WELFARE AND SANITARY FACILITIES ON CONSTRUCTION SITES

Regulation 17 of the 2006 Construction Regulations set out the requirements for welfare and sanitary facilities on construction sites. Safe access to facilities shall be provided and every such place shall be kept safe for those using the facilities. Suitable facilities for pregnant workers, nursing mothers and disabled workers must be provided where required.

WELFARE REQUIREMENTS

In the immediate vicinity of any construction site, shelters and accommodation for clothing and partaking of meals must be provided. This accommodation is required to take account of such factors as shelter during inclement weather, provisions to warm and dry wet clothing and facilities to boil water and heat food. There must be an adequate supply of wholesome drinking water.

In deciding on the suitability of accommodation provided, regard will be had to the factors outlined above, the number of persons using the accommodation, any transport provided to transport workers to and from the site – if for example accommodation for partaking of meals is provided off site and transport is available to convey workers to and from the site that will satisfy the Regulations.

CHANGING ROOMS AND LOCKERS

Changing rooms and lockers shall be provided for workers required to wear special work clothes and if, for reasons of health or propriety, they cannot be expected to change in another area. Any such changing room must be of sufficient size and be provided with seating. Where a danger of contamination exists, separate facilities are required to house personal clothing. Separate changing facilities must be provided for men and women. No changing facilities are required on sites where five or fewer workers are employed, however facilities must be provided to lock away clothing and personal effects.

WASHING FACILITIES

Adequate and suitable washing facilities are required to be provided at every construction site. Where there is reason to believe that construction will not be completed within thirty working days, adequate washing troughs or basins should be provided, together with a suitable means of washing and drying and an adequate supply of warm water. Where work on site is likely to extend beyond twelve months and one hundred or more employees are engaged on the site, a minimum of six wash basins must be provided with an addition of one extra basin per twenty workers thereafter. If dangerous substances are used on site, one wash basin per five workers should be supplied.

Washing facilities must be clean, convenient to accommodation for meals, well lit and ventilated, as a minimum requirement. Provisions should be made for separate use of facilities by men and women. Showers, where provided, must be adjacent to changing areas.

SANITARY CONVENIENCES

A minimum of one such convenience per twenty workers should be provided and, where practicable, such facilities should discharge into the main sewer. Every sanitary facility shall be well ventilated and not directly connected to a work or mess room. Each such unit, with the exception of urinals, shall be sufficiently partitioned and have a door that is capable of being fastened to ensure privacy. Where practicable, sanitary facilities should be convenient to washing facilities. They must be kept in a clean and hygienic condition and provision must be made for either separate access to or separate use of those facilities by women and men.

CONSTRUCTION SITE SAFETY

Regulation 17 of the 2006 Construction Regulations sets out further requirements for construction site safety.

ACCESS TO CONSTRUCTION SITES

The 2006 Regulations require contractors on site to ensure that:

- surroundings and perimeter of site be signposted and laid out in a manner that is clearly visible to all
- means of access and egress to and from the site be provided and clearly signposted
- precautions be taken to prevent injury to persons present or in the vicinity of the site, and, where necessary, barriers to prevent unauthorised entry erected.

EMERGENCY ROUTES AND EXITS

The 2006 Regulations require contractors on site to ensure that:

- all emergency routes be kept free of obstruction in order to allow quick and efficient evacuation in the event of an emergency
- entry and exit points be capable of taking account of maximum possible usage
- specific emergency routes be indicated by signs
- all emergency exits be kept free at all times of obstruction
- illumination, where required, be provided.

SITE TRAFFIC

The Regulations require that site machinery and traffic arrangements on construction sites be subject to a risk assessment. Details of all necessary control measures must be included in the site safety plan and those measures implemented on an ongoing basis. Site conditions such as temporary roadways, excavations, wet conditions and piles of debris all pose significant site hazards and, in terms of operating site traffic, hazards should not be tolerated just because the site is a temporary one. At the very least a hard surface is required for the safe movement of traffic, and this should be provided at the earliest possible time after the site opens. Roadways must be maintained in a safe condition and not be permitted to deteriorate.

All site machinery and vehicles must be checked regularly for defects in tyres, brakes and lights. The following rules need to be observed:

- avoid loading and unloading on other than flat surfaces
- always drive up and down a slope never across it
- never overload vehicles
- distribute loads evenly when loading
- if operating near overhead power lines with machinery, the ESB must be notified
- if possible, the reversing of vehicles should be avoided
- a one-way traffic system for vehicles should be introduced.

When reversing vehicles:

- use a one-way system only
- exclude pedestrians where reversing is unavoidable
- provide a banks man
- fit audible warning devices
- fit proximity indicators.

Employees driving or using site machinery must be both trained and qualified to do so. A driver must:

- have full responsibility for the safety of the vehicle
- never leave a vehicle unattended when the engine is running
- never enter or leave a vehicle while it is moving
- if possible, park only on level ground
- never carry passengers on moving vehicles
- strictly observe the site speed limit
- never overload vehicles
- avoid fast cornering and sudden braking with loaded vehicles
- never remain in the cab when a vehicle is being loaded.

In addition:

- straps securing loads must be removed with care
- a banks man must always be present when tipper trucks are loaded or unloaded
- the tipper body of a truck should be lowered as soon as possible
- tipper trucks should not move off with the body still raised
- dumpers, except when inching forward, should never travel with the body raised.

Pedestrians likely to come into contact with moving vehicles must wear high visibility vests.

SITE SIGNS

Prominent signs must be erected at the entrance to all construction sites clearly outlining the precautions to be taken by all entrants to that site. All site safety rules must be fully complied with.

OVERHEAD POWER LINES

The Construction Regulations 2006 (Regulation 41) require pre-planning and the carrying out of a risk assessment in any situation where the risk of contact with overhead power lines exists. Details of necessary safety procedures must be included in the site safety plan and these procedures must be monitored on an ongoing basis. Proper training in hazard identification and risk control must be given. Scaffolding, platforms or ladders should never be erected in the vicinity of power lines without prior consultation with the electricity supply company.

To ensure safe working practices:

- pre-plan and consult with the electricity authorities
- divert power via a safer route
- use access routes away from the danger zone
- where no work or movement is necessary under power lines, erect barriers not less than six metres from the lines
- determine the distance barriers are needed from power lines after consultation with the electricity company (voltage of electricity carried determines the distance of barriers from the lines)
- use coloured bunting to increase the visibility of barriers
- where access under power lines is necessary, the width should be restricted (ten metres maximum) and clearly signposted
- post notices highlighting the hazard at the site entrance and along the route to the lines
- indicate the safe working height of any jib or load
- do not disturb the ground at the base of either pylons or poles for a distance of three metres.

WORKING AT HEIGHTS

The Safety, Health and Welfare at Work (Working at Heights) Regulations 2006 apply to the construction industry and require that working at heights be properly planned and supervised and carried out safely without risk to the health, safety and welfare of employees. For these purposes, planning is required to take account of:

- selection of suitable work equipment
- appropriate assessment of risk
- planning for emergencies and rescue
- weather conditions, work at heights should only be carried out where weather conditions do not endanger the work.

Regulation 5 concerns the avoidance of risk when working at heights. Such work should only be undertaken where it is impossible to do otherwise. An employer shall take suitable measures to prevent an employee falling from a distance likely to cause injury. Measures here would include ensuring that work be carried out from an existing place of work or that access to the place of work be gained by existing means. If it is not feasible to carry out work in the manner indicated the employer must provide suitable work equipment to prevent falls occurring. Where these measures fail to eliminate the risk of falling, an employer is required to:

- provide sufficient equipment to minimise the distance of a potential fall
- provide additional training and instruction
- take additional measures to prevent as far as possible the risk of an employee falling a distance likely to cause injury.

The additional measures indicated above include selection of work equipment designed to work at heights that takes account of:

- working conditions including risks where the equipment is to be used
- where the equipment is designed for use in accessing heights, the distance and height to be negotiated
- distance of potential fall
- duration and frequency of use
- the need for timely evacuation
- any additional risk posed by either the installation or removal of equipment.

An employer shall select equipment that has suitable characteristics appropriate to the nature of the work to be performed and any foreseeable load. The equipment used must allow for the safe passage of employees and be in all other respects suitable for use.

Where guard rails are used as a means of protection, these must be of sufficient dimensions, strength and rigidity for the purpose used and be so placed and secured as to ensure that they do not become accidentally displaced. The purpose of guard rails is to prevent, as far as possible, the fall of any employee, material or object from any place of work. In construction work the top such guard rail is required to be a minimum of 950 millimetres above the edge from which an employee may fall.

SCAFFOLDING

Regulations 5 to 9 of the Working at Heights Regulations 2006 deal with the safe use of scaffolding. The stability of scaffolding will always be affected by how it is used. Prior to erection, therefore, an assessment must be carried out to evaluate its likely use. The most commonly used scaffolding is the independent variety without sheeting. This type must be tied to the building. A tie is generally required for every thirty-two square feet of scaffolding erected. Should the scaffolding be either sheeted or netted, additional ties are required. In addition:

- netting or sheeting is required where there exists either a danger of falling objects or the scaffolding is erected adjacent to a public place
- additional ties are required where chutes, hoists, lifting appliances or loading platforms are used
- ties should either be secured through a window to a wall or tied to a column
- all scaffolding must be braced, which necessitates the fixing of diagonals
- uprights should always stand on base plates
- ground, if soft, should be well compacted and levelled
- bricks or other loose materials are not suitable bases for scaffolding
- timber sole boards should be used to spread the load
- the working platform must be wide enough for safe use, the recommended width is four boards, however three boards may be used where no materials are lodged on the platform.

Scaffold platforms from which persons may fall more than two metres should be fitted with guard rails and toe boards. The top guard rail or other similar means shall be at least 950 millimetres above the edge from which an employee may fall. Any supporting structure for a working platform shall be stable and of suitable composition to support the structure, working platform and any intended load; mobile structures must be supported by appropriate devices to prevent accidental movement. Every working platform from which an employee may fall must be inspected within the previous seven days in that position. In the case of a mobile platform on the site, a report of that inspection must be compiled within twenty-four hours of that inspection and a copy handed to the employer and retained for inspection. Every fall protection measure should be visually inspected before use and thereafter at regular intervals.

Never:

- work from a platform not fully boarded
- overload a platform
- allow unauthorised access to platforms
- allow scaffolding to be erected by workers not certified and experienced enough to do so.

Always:

- deny unauthorised access by removing the method of access or by erecting hoarding
- inspect scaffolding before use and at least once weekly thereafter
- ensure ladders used are free from defects
- ensure that all scaffolding that is not the property of the user is inspected before use
- use competent persons only to erect and dismantle scaffolding
- use a chute to bring waste material to ground level
- prevent objects falling from platforms.

LADDERS

Regulation 6 of the Working at Heights Regulations 2006 deals with the safe use of ladders. In the construction industry one of the most common causes of fatal accidents is falling from heights, and a significant percentage of these accidents are caused by the incorrect use of ladders. Typical causes of accidents include:

- ladders not properly secured at the top or bottom
- climbing ladders with loads
- overreaching
- overbalancing.

These causes are indicative of the fact that ladders are being used in particular situations where either scaffolding or a raised platform would be a safer option. If the work is of long duration then scaffolding or a platform would be safer than a ladder.

When using a ladder, ensure that:

- the base always rests on firm level ground
- the base never rests on loose or makeshift material
- if possible, it is lashed at top and bottom
- if it is not possible to secure at the top, secure at the end or the ladder must be footed by a second person whilst in use
- the person footing the ladder remains there whilst it is in use, footing is not suitable if the ladder extends beyond five metres
- only suitable ladders are purchased
- manufacturer's instructions as to correct use are followed
- only one person uses a ladder at any given time
- it is maintained in good condition and stored properly when not in use

- it extends more than one metre beyond the work area
- the top rests against a firm surface (PVC chutes are not suitable).

Never:

- carry out work from a ladder that requires the use of both hands at the same time
- attempt to carry awkward loads up a ladder (a pouch should be used to carry tools).

When using a stepladder, ensure that it is properly secured on level ground before use and never use the top platform.

DANGER AREAS

Regulation 10 of the Working at Heights Regulations 2006 deals with danger areas. Any area where a risk of injury to employees exists from falling objects should as far as practicable be fitted with devices to prevent unauthorised access and should be suitably signposted. Work equipment, working platforms, scaffolding, fall arrest systems and ladders are required to be inspected at regular intervals in their work position. Details of such inspections should be retained at the employer's office.

ROOF WORK

Schedules 4 and 5 of the Working at Heights Regulations 2006 deal with roof work. Roof work continues to be the most hazardous occupation in the construction industry, with one in every five workplace deaths resulting from falls. Safety procedures are necessary for both routine and specialist repairs to roofs. Preventive measures include:

- all roof work must be subject to risk assessment
- prior to commencement of roof work, a detailed safety plan must be prepared which should be made part of the safety statement
- any risk assessment must fully address both human and material falls
- implementation of any detailed plan should be left to a competent person
- any extensive roof work will require barriers or guard rails, which must be strong enough to stop a human fall
- suitable purpose-built ladders or crawling boards are essential on sloping roofs
- never secure a roof ladder by lashing it to ridge tiles.

The level of risk will depend on:

- the pitch of the roof
- the nature of the surface
- prevailing weather conditions
- the surface (smooth surfaces made slippery are very dangerous).

Regulation 8 of the Working at Heights Regulations 2006 deals with fragile roofs:

- fragile roof materials are likely to shatter under pressure
- walking along the purlin bolt line on a roof is dangerous as it is akin to walking a tightrope
- roof ladders and crawling boards must always be used
- barriers should be erected around roof openings, or alternatively these openings could be covered
- where a roof covering is not substantial this fact should be clearly signposted.

Any initial risk assessment must consider the range of personal protective equipment required for roof work. A safety helmet with chinstrap would be essential. If a safety harness needs to be worn, only those trained in its use should wear one. Emphasis must be placed on the limitations of any such equipment and the manufacturer's instructions as to testing and maintenance must be fully followed.

Revision Questions

1. List the five additional categories of workers that skills certification is now required for by virtue of the Construction Regulations 2006.
2. What are the duties of the project supervisor design stage under the Construction Regulations 2006 with regard to the preparation of the safety file?
3. List five duties of the site contractor under the Construction Regulations 2006.
4. Outline the role and function of the mandatory safety representative under the Construction Regulations 2006.
5. Outline the legal requirements for the appointment of a safety officer on a construction site.
6. Outline the general duties imposed on employees by the Construction Regulations 2006.

7 List the principal provisions of the Working at Heights Regulations 2006.

8 What are the minimum legal requirements for the provision of sanitary facilities on construction sites?

9 Under the Construction Regulations 2006, what are the duties of contractors with regard to access to construction sites?

10 What are the safety requirements necessary for working on fragile roofs?

REFERENCES

Health and Safety Authority (2006), *Guidelines on the Procurement, Design and Management Requirements of the Safety, Health and Welfare at Work (Construction) Regulations 2006*, Dublin: Health and Safety Authority

Safety, Health and Welfare at Work Act 2005

Safety, Health and Welfare at Work (Construction) Regulations 2001

Safety, Health and Welfare at Work (Construction) Regulations 2006

Safety, Health and Welfare at Work (Work at Height) Regulations 2006

6
Welfare Issues in the Workplace

This chapter addresses the legal issues involved in workplace welfare issues such as equality in the workplace, bullying and violence at work, and the right to workplace leave including maternity, parental, carer's and force majeure leave. It examines relevant employment legislation and outlines the role and function of the state bodies involved in the enforcement of work-related rights. It also addresses the role of the employer and the employee in combating work-related harassment and issues arising from working in an increasingly diverse culture.

DISCRIMINATION

The Employment Equality Act 1998, in force since 1 January 2000, outlaws nine grounds of discrimination with regard to employment and training: gender, marital status, family status, sexual orientation, religious belief, age, race, disability and membership of the Travelling community. The Act defines a number of key terms, including discrimination both direct and indirect, sexual harassment, general harassment and disability.

Discrimination is simply treating one person in a less favourable way than another person would be treated. Indirect discrimination is different in the sense that the circumstances appear to be non-discriminatory, but in fact they affect a particular group; an intent to discriminate need not be shown here. For example, a workplace dress code that prohibits the wearing of head coverings may offend the sensibilities of particular religious groups. A way to overcome this problem would be to provide for a variety of styles in the dress code.

Section 23 of the 1998 Act defines sexual harassment as an act of physical intimacy other than an act that no reasonable person would consider offensive, any request for sexual favours and any other conduct that could with reason be considered offensive, humiliating or intimidating. The Act covers situations where A and B are employed at the same place by a common employer, or B is A's employer or B is A's customer or business contact. Under the Act, if the circumstances are such that the employer should have taken steps to prevent the conduct complained of, it constitutes discrimination on the ground of gender and the employer is legally responsible.

Section 32 of the 1998 Act prohibits general harassment in the workplace, which occurs where an employee suffers harassment because of his/her particular characteristics. The employer has a legal responsibility here if an employee, client or customer acts in circumstances that the employer should be aware of. An employer may have a legal defence to general harassment where he/she can show that reasonable steps were taken. The legislation places a legal onus on employers to promote a harassment-free environment.

Ireland's Defence Forces are now covered by the Act and may direct a claim to the Equality Tribunal provided internal procedures are first utilised and either twelve months have elapsed since the complaint was lodged or the complainant is unhappy with the outcome.

There are exclusions from the terms of the Act, including under the headings: artist's model, actress, pregnancy, maternity, care of the elderly, An Garda Síochána, Prison Service, citizenship, Irish language for the public sector, educational qualifications, posts where gender is an occupational qualification, employment in the family home, privacy, decency, and discrimination by religious to preserve their ethos.

This Act does not apply to those who have reached normal retirement age in Ireland (sixty-five years). It is not unlawful under the Act to set maximum age limits for entry to certain employments which take account of the period of training and the need for a reasonable period in that employment before retirement.

ACCOMMODATING DISABILITY

In March 2009 the Health and Safety Authority issued guidelines entitled *Employees with Disabilities Health and Safety Guidance*. It has been issued under guidance from the National Disability Authority. Its aim is to assist employers in providing a safe and healthy environment for workers with disabilities. The 2005 Health Safety and Welfare at Work Act states that employers must ensure as far as is reasonably practicable the health, safety and welfare of all its employees. The 2007 General Application Regulations in Regulation 25 states that an employer shall ensure that places of work where necessary be organised to take account of workers with disabilities, to include welfare facilities, access and workstations.

DISABILITY

About one in ten Irish people has some form of disability, ranging from physical impairment to mental health problems and including visual and hearing impairments. Some forms of disability are less obvious, such as epilepsy, asthma or mild hearing impairment. Frequently, employees with such disabilities will choose not to disclose it, as they fear that the focus will fall on their disability and not on their ability to perform the tasks for which they were employed. It is good health and safety practice to create a supportive environment and to communicate this openness to all employees thus enabling all employees with a 'hidden' disability to disclose it in the knowledge that they will not be judged on their disability. Studies have shown that workers who feel respected in their place of work are more productive and less likely to be absent from work, so a working environment that is inclusive and where all employees including those with disabilities feel comfortable makes good business sense. Advances in technology in particular have helped to ensure that workers with disabilities can work safely and effectively at many jobs provided their specific issues are dealt with and their needs built in to health and safety planning.

ACCOMMODATING DISABILITY AT WORK

The Employment Equality Acts 1998/2004 oblige employers to take all appropriate measures to provide reasonable accommodation to persons with disabilities to have access to employment, including both advancement and training. Employers, however, are not obliged to incur disproportionate costs in complying with this obligation. Measures to be undertaken may include training resources, and the adaptation of premises, work stations and equipment to make them more accessible to the disabled worker. Some practical examples might include hands-free telephone sets or distributing tasks in such a way that those hard of hearing need not take minutes. It should be noted that an employer is not obliged to provide any facility or treatment that employees can reasonably be expected to provide for themselves. In some cases, private sector workers may qualify for workplace equipment adaptation grants. Applications in this regard may be made to FÁS.

PLANNING AND MANAGEMENT

It is important to consider the different needs that employees may have so that health and safety planning can cater for their diverse needs. During induction and at job review meetings it is sound practice to ask the employee if s/he has any particular health or safety requirements. This should be done regardless of whether the employer is aware of an employee's disability.

DEVELOPING AN INCLUSIVE POLICY

Employers should prepare an inclusive health and safety statement. A policy on issues such as safety, bullying and health will form part of every safety statement. Developing this policy involves:

- risk assessment
- measures to control the risks identified
- consultation with employees with disabilities.

The risk assessment must take account of any particular risk for those with disabilities. It should identify any specific hazards for staff members with the following conditions:

- restricted mobility
- limited dexterity
- impaired vision
- impaired hearing
- mental disability
- health conditions such as heart problems, epilepsy or asthma.

Keeping in mind that workers may have undisclosed disabilities, it must be assumed that disability is a factor in your health and safety planning. Written records of risk assessments must be kept and include inputs from those competent to carry out the assessment of affected workers, these assessments must be updated as necessary for health and safety purposes. The next step is to consider what control measures are necessary based on your risk assessment. These are simply preventative measures put in place to protect their employees, which must take account of any worker with disabilities. These measures are, generally speaking, simple, involving little or no financial cost. It is advisable to consult both with employees and with organisations that provide services for the disabled to help to develop a policy of inclusion. It is important to ensure that your policies on safety are actually being implemented. Trip hazards, for example, pose a risk to both disabled and non-disabled workers. Regular reviews of safety policies should be undertaken, and it is good practice to have a worker with a disability on the safety committee to help with these reviews.

SAFE EVACUATION OF EMPLOYEES WITH DISABILITIES

Different disabilities pose different challenges to safe evacuation in an emergency, and any evacuation plan must take account of the needs of workers with disabilities. Individual consultations will be necessary to establish whether an individual needs a personal emergency evacuation plan. These plans should be modified or changed in response to any issue that arises during routine fire drills. Planning for safe evacuation should include the following steps:

- initial review of user needs
- develop an exit policy for the organisation
- plan safe evacuation
- implement the evacuation plan
- measure evacuation performance
- review your evacuation performance
- never presume that there is no staff member with a disability, as many disabilities are not apparent.

MATERNITY PROTECTION

The Maternity Protection of Employment Act 1994 provides protection for the following categories of workers: all pregnant employees, employees who have recently given birth and breastfeeding employees. No length of service at work is required to qualify for benefit under this legislation, employees on fixed-term contracts are also covered provided the pregnancy occurs before the expiration of the term of the contract.

Since 1 March 2007 the period of maternity leave qualifying for payment under the Act is twenty-six weeks; at the discretion of the pregnant worker, another unpaid period of a maximum of sixteen weeks is also provided for. During the twenty-six weeks of maternity leave an allowance is payable which is equivalent to 70 per cent of the aggregate income of that worker during the previous twelve months; this is subject to a minimum weekly payment, so workers who have no income for that period will still receive the allowance. Where the employer pays the employee during the period of maternity leave, as in, for example, the civil and public service, the maternity allowance will be paid to the employer.

Where a child is legally adopted, the mother is entitled to a maximum of fourteen weeks' adoptive leave with an allowance payable as with maternity leave; should the employer pay the worker during adoptive leave, he/she is entitled to be paid the adoptive benefit for that worker.

Pregnant workers are entitled without loss of pay to attend both antenatal and post-natal appointments with their doctor. In the case of post-natal appointments the provision only applies for a period of not more than fourteen weeks after birth. Written notice of the employee's intention to attend antenatal or post-natal appointments must be given to the employer not less than fourteen days from the date of that appointment.

It is very important that all notices given under the Act be in writing, for example a month's notice in writing must be given to the employer of the intention of the employee to avail of maternity leave and must be accompanied by a medical certificate confirming the pregnancy. Similar notice must be given of the worker's intention to resume her employment, otherwise the employer is not legally bound to hold her position pending her return. Copies of all correspondence with the employer and replies from him/her should be kept by the employee for a minimum period of twelve months.

Where health and safety risks are identified and it is not possible to give suitable alternative work to the employee, paid health and safety leave must be offered to that employee. Under the legislation the employer is obliged to make payment for the first three weeks of that leave, it should be noted that this is in addition to maternity leave and is not in any way to be considered a substitute for it. The leave in the first three weeks may be taken in shorter periods and need not be continuous. If the employee is on a fixed-term contract and the leave coincides with the end of the contract, the leave ends.

The Act imposes a legal duty on employees to notify the employer when they are no longer vulnerable to the risk identified.

All employment rights are preserved during maternity leave, adoptive leave and health and safety leave. During additional maternity leave, the employment relationship continues but rights based on reckonable service may be affected. Health and safety leave will cease when the employer either removes the risk or finds suitable alternative work and so notifies the employee; the employee must notify the employer when no longer vulnerable to the particular risk or when she has ceased breastfeeding. The employer is obliged in both instances to return the employee, in so far as it is reasonable to do so, to her previous job status.

If an employee is dismissed as a result of exercising her rights under the 1994 Act, such dismissal is considered automatically to be unfair by virtue of the Unfair Dismissals Acts 1977 and 1993. The 1985 case of Flynn *v* Power and the Sisters of the Holy Faith shows that a narrow view may be taken of what constitutes exercising your rights under the legislation. In this case, decided under the provision of the Maternity Protection of Employment Act 1981, the Employment Appeals Tribunal subsequently confirmed at Circuit and High Court levels that Ms Flynn was dismissed not for exercising her rights under the Act (even though she was in fact pregnant and had notified her employer of this) but because her private behaviour (living openly with a separated man in a small town) adversely affected the business of the employer (the provision of a Catholic education to secondary school girls).

Any disputes not pertaining to dismissal may be referred to a rights commissioner within six months of the dispute arising. Any decision by the rights commissioner may be appealed within four weeks to the Employment Appeals Tribunal.

GUIDE FOR THE PROTECTION OF PREGNANT, POST-NATAL AND BREASTFEEDING EMPLOYEES

In December 2007 the Health and Safety Authority published a guide to Chapter 2 of Part 6 of The Safety, Health and Welfare at Work Regulations 2007, which deals with the protection in the workplace of pregnant, post-natal and breastfeeding employees. The enactment of these Regulations replaces and revokes the Safety Health and Welfare at Work (Pregnant Employees, etc.) Regulations 2000. The 2007 Regulations are made under The Safety Health and Welfare at Work Act 2005.
Definitions:

- *employee*: an employee who is pregnant, breastfeeding or post-natal, having recently given birth
- *pregnant employee*: an employee who is pregnant
- *breastfeeding employee*: an employee who, having given birth not more than twenty-six weeks previously, is breastfeeding
- *post-natal employee*: an employee who gave birth not more than fourteen weeks ago

These regulations apply when an employee informs her employer that she is pregnant and provides an appropriate medical certificate of her condition. As the early stages of pregnancy are the most critical for the developing child, it is in the best interest of the employee to inform her employer of her pregnancy as soon as possible.

RISK ASSESSMENT

The employer must assess any risk of exposure to any agent, or any risk occurring during any process or in any working condition, determining the nature, degree and duration of any such exposure or risk. Having carried out this assessment the employer must take whatever steps necessary to avoid any adverse effect on the pregnancy or breastfeeding. By virtue of Section 18 of The Health Safety and Welfare at Work Act 2005 the employer is obliged to appoint a competent person to put into effect any control measures necessary for the health and safety of the pregnant or breastfeeding worker. The competent person appointed should if possible be a fellow employee. If the risk assessment identifies possible exposure to specified risks, the employer must ensure that pregnant and breastfeeding employees not be exposed to those risks and not be required to perform any task that would expose them to such risks.

PROTECTIVE OR PREVENTIVE MEASURES

Where the risk assessment reveals a risk to the health and safety of an employee or any possible adverse effect on the pregnant or breastfeeding worker and it is not possible to ensure the health and safety of that worker through either protective or preventive means, the working conditions or working hours, or both, should be adjusted to avoid risk to the worker. Where it is not feasible to adjust hours or conditions, measures must be taken to provide the worker with other work that does not pose any health and safety risk. When the risk assessment identifies a specific risk or risks to the pregnant or breastfeeding worker, the employer must establish if there are any practical ways that the risk can be avoided. There are three steps that may be taken in this regard.

- Step 1: adjust the working hours or conditions or both. If this does not work,
- Step 2: provide suitable alternative work. If this is not possible,
- Step 3: Health and Safety Leave under Section 18 1994 Maternity Protection of Employment Act should be granted by the employer.

It should be noted that Step 3 only applies where it is not possible to use the control methods outlined in Steps 1 and 2.

NIGHT WORK

Night work means working between 11 p.m. and 6 a.m. the following day and where a worker works a minimum of three hours during that period or where the worker spends a minimum of 25 per cent of working hours during a month working night hours. Should a registered medical practitioner certify it to be necessary for the health and safety of the employee, the employer shall not require her to perform night duty during pregnancy or for the fourteen weeks following childbirth. Should this occur, the employer must remove the employee from night work by transferring her to day work or, if this is not possible, grant the employee leave.

INFORMATION

An employer must by law ensure that employees be provided with information concerning the results of any workplace risk assessment undertaken on behalf of the employer and any control measures to be taken that concern the health and safety of employees.

SPECIFIC HAZARDS

Unless the risk assessment indicates that no health and safety risk exists, pregnant employees must not work in pressurisation chambers, with rubella, toxoplasma, lead and lead substances or in underground mine work. Where the worker is breastfeeding, unless the risk assessment indicates no health and safety risk, the worker should not work with lead or lead substances or in underground mine work.

AGENTS

Some physical agents are regarded as agents that can cause foetal lesions or disturb placental attachment or both, such as:

- shocks, vibration or movement
- manual handling
- noise
- ionising and non-ionising radiation
- extreme temperatures
- movements, postures and physical fatigue connected with the activity of the employee

- biological agents (other than toxoplasma and the rubella virus), in so far as it is known that these agents, or the measures necessitated by the presence of these agents, endanger the health of pregnant employees and/or the foetus.
- Chemical Agents that carry one or more of the following risk phrases:

  a R40 limited evidence of a carcinogenic effect
  b R465 may cause cancer
  c R46 may cause genetic damage
  d R49 may cause cancer by inhalation
  e R61 may cause harm to the unborn
  f R63 possible risk of harm to the unborn
  g R64 may cause harm to breastfed babies
  h R68 possible risk of irreversible effects

Other chemicals known to be harmful include carbon monoxide, mercury and cytotoxic drugs.

PARENTAL LEAVE

Parental leave is unpaid and, by virtue of the Parental Leave Regulations 2000, extends to the parents of natural and adopted children up to eight years of age. A period of fourteen weeks is permitted per qualified child and must in each case be availed of before the child reaches his/her eighth birthday. As a general rule an employee must have twelve months' service; however, employees with more than three months' service are entitled to a maximum of three weeks' parental leave. Section 7 of the Parental Leave Act 1998 provides that this leave may be taken in one block or, by prior agreement with the employer, even in days or hours. Section 8 of the Act provides that six weeks' notice must be given to the employer of the employee's intention to avail of this leave, this notice must be confirmed in writing at least four weeks before commencement of the leave. If an application does not fall within this procedure, the employer has the discretion to grant or refuse it. Once the employer has received a document confirming the taking of parental leave, the employer and employee may agree to vary, curtail or postpone the leave in any manner agreed.

Section 11 of the Act permits an employer to object to the granting of parental leave if he/she is of the view that granting the leave would have a substantial and adverse effect on his/her business. Reasons for objection include:

- seasonal work variations
- a substitute is not available
- nature of duties
- employee numbers
- other applications that coincide with that of the applicant.

In those circumstances the employer must give notice to the applicant, not less than four weeks before leave is due to commence, postponing the intended date of commencement for not more than six months. A period of consultation should always precede any such notice. Only seasonal variation allows postponement of parental leave more than once.

FORCE MAJEURE LEAVE

Force majeure leave is provided for by Section 13 of the Parental Leave Act 1998, here an employee is entitled to paid time off where the immediate presence of the employee is required for urgent family reasons owing to the injury or illness of an immediate family member. Paid leave up to three days in any twelve consecutive months or five days in any thirty-six consecutive months can be granted. The Irish Business and Employers Confederation (IBEC), which is the employers' representative body, for the purpose of this leave regard the taking of a part day as a whole day. IBEC prefers to refer to this leave as emergency leave and is concerned that it may be treated as additional paid sick leave by employees.

No service requirements are necessary to avail of force majeure leave and all employment rights are retained during the leave. The giving of prior notice to the employer does not arise as this leave by its very nature only arises in an emergency situation.

Immediate family member is defined as a child (biological or adopted), the spouse or the person with whom the employee lives as husband and wife, a person the employee is in loco parentis of, brother, sister, parent or grandparent of the employee. The scope of the Act in this regard is quite clear and categories outside the above definition are not covered by the Act.

Illness is not defined, but it must be substantial, and the employee's presence must be indispensable. This legislation is poorly drafted in this regard because its failure to define what constitutes illness under the Act has given rise to disputes concerning the essential presence of the employee.

Another area with the potential for problems is the requirement that employees notify their employer as soon as practicable of the leave to be taken, giving an outline of the reasons for availing of it. Problems can arise from the second part of this requirement, as employees may be reluctant to divulge details of the illness of a third party. Strictly speaking, the medical details of a person's illness may not be divulged without their consent and in any case it should not be necessary for the employer to be given full details of the illness.

A written formal notice of the availing of force majeure leave must be completed by the employee. Employers can tailor this notice to suit their individual needs provided it contains the essential requirements. This form of notice does not absolve the employee of the obligation to inform the employer of his/her absence as soon as possible in accordance with company rules. Independent evidence to support an application for force majeure leave is not required. An employer may however seek proof to establish that an employee did not take leave inappropriately or fraudulently, but there exists no mechanism for dealing with an abuse of force majeure leave.

Any dispute that arises about entitlement to force majeure leave (or parental leave) may be referred to a rights commissioner in writing within six months of the dispute arising. The decision of the rights commissioner may be appealed to the Employment Appeals Tribunal by giving written notice to the Tribunal within four weeks of the date the decision of the rights commissioner became known. The rate of appeal to date has been quite low. Redress may be ordered by either the rights commissioner or the Tribunal, and this may consist of either the granting of the leave sought or the payment of financial compensation up to a maximum of twenty weeks' pay.

In Carey *v* Employment Appeals Tribunal, Ms Justice Carroll in the High Court overturned the findings of the Employment Appeals Tribunal and directed the employer to pay the employee a day's wages under force majeure leave. Having discovered a rash on her child, the employee was concerned that her child could be seriously ill. Justice Carroll took the view that the rights commissioner and the Tribunal were overly restrictive and that it was reasonable in the circumstances then known for the employee to take the view that her presence with her child was indispensable. She was further of the view that Section 13 of the 1998 Act should not be interpreted based on facts that became known after the event as to whether the illness was serious enough to warrant leave. It should be noted that this is the first time a decision of both a rights commissioner and the Employment Appeals Tribunal has been reversed.

Where there is a refusal or failure to comply with the decision of the rights commissioner or the Employment Appeals Tribunal, the employee or the Minister for Justice may apply to the Circuit Court where the business of the employer is situated for a compliance order. The decision of the Circuit Court may be appealed to the High Court on a point of law only.

PROTECTION AGAINST DISMISSAL

An employee is protected against dismissal if they either exercise or propose to exercise their right to avail of either force majeure or parental leave. Protection is also available if an employee is not permitted to return to work following a period of either force majeure or parental leave.

CARER'S LEAVE ACT 2001

The Carer's Leave Act 2001 provides for the temporary absence from employment of employees for the purpose of providing full-time care to a person who requires it. The Act is designed to protect the rights of employees with more than one year's service with the same employer. Under this Act employers are prohibited from denying employees the right to avail of carer's leave. The key requirements of carer's leave are:

- the employee must be in continuous employment with the same employer for not less than twelve months
- the person in need of care must require full-time care
- the employee must provide the employer with a written decision from a deciding officer in the Department of Social and Family Affairs
- proof may be required that the employee will provide full-time care to the relevant person
- only one employee is entitled to carer's leave in respect of the same person
- during a period of carer's leave an employee may only engage in limited paid employment.

An employee who meets the legal requirements for obtaining carer's leave will be entitled to take that leave for a period not exceeding sixty-five weeks. It may be taken in one continuous block of sixty-five weeks or in a number of periods that in total do not exceed the permitted period. An employer may on reasonable grounds refuse a period of leave of less than thirteen weeks' duration, but the employee must be informed in writing of the reasons for that refusal. An employee must give a minimum of six weeks' notice to the employer of his/her intention to avail of carer's leave, though this notice may in exceptional circumstances be waived. The notice must include:

- the proposed commencement date of the leave
- the duration of the leave
- a copy of the deciding officer's decision or a copy of the application to the deciding officer.

Prior to receiving confirmation from the deciding officer, an application for carer's leave may be withdrawn. Both the employer and employee must sign a confirmation document not less than two weeks before the proposed commencement of carer's leave.

PROTECTING EMPLOYMENT RIGHTS

An employee's right to annual leave and public holidays is maintained only during the first thirteen weeks of carer's leave. This leave is expressly stated as not being part of any other leave to which the employee is entitled. A period of either probation or apprenticeship may be suspended during a period of carer's leave. During a period of carer's leave the employee may undertake limited employment either at home or outside for a maximum period of ten hours per week. A similar weekly period is allowed for further training, education or voluntary work.

A minimum period of four weeks' notice is required to be given to the employer of the employee's intention to return to work. As the 2001 Act provides for continuity of employment, the employee on return to work should enjoy the same conditions of employment that he/she enjoyed prior to availing of carer's leave.

DISPUTES AND REDRESS

A rights commissioner deals with disputes relating to the employer's interpretation of the 2001 Act, an employer penalising an employee for exercising his/her rights under the Act and employee disputes about entitlement. The deciding officer in the Department of Social and Family Affairs deals with the following disputed issues:

- an employer's opinion as to whether the relevant person is in need of full-time care
- an employer's opinion that the employee does not qualify for carer's leave
- an employer's opinion that an employee is undertaking work prohibited by the Act.

An employee may refer a dispute in writing to a rights commissioner within six months of the alleged breach; appeals against a decision of the rights commissioner may be taken to the Employment Appeals Tribunal within four weeks of the issue of that decision. Two forms of legal redress are available:

- confirmation of the employee's right to carer's leave
- financial compensation with a ceiling of twenty-six weeks' pay.

The Circuit Court for the area where the business is situated is the final legal arbiter on the facts arising from a dispute under this Act. Points of law arising from the interpretation of the Act may however be referred to the High Court.

ORGANISATION OF WORKING TIME

The Organisation of Working Time Act 1997 sets out basic standards for all workers with the exception of members of the Defence Forces and An Garda Síochána, sea fishermen, doctors in training, persons employed in the household of a relative, and the self-employed. The Minister for Enterprise, Trade and Employment is empowered to make regulations under this Act exempting further categories of employees from the provisions of the Act, and has to date also exempted the Prison Service, fire fighters and airport police.

In order to demonstrate compliance with the provisions of the 1997 Act, the employer must keep records of hours of work and holiday pay for his/her employees during the previous three years.

REST BREAKS AND INTERVALS AT WORK

A fifteen-minute rest break must be provided in a working period of four and a half hours, and a rest period of thirty minutes must be provided in any working period of six hours. An amendment introduced at committee stage of the Bill allowed shop workers to retain their traditional entitlement to a break of one hour. The 1997 Act provided for a maximum working week of forty-eight hours to be introduced on a phased basis over two years. Any agreement reached on the phasing in of this provision required the approval of the Labour Court. With regard to the working of night hours, a maximum average of eight hours per night over a two-month reference period with a weekly maximum of forty-eight hours is allowed. A collective agreement for a particular industry may extend the reference period beyond two months.

PROVISION OF INFORMATION

An employee is entitled to be notified in advance of the hours he/she is required to work if starting and finishing times of work are not contained in the contract of employment. The legal requirement is a minimum of twenty-four hours' notice unless the hours are already well known; in an emergency an employer may give less notice.

ZERO HOURS WORKING CONTRACTS

In the case of zero hours working contracts an employee is either asked to be available for work or informed that work will be available on a certain day or days. The 1997 Act provides that payment must be made for 25 per cent of contract hours or fifteen hours, whichever is the lesser, where the employer fails to employ the employee for 25 per cent at least of the required contract hours.

COMPLAINTS PROCEDURE

Complaints must be submitted in writing to a rights commissioner within six months of the dispute arising, this period can in exceptional circumstances be extended to twelve months. Within six weeks of the issue of the decision of the rights commissioner, an appeal can be lodged with the Labour Court. A determination of the Labour Court solely on a point of law may be appealed to the High Court. Any failure to implement a decision of a rights commissioner may be enforced through the Circuit Court of the area where the business is situated.

The Minister for Enterprise, Trade and Employment may prosecute for breaches of this Act. Decisions of the Labour Court include, for example, that:

- travelling time (a payment peculiar to the construction industry) is not a reckonable allowance for the purpose of holiday pay
- crane drivers employed on the docks are dock workers for the purpose of this Act and therefore not entitled to exemption from rest breaks under the Act.

More than 90 per cent of the cases that come before the Labour Court, relate to disputes over holiday entitlements, including disputes about leave arrangements, amount of leave and payment of leave.

THE EQUALITY AUTHORITY

The board of the Equality Authority is appointed by the Minister for Justice, Equality and Law Reform. It is a twelve-member board with an independent chairperson and vice-chairperson; all board members serve a four-year term of office.

The Employment Equality Act 1998 outlaws discrimination on the following grounds: gender, marital status, family status, sexual orientation, religion, age, disability, race and membership of the Traveller community. All aspects of employment are covered and the legislation applies to both public and private sector employment. It covers such matters as advertising, trade union and professional bodies and collective agreements in industry. An employer, an employment agency or a vocational training body will be liable for harassment of their employees, clients, customers or other business contacts unless reasonable steps are taken to prevent the harassment. Complaints under the Act must be brought within six months of the last act of discrimination; this time limit will not apply in equal pay cases. It is unlawful to penalise an employee for taking action to enforce this legislation.

If an employee is discriminated against, the Equality Authority recommends that he/she take the following steps:

- raise the complaint initially with his/her employer, which will provide an opportunity to resolve the issue within the organisation
- if he/she is not satisfied with the response of the employer, he/she should consider contacting the Equality Authority, a solicitor or a trade union
- persons who choose to contact the Equality Authority directly are advised of their general legal position. At this stage it is the practice of the Authority to ask the complainant to fill in a questionnaire, which assists the Authority in deciding on the best course of action to adopt in addressing the complaint
- if the complaint becomes the subject of an investigation by an equality officer (or an equality mediation officer of the Equality Tribunal), the complainant may represent him/herself, or be represented by his/her trade union or solicitor. This is a matter of choice for the complainant and legal representation is not necessary. The Equality Authority may in the first instance endeavour to achieve a settlement without invoking the legal process. The Authority may provide legal representation free of charge for a client. It is important to note that the Authority has no power to make an award for costs of private legal representation.

THE EQUALITY TRIBUNAL

The 1998 Act also established the Office of the Director of Equality Investigations (known as the Equality Tribunal). This office is not connected in any way to the Equality Authority; it is an office established by the Minister for Justice, Equality and Law Reform and has powers to investigate cases taken under the 1998 Act. It has two methods of operation: mediation and investigation. The Director may refer a claim to an equality mediation officer unless either party objects, in which case an investigation is conducted by an equality officer. Cases involving dismissal from employment are dealt with in the first instance by the Labour Court. In employment cases, decisions of the Director are enforceable through the Circuit Court. A person discriminated against on the gender ground may decide to seek redress in the Circuit Court, where the normal ceiling in civil cases of €100,000 does not apply. A decision of the Director may be appealed to the Circuit Court for the area where the business is situated not later than six weeks from the date of the decision. All decisions of the Director may be appealed to the Labour Court, the Labour Court will then issue legally binding determinations. Such determinations may only be appealed on a point of law to the High Court. The Labour Court is empowered to refer questions arising from the interpretation of the law of the European Union to the European Court of Justice for interpretation.

In cases involving equal pay, an award in respect of a period of not more than the preceding three years' pay may be made. In dismissal cases, the Labour Court is empowered to order reinstatement or re-engagement with or without financial compensation.

THE RIGHTS COMMISSIONER SERVICE

The Rights Commissioner Service, which is now part of the Labour Relations Commission, was established by the Industrial Relations Act 1969 and is empowered to deal with individual grievances arising in a wide range of areas, including parental, carer's and force majeure leave.

Hearings by rights commissioners are private and informal. Both parties to the dispute make a written submission setting out the points of their respective arguments. A rights commissioner then commences proceedings by confirming the legislation the claim is brought under and hearing the arguments from both sides. Having heard submissions, the commissioner may wish to see each party individually in order to assess whether a basis for settlement exists. If no basis for settlement exists, the commissioner will ask each party if they wish to advance further arguments and inform them that a written recommendation will be issued in the case. All recommendations of the commissioner are private to the parties in dispute. Any recommendation of a rights commissioner may be appealed to the Labour Court or Employment Appeals Tribunal as appropriate. The appeal must be made within six weeks of the issue of the determination.

THE EMPLOYMENT APPEALS TRIBUNAL

The Redundancy Payments Tribunal was renamed the Employment Appeals Tribunal by the Unfair Dismissals Act 1977. The Tribunal consists of a chairperson, 31 vice-chairpersons and a panel of 72 other members consisting of 36 nominees from the Irish Congress of Trade Unions (ICTU) and 36 representatives of employer organisations. The Tribunal acts in divisions consisting of either the chairperson or a vice-chairperson and one representative drawn from the employer and one from the employee panel. Members of the Tribunal are appointed by the Minister for Enterprise, Trade and Employment for a period of three years. The chairperson and vice-chairpersons must be solicitors or barristers; no special qualifications are expressed for the members of the employer and employee panels.

Claims before the Tribunal may arise on the termination of the contract of employment or during its continuation. A claim that arises on the termination of the employment contract is in general made directly to the Tribunal. Such claims include unfair dismissal, redundancy payments, minimum notice requirements and holiday entitlements. A claim for unfair dismissal can in the first instance be made either to the Tribunal or to a rights commissioner; the Tribunal cannot however hear a claim for unfair dismissal unless the employer or employee objects in writing to the hearing of the case by a rights commissioner (form TI-4 must be utilised to initiate a complaint or appeal before the Tribunal).

Both employers and employees should pay particular attention to the time limits set out in the various pieces of employment-related legislation as the Tribunal has no power to hear cases that are out of time. The unfair dismissals legislation, for example, provides for a six-month time period to commence proceedings, but the Tribunal may in exceptional circumstances extend that period to twelve months.

The Tribunal chairperson will conduct the hearing and outline the procedures to be followed. Hearings of the Tribunal are conducted in accordance with the laws of evidence, but a liberal view of the rules of evidence is adopted and matter that may not be introduced in a court of law may be allowed by the Tribunal. It is preferable if the parties before the Tribunal reach agreement in advance, at least on the non-controversial issues of the case, for example wages paid and length of service. If further issues can be agreed, that is all the better, as this leaves the Tribunal to deal only with the core issue(s) in dispute. Evidence before the Tribunal is usually given under oath and must be relevant to the matter at issue.

On completion of evidence, the Tribunal will ask the parties their attitude to the various legal remedies available. It is important to note that the remedy granted is at the discretion of the Tribunal and that no inference should be drawn as to the decision made from asking the parties their attitude to the remedies on offer. Tribunal remedies involve:

- *reinstatement*: this puts the claimant into the position he/she was in immediately prior to dismissal, preserves all statutory and employment entitlements and requires all wages and salary due be paid to that person from the date of dismissal
- *re-engagement*: this puts the claimant back into the same or a different position on such terms and conditions as the Tribunal sees fit and from a date to be decided by the Tribunal.

Compensation can be awarded as a remedy where neither of the above is considered suitable. The award is limited to actual financial loss up to a limit of two years' gross remuneration, which can include the cost of benefits to the employee provided by the employer. There is a caveat to the awarding of compensation and it is that the Tribunal will expect the dismissed employee to take all reasonable steps to obtain suitable alternative employment and any failure to do so will be taken into account by the Tribunal in arriving at the amount of compensation due.

It is important to note that bringing a claim to the Tribunal is a free service and if a party chooses to be professionally represented he/she is responsible for that cost. The legislation under which the Tribunal was established does not require that a party be represented at the hearing and no disadvantage will accrue to any party who chooses to represent him/herself.

A determination of the Tribunal may be appealed to the Circuit Court within six weeks of its receipt by both parties. If the determination is not appealed, the employee can take steps to have the decision implemented by the Circuit Court for the area where the business (employer) is situated.

A total of 3,113 claims were referred to the Tribunal and 2,908 were disposed of in 2006, the average waiting period from date of receipt of claim to hearing in the Dublin area was twenty-seven weeks and in provincial areas was forty-four weeks. In that same year the Tribunal disposed of 1,171 cases for unfair dismissal and a total of 261 appeals against the recommendations of rights commissioners.

The final report of the Employment Appeals Review Group, published in April 2006, accepts that there may be validity in the viewpoint that the procedures before the Tribunal have become more legalistic than envisaged by the Tribunal's original concept, which was to provide a simple procedure for dispute resolution without the intervention of a court of law. The problem with the Tribunal has always been that claimants have to meet their own legal expenses and many who come before the Tribunal believe that they need both legal advice and representation at the hearing, especially where they are employed in non-unionised employment. In its interim report, the review group recommended the introduction of an in camera preliminary proceeding which the group claim would speed up proceedings at the substantial hearing, this hearing would be chaired by an experienced member of the Tribunal. However, the holding of the preliminary hearing will not prevent the raising of a substantial issue not raised at preliminary stage at the substantial stage, a cynical observer might simply view this as an unnecessary additional layer to an increasingly complicated system. The review group, however, sees this preliminary hearing as a method of focusing the minds of parties on the issues involved and facilitating an early resolution.

Another recommendation of the review group is that the hearing process be underpinned by a process of formal training in procedures for both vice-chairpersons and Tribunal members, this recommendation may involve a programme of continuous professional development in employment rights and practice; best practice in the conduct of Tribunal proceedings; and the issuing of legally consistent determinations. If implemented, such a programme could only be seen as a welcome enhancement of the present process.

THE LABOUR COURT

The Industrial Relations Act 1946 is of considerable significance for two reasons: first, with some legislative amendment, it remains the key piece of industrial relations legislation in terms of dispute resolution; and second, it established the Labour Court.

The key function of the Labour Court is to settle industrial disputes. It has three divisions headed by a chairperson and two vice-chairpersons respectively; and it has six ordinary members: the Irish Congress of Trade Unions (ICTU) and the Irish Business and Employers Confederation (IBEC) nominate three members each, these nominees are then appointed by the Minister for Enterprise, Trade and Employment. Despite its title, the Labour Court is not a legally constituted court of law and its recommendations cannot be legally enforced, where found necessary to do so an order may be sought in the Circuit Court to enforce its findings. It has, however, power to summon witnesses, hear evidence on oath and, where the parties so agree, issue binding recommendations.

THE LABOUR RELATIONS COMMISSION

The Industrial Relations Act 1990 provided the legal framework for the establishment of the Labour Relations Commission. The Commission comprises a chairperson, representatives of employer and employee bodies and two independent members appointed by the Minister for Enterprise, Trade and Employment. The Commission has under its umbrella conciliation, rights commissioner and equality services. It is empowered to issue codes of practice and the minister may refer an industrial dispute affecting the public interest to either the Commission or the Labour Court.

Since the enactment of the 1990 Act, the Commission investigates and conciliates in industrial disputes. Before the Labour Court can now investigate an industrial dispute it must receive a report from the Commission stating that it cannot resolve the matter and that both parties to the dispute have requested that the Labour Court investigate. If there is a direct reference to the Labour Court in respect of an issue in dispute, agreement must exist between the disputing parties to accept the Court's recommendations.

VIOLENCE AT WORK

Violence at work occurs where persons are verbally abused, threatened or assaulted in circumstances that relate to their work. In 2006, over 5 per cent of all accidents reported to the Health and Safety Authority were violence-related.

In a booklet first published in 1996 and revised in November 2007, the Health and Safety Authority highlights the issue of work-related violence. Workplace violence occurs when persons in employment are aggressively verbally abused, threatened or assaulted. Every year more than 5 per cent of all workplace accidents in Irish workplaces are due to violence. The most vulnerable sector according to the Authority is public administration and defence at 17 per cent of all reported accidents, followed by health and social work at 16 per cent. Other sectors such as education, financial and retail are at 7 per cent followed by the transport and services sectors at 3 per cent.

THE EFFECTS OF VIOLENCE

The effects of violence on the victim are both immediate and longer-term. The physical injury caused may need first aid and medical treatment. The absence of the employee due to his/her injury can increase costs such as the employer's liability to increased insurance premium payments, compensation payments and hospital costs. In addition, those who experience violence frequently suffer a loss of self-confidence, feel insecure, no longer feel in control, and may be subject to panic attacks. The effects of violence on fellow employees cannot be underestimated, especially those who have witnessed the violent incident. It has been found that violence in the workplace can cause a lack of morale in the workforce and may make it difficult to recruit and retain staff.

WHAT THE LAW REQUIRES

Both the Health Safety and Welfare at Work Act 2005 and the General Application Regulations of 2007 place a legal onus on employers to ensure as far as is practicable the health and safety of employees. Thus all employers are required to carry out risk assessments of all workplace hazards, and, based on this assessment and workplace consultation, prepare a safety statement. The risk assessment will establish the potential for violence in the workplace and put in place appropriate safeguards. It must be remembered that violence is always a potential hazard where interaction occurs between people and it must be assessed accordingly. It may be necessary in some workplaces to look at arrangements made for getting to and from work or moving around the grounds of premises, and lone workers, those required to work late at night and those employed in areas with a history of violence are particularly vulnerable.

ESTABLISHING IF A PROBLEM EXISTS

The only way to establish if a problem exists is to examine all work practices under your control, discuss existing work practices with staff, and examine accident records, paying particular attention to previous attacks and especially the circumstances under which they occurred. Ongoing vigilance is crucial to avoid future incidents. Assessments can be carried out informally by asking staff at meetings, or formally, either through audits or questionnaires. Any assessment must include full consultation with all staff on all violence-related issues. Employees can be assisted in many ways in combating the problem of potential violence, and can be forewarned of the dangers where known.

HIGH-RISK AREAS

Experience has shown that workers engaged in the following activities are at higher risk of violence: providing care, advice or training, working with the mentally disturbed and addicts, inspection duties, handling money or valuables and working alone.

SITUATIONS THAT CAUSE OR WORSEN VIOLENCE

When reviewing your workplace for potential violence, it is useful to look at the situation from the perspectives of the attacker, the victim and the other workers, and to visualise how these perspectives might come together to create a violent incident.

THE ATTACKER

The attacker will frequently have a history of violent behaviour. Some aggressive personalities may interpret ordinary, non-threatening situations as threatening. Others may suffer from mental illnesses that manifest themselves in aggression. It is important in these situations to remain calm and under no circumstances challenge the individual while attempting to lead the situation back to a state of relative calm. Alcohol and drugs are major factors in violent behaviour, and any risk assessment should take this into account, for example in casualty departments in hospitals, night clubs and public transport. Other potential problem areas can be public offices charged with disseminating sensitive information, including housing, social welfare and personal finances, where members of the public may seek confrontation, which in turn can lead to violence. For that reason, staff in such workplaces should receive training in dealing with the public in difficult situations and be adequately protected by barriers and screens. It should be noted that young persons may be less restrained in their behaviour especially where alcohol or drugs are involved, and extra precautions may be necessary where groups of youths gather.

THE VICTIM

Potential victims of violence may be in a position to avoid or influence the outcome of a violent situation by being sensitive to changes in the body language of their assailant and by altering their own body language. Female staff may be better in calming potentially violent situations that involve men, but women may be more vulnerable where money is the motive for the assault. Training in dealing with potential violence helps staff to deal calmly with situations that have the potential for violence. A sensible approach is to ensure that the aggressor knows that you have back-up available to you, remain calm, never turn your back on a potential assailant, use an appeasing tone and agree with the would-be assailant until you are safe.

WORK ENVIRONMENT

The work environment includes both the place of work and work practices. A number of issues such as the isolation of lone workers, job location, handling cash, time spend waiting, and opening and closing times require special attention. All high-risk areas and times of day must be identified for employees and additional security measures taken to ensure their safety.

ENSURING ADEQUATE SAFEGUARDS

Having identified potential areas of violence it is equally important to identify the reasons for this potential behaviour. Once these reasons have been established the most appropriate safeguards can be put in place. It is crucial, however, that safety measures not irritate customers by, for example, forcing them to raise their voices in order to be heard through protective screens. Preventative measures can include screens and partitions to prevent physical assault, the exclusion of the public by using coded door locks, a dress code that excludes necklaces, ties and scarves (a clip-on tie can be worn where required), and stab-resistant vests can be worn under normal clothing in areas with a history of knife crime. The installation of video surveillance, personal alarms and static panic buttons can all deter would-be assailants. Any workplaces that use interview rooms should be equipped with an exit behind the staff member conducting the interview, and glass or Perspex panels can be installed so employees can have visual contact with each other. Having a cash-free system and time-lock safes can also safeguard employees. Waiting rooms should be equipped with reading material, chairs and an orderly system of queuing that uses either numbered tickets or displays with expected waiting time. Signs should be erected in the waiting area signed by senior management stating that no level of violent behaviour will be tolerated, and that if violence occurs, the Gardaí will be notified.

TRAINING AND SUPPORT

Employers can offer training in recognising and avoiding potentially violent situations. This can include identifying signs of potential violence, such as fixed gaze, rapid breathing, loud talk and restlessness. Techniques such as distraction and empathising with the assailant, in addition to break-away and physical restraint techniques. It is crucial in the resolution of conflict that employees remain calm and provide alternative routes of appeal for disappointed customers. Staff must be trained in the use of appropriate security technology such as silent alarms or intercoms. No resistance should be offered where cash or goods are the objective of the assailant.

Should violence in the workplace occur, facilities should be provided for the victims, such as treatment and counselling, if required. It is advisable for all victims of violence to seek help, even if this is of an informal nature from his/her colleagues. Frequently, problems will not arise with the victim until some time after the occurrence when symptoms akin to post-traumatic stress disorder may manifest themselves, hence the need to seek assistance (be it professional or otherwise) as soon as possible after the incident.

REPORTING OF VIOLENCE

As well as completing an accident report form or reporting the incident online to the Health and Safety Authority, a suitable format should be devised internally to record all violent incidents in the organisation. Useful data in such a report would include a detailed account by both the victim and assailant, recorded separately, of when, where and how the incident occurred. Questions need to be asked as to what security system failed, and whether procedures were bypassed. This record should be signed by the victim and his/her immediate superior and should be used as a basis for discussion and for devising suitable security measures. It is probably not possible to eliminate violence totally from the workplace, but it should be possible to reduce its occurrence and to minimise the consequences of violence when it does occur. A checklist is a useful tool in prevention, and should include issues like the potential for violence from clients, the likelihood of violence from interaction with the public, the safety of the work environment, whether employees work alone, whether emergency procedures are in place, and whether all violent incidents are followed up.

ADDRESSING WORKPLACE BULLYING

Bullying at work is repeated inappropriate behaviour, direct or indirect, whether verbal, physical or otherwise, conducted by one or more persons against another or others, at the place of work and/or in the course of employment, which could reasonably be regarded as undermining the individual's right to dignity at work.

The following are examples of what constitutes bullying at work:

- unnecessary exclusion from work-related activities
- verbal abuse/insults
- physical abuse
- being treated less favourably than colleagues
- intrusion: pestering, spying or stalking
- menacing behaviour
- intimidation
- aggression
- undermining behaviour
- excessive monitoring of work
- humiliation
- withholding work-related information
- repeatedly manipulating a person's job content and targets
- blame for things beyond the person's control.

It is important to note that a once-off incident of bullying behaviour may be offensive to an individual but it is not considered to be bullying.

Bullying at work does not include reasonable and essential discipline arising from the good management of the performance of an employee at work or actions taken which can be justified as regards the health, safety and welfare of the employees.

Bullying at work can arise in many different situations and at all levels of employment and may include the following situations:

- manager/supervisor to employee
- employee to supervisor/manager

- one employee to another (or group to group)
- customer/business contact to employee
- employee/supervisor/manager to customer/business contact.

ANTI-BULLYING POLICY

The purpose of an anti-bullying policy at work is to prevent improper work-related conduct and also to encourage best practice and a safe and harmonious workplace where this behaviour is unlikely to occur.

An employer should be committed to ensuring that the workplace is free from bullying and that the work environment is aimed at providing a high-quality service in an atmosphere of respect, collaboration, openness, safety and equality. The employer should ensure that all employees have the right to be treated with dignity and respect at work, and that the risk of bullying has been assessed and preventive measures prepared. All employees should be fully consulted in relation to the implementation of the organisation's anti-bullying policy.

WORKPLACE RESOLUTION OF BULLYING

Each employer should have put in place an informal and formal process for the investigation and resolution of complaints of bullying at work. The aim of these procedures is to ensure that the behaviour complained of, if in fact established, is eliminated and that good working relationships are restored.

The informal process will be in place within three weeks of the complaint being made and will have the following objectives:

- to assess and address the allegation
- to use agreed procedures, be consistent and fair
- to restore the harmony of the workplace over the medium to long term.

In order to implement this policy, a senior employee should be appointed as a facilitator of informal complaints, the policy being to try and reach an acceptable resolution through dialogue between the alleged bully and the alleged victim. Should it be necessary, as in the case of a complaint against a senior person in the organisation, the services of an independent professional body will be utilised to access mediation or conciliation, such as the mediation services of the Labour Relations Commission. In cases where there is no conflict of interest, the employer will attempt informally to resolve the issue provided objectivity is not compromised.

Any employee who believes that he/she is being bullied should tell the person complained of that their behaviour is unacceptable. Where the person alleging bullying finds it difficult to approach the person complained of, he/she can seek the help of the senior employee nominated for this purpose or a fellow colleague. A complaint of bullying can be made verbally or in writing. If the complaint is made verbally, the nominated senior employee will take a written note of that complaint and give a copy of that note to the complainant. The facts of the complaint will then be established and the person complained against will be presented with a copy of the complaint. At this point every effort will be made to resolve the complaint and to return the workplace to a harmonious working environment.

If the issue cannot be resolved through an informal process, or should the bullying continue after informal intervention, a formal process will be invoked. This will include a formal complaint which will be in writing and signed and dated by the complainant. The complaint should be confined to details of alleged incidents of bullying, including when they occurred and the names of any witnesses. Where a written statement of complaint has not been made, a written record will be taken by the senior manager nominated to conduct the formal process and must be signed by the person making the complaint. At this point the senior manager nominated will advise the complainant of the aims and objectives of the formal process, including procedures and timeframe involved and any possible outcome. That person will be assured of the support of the organisation throughout the process and will be given a copy of the organisation's bullying prevention policy.

The person complained against will be notified in writing that an allegation of bullying has been made against him/her. The organisation will assure that person that it presumes him/her to be innocent of any wrongdoing at this point, and advise that person of the aims and objectives of this process, the timeframe involved and the possible outcomes.

The nominated senior manager will conduct the formal investigation into the complaint, a timeframe for dealing with the complaint will be outlined and agreed between the parties. The senior manager will then consider whether the complaint falls within the definition of bullying at work and whether this complaint has been upheld. Statements in writing will be taken where possible as this will make matters clearer and maintain clarity in the investigation. If a conflict of interest arises, the mediation services of the Labour Relations Commission will be utilised. The senior manager will meet with both the complainant and the person complained against and any witnesses, the aim being to establish the facts of the case.

This will be done on an individual basis and the right to confidentiality of each party will be respected.

On completion of the investigation, the senior manager will submit to the employer a report on the complaint. The complainant and the person complained against will, as soon as practicable, be given a copy of this report by the employer and will then within a two-week timeframe be given an opportunity to comment on the contents of the report. The employer will then decide, in the light of this report and the responses from the parties concerned, what action requires to be taken.

Bullying behaviour is recognised as having the potential to damage both the health of the victim and the integrity of the organisation, therefore eliminating this hazardous behaviour and controlling the risks arising from it is part of the duty of care owed by the employer to his/her employees. As a consequence of this legally imposed duty it will be necessary for the employer to invoke disciplinary proceedings to resolve a complaint. In any disciplinary proceedings the employer will follow the Labour Relations Commission's Codes of Practice on Grievance and Disciplinary Procedures and on Voluntary Dispute Resolutions.

Where a person complained against wishes to make an appeal against the formal resolution of the complaint, the employer will seek the advice of the mediation services of the Labour Relations Commission.

Where the complaint is not upheld, both parties will be treated sympathetically by the employer and will be informed that the complaint has not been upheld and that no wrongdoing has been found. If, however, the complaint is found to be malicious, the employer will invoke disciplinary proceedings to address this issue.

Where internal procedures fail to resolve a bullying complaint, despite having fully utilised both of the internal procedures, complainants may access the Rights Commissioner Service of the Labour Relations Commission directly. A rights commissioner can assess how procedures were applied in individual bullying cases and can intervene in the process in a number of ways including carrying out a new investigation. Those wishing to access the system must apply directly to the Rights Commissioner Service and these applications can be made either online (www.lrc.ie) or by contacting the Commission. Any recommendation of a rights commissioner in bullying cases can be appealed to the Labour Court.

MANAGING DIVERSITY IN EMPLOYMENT

The Employment Equality Act 1998, as well as covering discrimination on grounds of recruitment and selection for employment, addresses such issues as discrimination in training, development and promotion within the workplace.

TRAINING AND DEVELOPMENT

Training and development processes will be less formal and a great deal may be taken for granted, especially where parties are known to each other over a long period of time. If management perceive that a particular worker has considerable potential that worker may be given greater challenges by management, whereas a worker perceived as having little potential will not be given challenges and much less effort will be put into training or developing that worker.

As the legislation requires employers not to discriminate against an employee on the grounds protected by the Act, it is important that managers make clear the reasons why individual workers are being treated differently than others if that is the case. Checklists should be established for accessing entry to training and development courses and for training course documentation and trainer behaviour. The design of a checklist for training and development should ensure that:

- managers have a key role in developing all their staff
- a range of training and development opportunities be available to all staff
- managers be aware of the range of ways in which development can occur
- managers be assessed on how they treat their staff
- every staff member have a development plan
- all plans be designed to meet specific needs
- the purpose of any development plan be to increase workplace performance by that worker
- any development plan seek to develop both skill and knowledge
- access to training be related to the job-related individual need of the worker
- provision be made for ready access of disabled workers
- transport, if needed, to the training venue be provided
- for those with sensory disability, visual and aural aids be provided
- monitoring of the sex, age, race and disability of applicants be carried out; as a result of monitoring this data, a relevant mix of persons based solely on their training needs attend the course.

A checklist for course documentation and trainer behaviour should ideally ensure that:

- the language used in documentation be non-sexist and non-offensive throughout
- case studies and scenarios referred to contain a good mix of persons
- case studies portray people in non-stereotypical roles as well as in traditional roles
- pictorial information show a good mix of persons
- explicit reference be made to diversity/equality policy and legislation where relevant
- potential for bias and ways of dealing with bias be mentioned in all aspects of dealing with people
- all trainers on management people-related courses be possessed of sufficient information to address relevant equality and diversity issues
- only non-sexist, non-offensive language be used by trainers
- stereotypes not be reinforced by the example of the trainer
- trainers pick up on equality and diversity issues when participants raise them
- trainers not spotlight minority participants and seek their experience as a member of an under-represented group
- the discussion not be dominated by one or other group of participants
- sexist or offensive language used by participants be challenged in a positive way.

PROMOTION

In some organisations a formal process for selecting workers for promotion may not exist because it is felt in the case of internal promotions in particular that enough is already known about the applicants for the post. Nevertheless, it is important that a systematic approach is adopted when dealing with promotion in the workplace and that decisions made on the suitability of the candidate selected are both clear and objective. A checklist outlining the criteria for the post should be prepared and cover the following issues:

- clear and accurate description of the role of the position on offer
- all criteria for promotion should be written down in a clear and unambiguous way
- promotion criteria are justified by the position on offer
- promotion criteria are at a level suitable for the position on offer

- promotion criteria must not cause unlawful direct or indirect discrimination
- if a competency framework is used it should include an indication of the role and responsibility of the position offered
- sex, race, age and disability monitoring is undertaken at each stage of the promotion process
- the data monitored is analysed and action follows the analysis
- the promotion process in the organisation needs continuous monitoring to ensure its continued objectivity and fairness.

Revision Questions

1. List the nine grounds of discrimination outlawed by the Employment Equality Act 1998.
2. Define sexual harassment.
3. How is disability defined under the Employment Equality Act 1998?
4. List the categories of worker covered by the maternity protection of employment legislation.
5. Outline the circumstances under which parental leave may be granted.
6. Define the term 'force majeure leave'.
7. List the conditions that must be met by an applicant before carer's leave may be granted.
8. What are the rest breaks in the working day provided for in the Organisation of Working Time Act 1997?
9. Briefly outline the role and function of the Rights Commissioner.
10. What are the remedies that may be granted by the Employment Appeals Tribunal?
11. What are the principal causes of work-related violence?
12. What is workplace bullying?

References

Carer's Leave Act 2001

Carey *v* Employment Appeals Tribunal (unreported, High Court, 2001)

Costigan, L. (1998), *Bullying and Harassment in the Workplace*, Dublin: Columba Press

Employment Equality Act 1998

Flynn *v* Power and the Sisters of the Holy Faith 1985, ILRM 336

Fullerton, J. and Kandola, R. (1999), *Managing Diversity in Ireland: Implementing the Employment Act*, 1998, Dublin: Oak Tree Press

Health and Safety Authority (2007), *Code of Practice for Employers and Employees on the Prevention and Resolution of Bullying at Work*, Dublin: Health and Safety Authority

Health and Safety Authority (2007), *Guide to the Health Safety and Welfare at Work (General Application Regulations) 2007, Chapter 2 of Part 6*, Protection of Pregnant, Post Natal and Breastfeeding Employees, Dublin: Health and Safety Authority

Health and Safety Authority (2007), *Violence at Work*, Dublin: Health and Safety Authority

Health and Safety Authority (2009), *Employees with Disabilities Health and Safety Guidance*, Dublin: Health and Safety Authority

Industrial Relations Acts 1946 and 1990

Labour Relations Commission (2000), *Code of Practice: Grievance and Disciplinary Procedures*, Dublin: Labour Relations Commission

Labour Relations Commission (2004), *Enhanced Code of Practice on Voluntary Dispute Resolution*, Dublin: Labour Relations Commission

Maternity Protection of Employment Acts 1981 and 1994

Meenan, F. (2006), *EAT Guidelines and Working Within the Law: A Practical Guide for Employers and Employees*, Report of the Employment Appeals Tribunal Working Group, Dublin: Oak Tree Press

Organisation of Working Time Act 1997

Parental Leave Act 1998

Unfair Dismissals Acts 1977 and 1993

7
Safety Culture

This chapter addresses how a safety culture or the lack of it in an organisation can affect not only the health, safety and welfare of employees but also their levels of efficiency. The distinction between a positive and negative approach to safety, ergonomics at work and the diversity model of workplace culture will be considered.

SAFETY CULTURE

There are two distinct components in organisational culture: formal and informal. The formal incorporates positions, roles and group relationships with the objective being to achieve outcomes that are both efficient and effective. The informal relationship develops over time when the formal approach is considered either ineffective or simply fails to meet the needs of particular groups, it involves relationships between individuals and relationships between groups of individuals.

The Stranks study of 1994 identified a number of weaknesses in formal components. They:

- experience many communications problems
- ignore factors that arise from human emotions
- may be either unwilling or unable to detect errors.

Positive characteristics in workplace organisations in health, safety and welfare terms include:

- promotion of a conscious health, safety and welfare policy by top management
- health, safety and welfare policies allow for human error
- management promotes higher standards in health, safety and welfare performance
- top management shows an active involvement in health, safety and welfare on a continuous basis
- management provides leadership on health, safety and welfare issues in the workplace.

The Du Pont Corporation is considered to be a leader in workplace health, safety and welfare. It has developed the following effective safety principles:

- all accidents and injuries are preventable
- management is directly responsible for preventing workplace accidents and illness
- safety is an essential feature of employment
- management must both train and motivate staff in health, safety and welfare issues
- safety audits must be conducted
- all defects discovered must be promptly corrected
- all unsafe practices and incidents are promptly investigated
- the establishment of the principle that safety is paramount on and off the job
- preventing workplace injury and illness is good for business because the cost savings are enormous
- people must be recognised as the critical element in any safety policy.

All attitudes and perceptions are grounded in the culture of the organisation, and the reality for management is therefore that prevailing attitudes to work-related safety demand the attention of the organisation. The majority of workplace accidents occur when a worker using the correct equipment and in possession of the correct information fails to carry out the assigned task correctly. An organisation that has serious concerns about safety must look at both the physical and cultural environments of the workplace because hazards are both behavioural and cultural and are influenced for better or worse by the culture prevailing in the organisation.

The culture of an organisation can best be defined as a set of values that helps the members of that organisation understand what the organisation stands for. Culture is not easily measured due to its intangible nature. Culture can guide employee behaviour and a strong organisational culture can be used to support health, safety and welfare issues. A great deal of the behaviour in organisational settings is moulded by socially based factors, employees' expectations of what is expected of them are based on the context within which they work, these expectations can be said to be a function of and shaped by their social group, that is the persons with whom they work.

Cultural features are complex and include shared characteristics such as beliefs, values, attitudes, opinions and motivation. More tangible aspects of a culture could be said to be buildings, uniforms, documents, logos and designs.

Rousseau's study conducted in a two-year period from 1988 to 1990 considers that an organisation's culture may be expressed at five levels:

- artefacts such as a company logo
- patterns of behaviour
- behavioural norms
- values
- fundamental assumptions.

An effective safety culture should help to communicate a sense that safety is valued and that effective safety behaviour will be valued. Any behaviour by an individual worker is likely to change if the organisation's safety culture is also changed. Erickson's study in 1997 identified two ways in which a high safety rating can be achieved:

- by continuous management support for the health, safety and welfare programme
- by management concern and support for the welfare of employees.

The study suggests that these ways may be further divided into management support, management concern and employee setting. An example of management concern would be the provision of adequate resources for health, safety and welfare; a positive employee setting would be the provision of a clean and safe working environment.

Pidgeon's study conducted in 1991 identified three essential aspects of a safety culture:

- standards for handling work-related hazards
- a positive approach by employees to workplace health, safety and welfare
- a capacity to reflect on safety practice.

MEASUREMENT OF SAFETY PERFORMANCE

In a proactive safety culture (see Garavan, p. 555), key elements of the safety system are identified and a numerical rating system is devised for hazards. In the investigation of workplace accidents, accidents may be dismissed as isolated incidents not involving a breakdown in management systems. The result of such an approach is that system deficiencies may go undetected and as a consequence remain free to be the source of further workplace accidents. A proactive safety culture sets health, safety and welfare goals, all of which focus on improving the system; allocating blame to individual workers is not part of this culture. A reactive approach to safety is driven by incident investigation that focuses on unsafe acts and conditions.

Proactive characteristics of a safety system include:

- incident investigation that focuses on the root causes of accidents
- any safety evaluation conducted is based on improving safety systems
- behaviour-based safe practices are developed following the identification of hazards in the workplace.

Examples of the characteristics of a reactive safety policy include:

- incident investigation simply focuses on unsafe acts and conditions
- safety, health and welfare training is conducted mainly in response to legally enforced requirements
- safe practices are developed in response to either workplace accidents or legislative requirements.

A proactive approach to workplace safety recognises that the occurrence of an accident at work is most likely the result of a failure in the safety system rather than a mistake by an individual worker. In order to address accident prevention in the organisation in a satisfactory manner, factors such as a reward and punishment system, safe-practice enforcement, engineering inspection programmes, maintenance schedules, purchasing and training must be addressed. In order to be proactive, the organisation is required to look beyond the single-cause concept in accident prevention.

An organisation that claims, for example, that absence of injury in the workplace is equivalent to safe work practice can de-motivate its management, causing line management to devote little time to the supervision of safe working practices. In contrast, a proactive safety culture evaluates and rewards a manager's safety performance based on the contribution he/she has made to the organisation's safety system.

In a reactive safety culture the safety system itself is badly defined, and efforts here are oriented towards hazards, workplace contests and gimmicks. Most managers asked to outline their safety strategy in such an organisation are unable to do so. Safety, health and welfare goals in a reactive safety culture are either not established or based solely on the reduction of injury.

Proactive safety culture activities focus on workplace behaviour and on improving safety in the existing system. The key elements of a proactive safety culture are structured to reflect a behaviour bias, which bias must be reflected in management and staff alike. Examples of such behaviour would include safe-behaviour coaching and goal-setting that focuses on system safety improvement. Goals are established at both departmental and plant levels and focus on improving key elements in the existing safety system and on encouraging action. The progress made is monitored by top management, periodic reviews of the system are conducted and achievements are recognised and celebrated.

SAFETY MEETINGS

In a reactive safety culture employees' response to the holding of safety meetings will be negative, the prevailing feeling being that management do not really care about safety and the meetings, when held, are generally viewed as a drain on production time. Little if any planning will go into the holding of those meetings.

In contrast, a safety meeting in a proactive safety culture can be an interesting educational event, such meetings are properly planned and focused on improving understanding of work-related safety, actively involving the workforce as partners in safety with management.

SAFETY AND HEALTH TRAINING

In a reactive safety culture little if any safety training is provided beyond what the law requires. To make a full contribution to workplace safety, employees must understand the scope, context and objectives of the safety system as well as how that system functions. If a department in the organisation has a behavioural observation system, employees should both participate in and lead such a system, though training in the operation of the system will be required. A proactive safety culture in an organisation will recognise that training needs to go beyond what the law requires and will schedule both time and resources to meet this requirement. The primary learning focus of this culture is the key element of the safety system. Safety leaders will need appropriate training to discharge their functions.

SAFETY PRACTICES

A reactive safety culture, if it has written safety practices, will use written phrases such as 'be careful', 'be alert' and 'watch out'. It should be noted that none of these phrases convey information, they are merely used to emphasise a point. In contrast, a proactive safety culture develops its safety practices based on a thorough assessment of hazards in a work area and implements safeguards before an accident occurs. All safe practices: are written down in clear, concise language; are known, understood and easily available to all affected; are updated where necessary; and are reviewed and used in safety training and employee evaluation.

SAFETY MEASUREMENT

The correct type of safety culture is based not on a celebration of accident-free days but on a high safety rating achieved through a system such as behavioural observation. Such a system helps to achieve continuous improvement in safety systems, the net consequence being a reduction in workplace costs achieved through driving down accidents. Ryan's study in 1991 identified four critical indicators of a safety culture:

- effective communication
- good organisational learning
- the organisation is focused on health, safety and welfare
- external factors including the financial health of the organisation.

A report by the Confederation of British Industry in 1991 recognised five factors as being important in assessing the safety culture of an organisation:

- the critical leadership role of the chief executive officer
- the safety role of line management
- employee involvement
- open communication
- demonstration of care and concern by management.

The United Kingdom's Institute of Occupational Health and Safety (the equivalent of the Health and Safety Authority in Ireland) maintains that organisations with a positive safety culture have competent people strongly committed to safety who put their values into practice. The view on safety culture of the Irish Business and Employers Confederation is that safety policies in the workplace need to be supported by a culture that supports occupational health, safety and welfare. A total safety culture at work will be underpinned by a number of general principles that concentrate on behaviour, attitudes and perceptions.

The basic factors found to motivate employees' interest in safety are:

- fear of personal injury
- fear of economic loss
- desire for reward
- desire for leadership
- desire to excel
- desire to protect others
- desire to create a favourable impression.

ESTABLISHING A WORKPLACE DIVERSITY STRATEGY

The Employment Equality Act 1998 prohibits discrimination on nine grounds and it is essential that employers examine workplace practices in their organisation to check for compliance with the terms of the Act. What is crucial here is that the organisation have a clear vision of what it wants to become. Measuring the present position against the organisation envisaged will give a clear idea of the steps to be taken to achieve that vision.

The Mosaic Model provides a view of an organisation that has its roots in workplace diversity. Mosaic stands for:

M   mission and values
O   objectivity and fair processes
S   skilled workforce that is both aware and fair
A   active flexibility
I   individual focus
C   culture that empowers.

The organisation must have core values that make managing diversity a business objective. Its diversity policy must be clearly explained to all and must reflect the values and needs of the workforce. All workplace systems such as recruitment, selection and training should be audited on a regular basis to ensure that no one category of worker have a predominant position. Employees should be trained to recognise that bias and prejudice can influence their actions and decision-making. In this regard managers should be constantly developing new skills where appropriate. All managers need the requisite skills to make workers feel valued and this should be so regardless of gender, race or ethnic background.

Diversity means that the organisation has accepted that cultural differences exist and that workers are not expected to conform to the culture of the majority employed by an organisation. One of the keys to diversity is flexibility in management approaches to problem-solving; a flexible approach would, for example, concentrate on workplace output rather than on the number of hours worked per day. The individual focus in this regard should be concentrated on the development of skills based on individual need, not on the group to which they belong (men, women or ethnic group).

Where an organisation values diversity, the culture of that organisation will be consistent with the management of diversity. This type of organisation will understand the importance of its culture and how that culture impacts on individual workers. As a result it will ensure that its employees understand how as an organisation it operates, what its core values are and how it expects its employees to behave.

A culture that empowers both the organisation and its workforce should include the following elements:

- an open environment, free of harassment, prejudice and discrimination
- jobs, promotion and access to income are equally distributed, and merit alone will determine advancement
- management structures should be flattened where possible
- employees are encouraged to participate in decision-making
- an employees versus management culture is discouraged
- employees are allowed to experiment and fail
- innovation and creativity are encouraged.

AUDITING THE SYSTEM

Any audit of a diversity culture will concentrate on the organisation's written guidelines, what happens in reality and how the system is perceived. As in any other audit there are key issues that need to be addressed, including:

- clarification of the purpose of the work
- identifying the sources of information that can be used
- analysis and interpretation of the data obtained.

As audits will inevitably include recommendations for change, persons in the organisation with the power to effect change should be involved from the earliest stage. Without the early involvement of such persons, little or nothing can be achieved by the audit.

Various methods of obtaining information can be used, such as the one-to-one interview, group discussion (care should be taken to ensure the group is not too large – a group of eight to fifteen people has been found to be the most effective) or a questionnaire-type survey (care should be taken to frame the questions in such a manner as to obtain informative answers).

It must be accepted at the commencement of the audit that changes may have to be made resultant on that audit, therefore the organisation should be prepared to effect those changes. As a general rule, when people have been involved in helping to identify issues they will be anxious to find out what is being done to address those issues. Any failure on the part of management to take positive action or to communicate details of the action proposed will only serve to increase levels of cynicism and negative perceptions of the organisation.

PRINCIPLES OF SYSTEM SAFETY

System safety techniques primarily come from the aviation industry, where the overriding concern is for the complete system to work as designed to avoid injury resulting from the malfunction of that system. These techniques can therefore be used to eliminate machine malfunction or mistakes in machine design that could have serious consequences for employees. They are used where a need exists to analyse critically the complete system in order to anticipate risks and to estimate the maximum potential loss associated with those risks.

The basic principles of any safety system are pre-planning and organisation of action designed to conserve all resources associated with the system under review. According to a study conducted by Bird and Loftus in 1976, the four stages associated with system safety are:

- pre-accident identification of potential hazards
- timely incorporation of effective safety-related designs and criteria
- early evaluation of the system's design and full compliance with relevant safety requirements
- continuous surveillance over the entire life span of the system including its safe disposal.

System safety may therefore be seen as the ordered monitoring programme of the system from a safety standpoint.

The elements within a system will include manpower, materials, machinery and methods. Each system will have a series of phases that follow a chronological pattern, the sum of which is equal to the life span of the system:

- *conceptual phase*: this stage considers the basic purpose of the system and formulates its preliminary design, methods of operation and hazards; operability studies should be conducted at this stage

- *design and engineering phase*: this stage develops the basic idea from conception and will include testing and analysis of the various components of the system to ensure compliance with the specifications of the system; job safety analysis needs to be undertaken at this stage
- *operational phase*: this stage brings the various components of the system together; as a matter of practice, safe work systems should be both developed and communicated at this stage
- *disposal phase*: disposal commences when machinery or manpower are no longer needed to achieve the purpose of the system; all components must be effectively disposed of, transferred, relocated or placed in storage.

ERGONOMICS

Ergonomics is the study of people at work focusing on how they cope with their working environment. It can be cogently argued that an understanding of how employees behave in the work environment and how they act at a physical and emotional level makes it possible to design suitable places of work. Oborne's study in this area, conducted in 1995, suggests that by designing the place of work to suit the capabilities of employees, safety, efficiency and worker comfort can be maximised. A narrow definition of ergonomics would be the study of the human/machine interface, which is beyond doubt a crucial factor in designing workplace layouts, safe systems of work and setting work rates. A broader view of ergonomics, which it is suggested is the better view, focuses on the work system as a whole.

PERSON-CENTRED ERGONOMICS

A person-centred view of ergonomics claims that the employee controls the system, operates it and evaluates its effectiveness. Sanders and McCormick argue that for the work system to be effective it should be designed from the employees' point of view. Employees can be said to bring to the work system a complex set of characteristics that they use to interact with the system and change it. The central tenet of person-centred ergonomics is the need to accommodate human attributes and to design the system to suit those attributes.

Four characteristics of employees are said to fit a person-centred approach to ergonomics:

- *purposiveness*: employees have a specific purpose in their interaction with the system and this must be recognised when designing workplace systems
- *uncertainty reduction*: employees can be said to have a desire to control, it is this desire that reduces the uncertainty about work-related outcomes
- *responsibility and trust*: employees will act responsibly to achieve success, a lack of trust however in new technology or over-reliance on technology can create difficulties
- *interest and commitment*: increased interest leads to a reduction in boredom, errors and accidents; reduced interest may increase work-related stress thus leading to panic, followed closely by errors and accidents.

Human characteristics include body dimensions, physical and mental strength, mental and physical limitations, perceptions, ability to learn and reaction. Environmental factors that affect humans are temperature, humidity, light, ventilation, noise, vibration, and at the machine interface the worker will be confronted by displays, controls, means of communication and automation. Possible work-related outcomes include fatigue, slower work rate, poor posture, stress, reduced productivity and accidents.

Two studies that were conducted between 1960 and 1971 (see Chapanis and Murrell) suggest that humans are better decision-makers than machines, are more flexible and can deal more efficiently with unexpected events. Humans are said to have the ability to improvise, to draw on past experiences and to perceive and interpret complex forms. On the other hand, machines are said to be highly efficient at computing, differentiation and dealing with predictable events.

The advantages of humans over machines could be said to be that people are adaptable and flexible and are capable of detecting minute stimuli. In assessing small changes, they can interpolate and use judgment, can synthesise and learn from past experience. The disadvantages of people over machines in the workplace include that people are slower in capability and response, easily distracted from the task in hand, have limited short-term memory, compute slowly and often inaccurately, tire easily and have a relatively low boredom threshold.

The advantages of using machinery are capability of operation in a hostile environment and the ability to respond quickly to an emergency signal, apply large force, store information, perform repetitive tasks efficiently and operate without maintenance for considerable periods of time. A machine's disadvantages include relative inflexibility and that it can only detect errors if programmed to do so, cannot assess errors, is incapable of using judgment and cannot learn from experience.

EMPLOYEES' VISUAL CAPABILITIES AND AVOIDANCE OF ACCIDENTS

The accommodation of the eye is defined as the ability of the lens of the eye to focus light rays on the retina, which allows object details to be seen. Where the accommodation capacity of the eye is inadequate it causes either near-sightedness or long-sightedness, the former is an inability to see distant objects clearly and the latter is an inability to see objects close up. The ageing process tends to develop long-sightedness through changes in the eye muscles and the eye lens.

Visual acuity is the ability of the eyes to discriminate fine detail and depends on the level of accommodation of the eyes; as a general rule the visual acuity of older workers is not as good as that of their younger counterparts.

Contrast sensitivity is simply the ability to discriminate between different objects and signs. Studies carried out by Evans and Ginsburg between 1980 and 1985 showed that this is a more important capability than visual acuity in two important respects: the ability to see in air to ground searches and the identification of highway signs. Six variables are seen as significant here:

- *luminance level*: visual acuity and contrast sensitivity increase with increasing light or background light and then level off
- *contrast*: when the contrast is low between a visual target and its background, the target needs to be larger to be readily identified
- *exposure time*: movement of the target or the observer tends to increase visual acuity
- *age*: visual acuity and contrast sensitivity decline with age; a study conducted by Owsley, Sekuler and Siemsen in 1983 demonstrated that contrast sensitivity declines from the age of forty
- *training*: training can improve both visual acuity and contrast sensitivity
- *colour perception*: the most common deficiency in eyesight is colour blindness, the inability to distinguish between the colours red, green and blue. There is some evidence to suggest that workers with normal eyesight may also have vision problems because they are suffering from a particular illness. For example, a person with vitamin A deficiency will have problems in identifying most colours, and diabetics will have problems with the colour blue.

WORKPLACE LIGHTING

Effective lighting facilitates effective performance of the task in hand. The quality of light from its source is known as the light flow or lux, most commonly known as luminance. The lux is the metric unit of measurement for light. As a general rule the lighting standard for working interiors varies from 200 to 2,000 lux. A task that requires limited vision requires 200 to 500 lux, whereas tasks with special visual requirements may need 1,000 to 2,000 lux. For example, electronic watch assembly needs 1,000 lux and micro-electronic assembly needs 2,000 lux.

Glare is the effect of light that causes discomfort or impaired vision and it occurs when part of the field of vision is excessively bright relative to the background. There are three types of glare. The first is disability, which is caused by bright light directly in the field of vision, the effect is to dazzle and is particularly dangerous when either driving or working at heights. The second is discomfort, which can cause eye strain, headache and fatigue; here there is too much contrast of brightness between an object and its background. The third is reflective, which can best be described as the reflection of bright light on shiny surfaces; its effect can be to conceal detail behind the glinting object.

Glare is particularly relevant in the context of the use of visual display units, where significant luminance contrasts exist between the display screen and its surroundings and where characters on display vary in brightness. This can lead to irritation and reddening of the eyes. Glare in this instance can be reduced by the correct positioning of the visual display unit, putting blinds on windows and using screen filters and matt surfaces surrounding the unit. It is suggested that the following measures will reduce glare:

- ensure that the working area is uniformly lit
- ensure that the source of light is correctly positioned; several low-powered sources are better than one high-powered one
- the task in hand should be brighter than its surroundings
- all light sources need to be properly shielded
- the use of reflective surfaces should be avoided
- fluorescent lighting tubes should be mounted at right angles to the line of sight.

Some debate has taken place about the use of windowless offices, but research has shown that employees would complain of lack of awareness of daylight and the weather and of having no external view.

Distribution refers to the spread of light. Poor light distribution may cause shadow areas which in turn increase the risk of accidental injury. Brightness is a subjective sensation on the part of the employee and for that reason it is difficult to quantify. Stranks' 1994 study found that the work should be illuminated to a level three to five times greater than the surrounding floor. Where light is diffused it is projected in many directions with no one direction predominating. The direction of the flow of light can determine the density of shadow which in turn can cause accidents in the workplace.

Research indicates that visual fatigue and eyestrain can occur from inadequate illumination, glare or attempting to decipher poor handwriting, the visual display unit in use may also have unstable images. A report published in 1982 (see Murray) found that the most severe form of visual fatigue had four symptoms:

- eyes were sore, dry and itchy
- eyesight that blurred temporarily
- an acute sensitivity to light
- headaches that spread to both the neck and shoulders.

Any working activity that makes excessive demands on eye muscles is likely to be a source of strain, for example prolonged close work, poor lighting, blurred images and glare. It is generally accepted that no permanent damage to eyesight is caused by visual fatigue.

THE IMPACT OF TEMPERATURE CHANGE

Room temperature influences work performance: at 18 degrees Celsius, active persons are comfortable at work, and 21 degrees Celsius is considered best for mental activity. At 0 degrees Celsius there exists a risk of frostbite to exposed flesh, and 26 degrees Celsius is extremely fatiguing to work in.

The temperature of the human body is regulated by a section of the brain and must be maintained at close to 36.8 degrees Celsius. When the body needs to lose heat it produces sweat; conversely in cold conditions shivering occurs, thus maintaining the mean body temperature.

At 40 degrees Celsius an individual will be prone to heat stroke, the likely outcome being loss of consciousness and, unless corrective action is taken, death will follow. Oborne's 1995 study suggests that there are three reasons why the body may have difficulty getting rid of excess heat:

- the person may be subject to excess humidity due to circumstances in his/her environment, therefore the body cannot reduce heat by evaporation
- the wearing of protective clothing can cause excess heat due to the heat-retaining properties of that clothing
- hyperthermia can occur in conditions that are not excessively hot but may still interfere with the ability of the body to produce sweat.

Heat acclimatisation is the adaptation of the human body to a hot environment. Generally it consists of an increased capacity to sweat, which enhances the skin's cooling capacity. An individual's capacity to sweat depends on his/her climate experience in the early years of life. The risk of dehydration and salt depletion is significantly reduced in a worker acclimatised to the hot environment, but the human body does not possess the ability to acclimatise to dehydration. Several factors influence the ability of the body to tolerate hot conditions:

- work rate, rest pauses, protective clothing
- environmental features such as humidity, wind speed and temperature
- age; in this regard it should be noted that the very young and the old have the least tolerance to heat
- sex; women begin sweating at a higher skin temperature and sweat less than men
- fitness level; people who are physically fit are, as a general rule, the least stressed by hot conditions
- fat tissue contains less water than other tissue and has a lower heat capacity, therefore those carrying excess body fat will suffer more than those who do not
- radiation is emitted by the heat source through electromagnetic waves, if this is at a high level it can burn skin
- humidity is the index of the amount of water vapour in the air, excess vapour in the air is likely to interfere with the evaporation of sweat from the skin.

The body will be in a state of hypothermia when its temperature falls below 35 degrees Celsius. Studies conducted in 1961 (Clarke) and between 1982 (Ellis) and 1993 (Ginsbreacht) found that the longer that workers were subjected to cold conditions the more their work performance decreased and that the cold can act as a source of workplace stress.

REVISION QUESTIONS

1 List the Du Pont safety principles.
2 What are the five levels at which the culture of an organisation may be expressed?
3 Give three examples of proactive characteristics in a safety system.
4 In a reactive safety culture, how is the safety system defined?
5 What are the four critical indicators of a safety culture?
6 What does the term 'Mosaic' stand for in the context of defining workplace diversity?

7 List the key issues that must be addressed when auditing an organisation's diversity culture.
8 List the four stages associated with system safety.
9 Describe the four principal characteristics of person-centred ergonomics.
10 What is meant by visual acuity?

REFERENCES

Bird, F.E. and Loftus, R.G. (1976), *Loss Control Management*, Loganville, GA:
   Institute Press

Chapanis, A. (1960), *Human Engineering*, Baltimore: John Hopkins University
   Press

Clarke, R. (1961), 'The Limiting Hand Skin Temperature for Unaffected
   Manual Performance in the Cold', *Journal of Applied Psychology*, vol. 45,
   pp. 193–194

Confederation of British Industry (1991), *Safety Culture in Organisations*,
   London: Confederation of British Industry

Ellis, H.D. (1982), 'The Effects of Cold on the Performance of Serial
   Choice Reaction Time and Various Discrete Tasks', *Human Factors*, vol.
   21, pp 161–168

Erickson, J. (1997), 'The Relationship between Corporate Culture and
   Safety Performance', *Professional Safety*, May

Evans, D.W. and Ginsburg, A.P. (1985), 'Contrast Sensitivity Predicts Age-
   Related Differences in Highway Sign Discriminability, *Human Factors*,
   vol. 27, pp. 637–642

Fullerton, J. and Kandola, R. (1999), *Managing Diversity in Ireland: Implementing
   the Employment Act*, 1998, Dublin: Oak Tree Press

Garavan, T.N. (2002), *The Irish Health & Safety Handbook*, 2nd edn, Dublin:
   Oak Tree Press

Ginsbreacht, G.G. (1993), 'Effects of Task Complexity on Mental
   Performance during Immersion Hypothermia', Aviation Space and
   Environmental Medicine, vol. 64, pp. 206–211

Irish Business and Employers Confederation (1986), *Safety Culture Policy*,
   Dublin: IBEC

Murray, B.D. (1982), 'Promoting the Healthy Banker', *Journal of the Institute
   of Bankers*, December, pp. 199–200

Murrell, K.F.H. (1965), *Ergonomics. Man in his Working Environment*, London:
   Chapman and Hall

Oborne, D.J. (1995), *Human Factors in Design and Development: Ergonomics at
   Work*, 3rd edn, New York: Wiley

Owsley, C., Sekuler, R. and Siemsen, D. (1983), 'Contrast Sensitivity throughout Adulthood', *Vision Research*, vol. 23, pp. 689–699

Pidgeon, N.F. (1991), 'Safety Culture and Risk Management in Organisations', *Journal of Cross Cultural Psychology*, vol. 22, pp. 129–140

Rousseau, D. (1988), 'The Construction of Climate in Organisational Research', cited in T.N. Garavan (2002), *The Irish Health & Safety Handbook*, 2nd edn, Dublin: Oak Tree Press

Rousseau, D. (1990), 'New Hire Perceptions of their own and their Employers' Obligations', cited in T.N. Garavan (2002), *The Irish Health & Safety Handbook*, 2nd edn, Dublin: Oak Tree Press

Sanders, M.S. and McCormick, E.J. (1993), *Human Factors in Engineering and Design*, 7th edn, New York: McGraw-Hill

Ryan, G.A. (1991), 'Perspectives on a Safety Culture', *Safety Science*

Stranks, J.W. (1994), *Human Factors and Safety*, London: Pitman

Stranks, J.W. (1994), *The Handbook of Health and Safety Practice*, London: Pitman

8
Health and Safety Authority

Almost from its inception the National Authority for Occupational Health and Safety has been known by its more common name – the Health and Safety Authority – the latter being more easily understood. This chapter addresses the legal role and function of the Health and Safety Authority, the role of the Authority's personnel, its most recent (2006) annual report and its strategy statement for the period from 2007 to 2009.

LEGAL ROLE AND FUNCTION

Part III of the Health, Safety and Welfare at Work Act 1989 (Sections 14 to 26) now contained in Part V of the Safety, Health and Welfare at Work Act 2005 (Sections 32 to 51) provides for an Authority with the responsibility to:

- enforce the provisions of the Act
- promote and encourage accident prevention in the workplace
- foster activities designed to promote workplace safety
- provide relevant information and advice
- make suitable arrangements to publish the results of surveys and research designed to improve workplace safety and health.

The Authority is obliged to supply the relevant government minister with any information regarding the discharge of its functions from time to time. The Authority in fact publishes an annual report on its activities, covering such matters as inspections made, number of notices issued by inspectors and prosecutions taken.

The Authority is a legal person with the authority to sue and be sued in its own name and with a right to perpetual succession. It consists of a chairperson and ten other members, and all such members are appointed by the Minister for Enterprise, Trade and Employment. In arriving at the composition of the Authority, the minister appoints three employee representatives, three representatives of employers and four representatives of relevant government departments and state agencies. Where a member of the Authority is nominated or elected to either the national or European

Parliament that person ceases to be a member of the Authority; members of the staff of the Authority shall cease to be remunerated by the Authority on nomination or election to either the national or European Parliament.

The chairperson of the Authority may serve in a whole-time or part-time capacity and may not serve for more than three years; salary and expenses are determined with the consent of the Minister for Finance. All ordinary members of the Authority shall hold office in a part-time capacity for a period of not more than three years, however all members including the chairperson are eligible for reappointment.

With regard to the appointment of the employer and employee members, the practice has been for the Irish Congress of Trade Unions to nominate the employee representatives and for the Irish Business and Employers Confederation (incorporating the Construction Industry Federation) to nominate the employer representatives, and the minister then simply appoints those nominated. The remaining appointees are senior civil servants and management from state agencies relevant to health and safety. The minister is authorised under this legislation to remove any ordinary member from the Authority, an ordinary member may also resign by letter addressed to the minister. A member of the Authority may be disqualified from membership if he/she:

- has been declared bankrupt
- makes a compromise with creditors
- is sentenced to a term of imprisonment
- ceases to be a resident of the state.

Salaries of members are paid from state funds and any expenses paid are regulated by the Department of Finance. Casual vacancies are filled on invitation by the minister to the original nominating body to make a fresh nomination.

The legislation also deals with procedures for the holding of meetings by the Authority and includes nomination by the minister of a member of the Authority as vice-chairperson, voting rights of members and what constitutes a quorum at such meetings.

The aims of the Authority may be summarised as to:

- enforce standards in health and safety
- provide advice and information
- promote higher standards in health and safety practice
- advise on and assist in the development of health and safety laws and standards.

ENFORCEMENT

The Authority is authorised under Part VI of the 2005 Act (Sections 62 to 71) to appoint suitably qualified persons to act as inspectors for the purpose of enforcing the legislation. Inspectors on appointment will be furnished with a certificate of authorisation by the Health and Safety Authority and when exercising their powers shall produce this authorisation and a form of personal identification. Inspectors appointed under this legislation have the following powers:

- to enter, inspect and examine any place believed to be a place of work
- should he/she believe that resistance to entry will be experienced, to take with him/her a member of An Garda Síochána
- to take with him/her any other person or equipment necessary to the purpose of entry
- provided the inspector is authorised by warrant of the District Court, reasonable force may be used to effect entry to any place where an offence under the Act is believed to be taking place
- having entered the place of work he/she may make whatever enquiries are deemed necessary to establish compliance with the legislation
- to require the production of any records or other material required to be kept to comply with the Act and to examine and where considered necessary to takes copies of any such records or materials
- to require any person to answer any questions in respect of matters under the Act provided he/she has reasonable cause to believe that the person questioned has possession of information relevant to his/her enquiry
- to order that a place of work be left undisturbed for a reasonable period of time in order to facilitate examination and enquiry
- to require any person in possession of any materials or substances to supply to the inspector free of charge for the purpose of test or analysis a sample of that material or substance
- to cause any article or substance found in the place of work and likely to pose a threat of injury to any person to be dismantled or tested
- where an article or substance found at a place of work is believed to have the potential to cause injury, he/she is authorised to take possession of and retain it for the following purposes: to examine or cause it to be examined by another expert and to ensure the item is not tampered with pending its production in any subsequent court proceedings
- to take samples of the atmosphere in the workplace
- to photograph or measure the place of work
- to require any person to afford reasonable facilities and assistance to exercise any power under this legislation.

In summary the role of the inspector is to carry out routine and reactive inspections to enforce actions, to give both information and advice, investigate complaints and accidents and give evidence in court proceedings initiated by the Authority.

Inspectors visit places of work to assess compliance with health, safety and welfare requirements; to investigate accidents and complaints in the workplace; to assist in the resolution of complaints; and to advise on and plan improved services.

The frequency with which inspectors carry out visits to places of work depends on the seriousness of the hazards encountered, the level of hazard control and the degree of risk from hazards. During 2006 inspectors of the Authority carried out a total of 15,365 inspections of which 7,616 were in the construction sector, 2,446 in the manufacturing sector and 1,457 in the agriculture sector. In the course of these inspections compliance with the new legal requirements was monitored, in particular with regard to the legal requirements of the updated risk assessment and safety statement procedures.

In 2007 the Authority employed a total of 115 inspectors, who carry out a range of duties including:

- developing proposals for legislation at national and European Union levels
- developing guidance
- liaising with other bodies
- inspecting
- promotion, information and advisory activities
- investigating complaints and accidents
- prosecuting offenders.

NOTICES AND DIRECTIONS ISSUED BY THE AUTHORITY

Notices and directions are covered by Sections 65, 66 and 67 of the 2005 Act.

DIRECTIONS AND IMPROVEMENT PLANS

If an inspector is of the opinion that in any place activities are being carried on that are likely to involve risk to the safety or health of persons, he/she may serve a direction in writing on the person in charge of that place requesting the submission of an improvement plan to the inspector within a time specified in the notice. This plan must set out the remedial action proposed. The inspector will have indicated in the notice the matters that require attention and the person affected by the notice can consult with the inspector on remedial issues. Where an improvement plan is submitted and found to be inadequate the inspector may insist on the plan being revised, and a further period (usually of fifteen days) is allowed by the inspector for the submission of the revised plan.

IMPROVEMENT NOTICES

An improvement notice will be issued by the inspector where either a clear breach of the legislation is shown or where a failure has occurred to submit an appropriate safety plan. This notice, in writing, shall specify the legal breach, or where appropriate state that the person named in the notice has failed to submit an appropriate improvement plan when requested to do so. Improvement notices, as a matter of practice, usually contain directions as to the measures necessary to remedy the breach alleged. According to the wording of the legislation, however, the inspector has discretion as to whether the improvement notice should contain this information.

A person aggrieved by the issue of an improvement notice may appeal to a judge of the District Court in the District Court Area in which the notice was served. An aggrieved person has fourteen days from the date of service of the notice to make such an appeal. The judge has the following powers in relation to the holding of the appeal: if he/she considers this course of action reasonable, he/she may either confirm the notice (but may order modification) or cancel the notice. The Health and Safety Authority has a right to attend, be heard and if necessary produce evidence at any such appeal. Where an appeal is taken against the issue of an improvement notice, that notice shall not have legal effect until it has been confirmed by the District Court. An inspector may withdraw a notice before it takes legal effect or can extend the time allowed for that notice to take effect if no appeal is pending.

PROHIBITION NOTICES

Where activities are being carried out in any place that is under the control of any person(s) and those activities involve a threat of serious personal injury to those employed at that place of work, the inspector may serve a prohibition notice on that person. This notice prohibits the carrying on of work-related activities at this place of work until the matters specified by the inspector have been remedied. The notice, unless it states to the contrary, will come into effect immediately. The aggrieved person has seven days to appeal against the notice to a judge of the District Court in the District Court Area in which the notice was served. Unlike the improvement notice, the prohibition notice is not automatically suspended pending the appeal. If the aggrieved person wishes to have the notice suspended, he/she must make a specific application to the court for such a suspension. The Health and Safety Authority has a right to attend and be heard at any such application. The judge hearing the appeal may either confirm or cancel the notice with or without modification to that notice.

An inspector is empowered to withdraw a prohibition notice where, for example, the inspector is satisfied that the circumstances that originally warranted the issue of that notice no longer exist. It is important to note here that prohibition notices are only issued where a serious risk of injury is likely to arise from the workplace activity. This is reflected in the fact that inspectors issue on average only fifty such notices annually.

Where a prohibition notice has been served and activities are still being carried on in breach of that notice, an inspector may seek an order from the High Court prohibiting further work activity at that place of work. On average only three or four such orders are sought on an annual basis as the level of compliance with prohibition notices is generally speaking very high.

The customs and excise authorities are authorised to detain articles imported into Ireland in order to allow them to be examined by a health and safety inspector where requested to do so by the Health and Safety Authority. The legislation permits the customs and excise authorities to detain the article or substance for not more than forty-eight hours.

ORDER OF THE HIGH COURT

Where the Health and Safety Authority considers that the nature of the threat to a particular workforce is so great as to pose a serious risk to their health and safety, it may apply to the High Court for an order either prohibiting or restricting further work activities at that place of work. The presence of the aggrieved party at this application is not essential and such an application may be made in the absence of that person. Under this legislation the High Court is entitled to make whatever order it considers to be appropriate in the circumstances.

OFFENCES, PENALTIES AND LEGAL PROCEEDINGS

A number of criminal offences are created by Part VII of the 2005 Act (Sections 77 to 85), including such matters as failing to provide and revise a safety statement as necessary, obstructing or impeding an inspector in the course of his/her duties, contravening any requirement of either an improvement or prohibition notice, making a false statement in relation to any duty imposed under the Act, or forging or altering any document required to be kept by the legislation.

The 1989 Act provided for penalties on conviction in the District Court to a fine of not more than £1,000 or on conviction on indictment in the Circuit Court to a fine and/or, at the court's discretion, to a term of imprisonment of not more than two years. The 2005 Act provides for a wider range of offences, and penalties in the District Court have been increased to a maximum €3,000 fine and/or imprisonment for six months; on indictment in the Circuit Court an unlimited fine may be imposed and the maximum custodial sentence remains two years. All proceedings in the District Court may be conducted by the Authority and a maximum period of twelve months to commence proceedings is provided for.

In any prosecution by the Authority for failure to comply with a duty imposed by this legislation it shall be for the accused person to establish that in all the circumstances of the case it was not reasonably practicable for him/her to do more to satisfy the requirement of the duty imposed or that there was no better practical means than were in fact employed to satisfy that duty.

ANNUAL REPORT YEAR ENDING 2010

The Health and Safety Authority annual report for the year ending 2010, which was published in June 2011, points out that the Authority, in addition to being the statutory body charged with the responsibility for enforcing health, safety and welfare legislation, is also the national competent authority for the implementation of reach, which is the registration, evaluation, authorisation and restriction of chemicals and the implementation of other chemical legislation. It is the responsibility of the authority to deal with all business enterprises regardless of size. In its strategy statement for 2010 to 2012, the authority aims to achieve six goals:

- to reduce risks to the safety and wellbeing of office holders, employers and employees
- to motivate a commitment to healthy and safe workplaces
- to support the Minister in the development of appropriate legislation

- to hold accountable those who flout health and safety requirements
- to promote safety in chemical management
- to ensure the effectiveness of the authority in delivering its goals.

COURT PROSECUTIONS

A total of 100 prosecutions were undertaken: 33 conducted in the district court and 67 on indictment in the circuit court.

ENFORCEMENT PROCEDURES

In total, the authority carried out 16,714 inspections and investigations ranged over the entire work area. Compliance with the legal requirement to have a safety statement in place was highest at 93 per cent in electricity, gas, steam and air conditioning supply sectors, and lowest at 48 per cent in other service activities. The appointment of safety representatives was again highest in the electricity, gas and steam sector and lowest at 10 per cent in other service activities. A disappointing feature of the report is the increase in fatalities from an all-time low in 2009 of 43 to 48 in 2010.

INSPECTION PROGRAMMES BY SECTOR

CONSTRUCTION

A total of 5,930 inspections were conducted in the construction sector. In addition, investigations were conducted into ten fatal accidents and 448 other accidents and complaints. A worrying trend was the increase in the issue of prohibition notices from seven in 2008 to fourteen in 2009.

AGRICULTURE

A total of 1,558 inspections completed in the agricultural sector in 2009. In addition, investigations were carried out into eleven fatal accidents and 43 other accidents and complaints. Whilst there was a welcome increase in compliance on the 2006 figures, the Health and Safety Authority continues to be concerned about the quality and implementation of controls identified in safety statements in this sector.

MINES AND QUARRIES

The inspectorate carried out a total of 530 inspections in mines and quarries. In addition, two fatal accidents and twenty-two other accidents and complaints were investigated by the inspectors. This sector had a high level of compliance with the Health Safety and Welfare Act, as 90 per cent of the places of work inspected had safety statements, and of those statements inspected, 90 per cent had identified relevant hazards and had put in place appropriate control measures.

MANUFACTURING

In the manufacturing sector, the inspectorate completed 2,563 inspections. In addition, one fatal accident and 151 other accidents and complaints were investigated. Despite the existence of safety statements in 84 per cent of workplaces inspected, action was required by the inspector in 40 per cent of the cases examined. Particular difficulties arose in the areas of machine safety, forklift use and maintenance, and working at heights.

WHOLESALE AND RETAIL

A total of 2,179 inspections were completed in wholesale and retail. In addition, the inspectorate investigated two fatal accidents and seventy-five other accidents and complaints. Sixty-seven per cent of places inspected had a safety statement, of which approximately 75 per cent contained risk assessments that identified hazards relevant to the place of work and had identified necessary control measures. The inspections, however, reveal two worrying trends:

- 40 per cent of the employers in this sector were not aware of their legal duty to report all reportable accidents and incidents
- levels of awareness of duties under Health Safety and Welfare Legislation was low at 45 per cent

ACCOMMODATION AND FOOD

The inspectorate conducted 977 inspections in the accommodation and food sector, and in addition investigated one fatal accident and twenty-seven other accidents and complaints. Safety statements were available in 63 per cent of workplaces visited, and of these statements 77 per cent correctly identified relevant hazards with risk assessments and appropriate control measures addressed. However, there was a failure to implement those controls fully in 60 per cent of the workplaces examined. Only 23 per cent of the workplaces inspected had a safety representative, and advice on safety consultation was required in 52 per cent of the inspections made. A total of 42 per cent of employers were found to be unaware of their legal duty to report accidents and incidents to the Authority, and more than 50 per cent of the senior managers were not fully aware of their duties under Health, Safety and Welfare Legislation.

EDUCATION

Education was a new area of inspection and a total of 250 inspections were conducted. In addition, the inspectorate investigated nineteen accidents and complaints. Safety statements were available in 89 per cent of the inspections in this sector but only 66 per cent of those inspected correctly identified hazards and only 55 per cent contained an appropriate risk assessment that correctly identified control measures. The risk assessments revealed a significant requirement by the inspectors to take action, as health and safety controls were not fully implemented in 62 per cent of the workplaces, safety representatives were present in 63 per cent of the workplaces and advice on safety consultation was required in 49 per cent of the inspections.

ENFORCEMENT ACTIVITIES

Enforcement activities in 2009 included:

- 6,874 instances of specific written advice was issued this represented 37 per cent of all workplaces inspected
- 1,394 improvement notices were issued to ensure compliance with statutory provisions
- 633 prohibition notices were issued where activity likely to result in serious injury was observed
- 17 places of work were deemed so poor as to warrant immediate closure

Inspectors also investigated 350 serious accidents and seventy-eight dangerous occurrences. A further 593 investigations were undertaken on the foot of complaints received by the contact unit of the Authority. All forty-three fatal accidents reported were fully investigated.

PROSECUTIONS

The Health and Safety Authority initiated thirty-eight prosecutions in 2009, fifteen of which were conducted at summary level in the District Court and twenty-three on indictment in the Circuit Court. Fines totalling €705,850 were imposed. One prohibition notice was successfully appealed to the District Court, and a further two such notices await the outcome of judicial review in the High Court.

HEALTH AND SAFETY STRATEGY 2010 TO 2012

In March 2010 the Health and Safety Authority launched its strategy document for the period 2010 to 2012. In the document, the Authority commits to a national culture in which everyone commits to workplaces that are both safe and healthy and to the safe and sustainable management of chemicals. The strategy undertakes to support the delivery of the following goals:

- to enable employers, employees and others to reduce risks to safety, health and welfare in the workplace
- to gain commitments towards achieving safe and healthy workplaces, which support success in all enterprises
- to support the Minister for Enterprise, Trade and Employment in the initiation and development of appropriate legislation and policies
- to hold accountable those who disregard their obligations in occupational health, safety and welfare
- to promote the safe management of chemicals
- to ensure that the authority deliver value for money in the conduct of its activities

The enactment of the Chemicals Act in 2008 as amended by the Chemical Amendment Act 2010 has changed significantly the remit of the authority because Sections 7 and 8 of the Act as amended state that the Health and Safety Authority is the enforcing authority for the Act's provisions. In Section 7 of the Act as amended, the Authority is authorised to issue codes of practice setting out practical guidelines in the management of chemicals.

REVISION QUESTIONS

1 List the legal responsibilities of the Health and Safety Authority.
2 Outline in brief the powers of a health and safety inspector.
3 How many inspections were conducted by the Health and Safety Authority in the agriculture sector in 2009?
4 Under what circumstance will a health and safety inspector issue an improvement notice?

5   Outline the circumstances in which the Health and Safety Authority
    will seek an order of the High Court in relation to a place of work.
6   How many non-fatal work-related accidents were reported to the
    Health and Safety Authority in 2009?
7   How many non-fatal work-related accidents were reported to the
    Health and Safety Authority for the manufacturing sector in 2009?
8   Outline the role of the Health and Safety Authority in the enforcement
    of the Chemicals Act 2008 as amended.

REFERENCES

Chemicals Act 2008

Chemicals Amendment Act 2010

Health and Safety Authority (2006), *Working to Create a National Culture of
    Excellence in Workplace Safety, Health and Welfare in Ireland*, Dublin: Health
    and Safety Authority

Health and Safety Authority (2008), *Guide to the Chemical Act*, Dublin: Health
    and Safety Authority

Health and Safety Authority (2010), *Annual Report 2009*, Dublin: Health
    and Safety Authority

Health and Safety Authority (2010), *Health and Safety Authority Strategy
    Statement*, Dublin: Health and Safety Authority

Health, Safety and Welfare at Work Act 2005

9
Farm Safety

Farm safety is an issue of increasing concern. This chapter examines: farm safety; farm health; safety precautions that address farm-related hazards, in particular hazards arising from the use of farm equipment and chemicals; and safety precautions necessary in the handling of farm animals, including the issue of infections transmitted from animals to humans.

THE DUTIES OF FARMER EMPLOYERS

Farmer employers are obliged to provide:

- a safe place of work, including farm buildings
- safe working procedures
- safe plant and equipment
- safe ingress to and egress from the farm
- relevant information and training for farm workers
- personal protective equipment, issued and used as appropriate
- emergency planning
- safe systems of using hand tools, chemicals and pesticides
- adequate toilet and washing facilities.

Farmer employers must also take care in the spreading of slurry and in crop-spraying. They must take care of visitors to their farms.

Farmers must prepare a safety statement and review it annually. As with other employers, consultations on safety must take place with the farm workers. Based on those consultations, a risk assessment of the farm must be prepared.

Farmers are obliged to report all accidents involving the absence from work for more than three days of any employee and any dangerous occurrence to the Health and Safety Authority.

THE DUTIES OF FARM EMPLOYEES

The duties of farm employees are to:

- take care of themselves and others
- give full cooperation with the implementation of the farm safety plan
- use personal protective equipment as required
- report any hazard encountered.

TRAINING

Because of the high labour input in farming the importance of training cannot be overemphasised. Teagasc, the farm training agency, provides a number of comprehensive courses including farm apprenticeships and a certificate course in farming. All such courses have a specific health and safety module included and place considerable emphasis on the legal responsibilities of farmers for health and safety issues on their farms.

Existing farmers may avail of a number of specific courses of at least twenty hours' duration that are run throughout the year at various locations. An example of this type of course is one based on modern spraying techniques, with particular emphasis being placed on operator health and safety and environmental protection. The spraying system adopted by each participant is examined and successful applicants receive a certificate of competency in spray applications.

FARM SAFETY

The *Farm Safety Handbook* was first published in September 1994. During the initial years of publication farm accidents decreased significantly, but from 1997 onwards the position has deteriorated. In response, the Health and Safety Authority issued the *Code of Practice for Preventing Injury and Occupational Ill Health in Agriculture*, effective from 1 November 2006.

Of all fatal workplace accidents, 28 per cent occur in the agricultural sector even though only 6.5 per cent of the workforce is engaged in agriculture. The statistics show that the level of farm accidents is not decreasing and that similar types of accident occur every year. This suggests that farmers take unnecessary risks in carrying out work-related tasks. Research by the Farm Safety Action Group also indicates that it is only after a serious accident occurs that farmers' attitudes to safety change. Health and safety must become a priority in farming, as it is the only way to reduce the levels of pain and suffering caused by farm-related accidents.

SAFETY OF FARMERS AGED 65 YEARS AND OVER

In the period from 1996 to 2005 there were fifty-eight work-related deaths of farmers aged 65 years and over; the use of tractors and machinery accounted for 29 of those deaths, animals 11, falls and struck 11, and electricity, fire and drowning accounting for the other six deaths.

Accidents and ill health amongst those aged 65 years and over can be avoided if the health and safety hazards to which this group is most vulnerable are identified. The ten-year review of fatal accidents shows that most fatal farm accidents were connected with the use of tractors and other machinery, handling livestock and falling from heights. Work practices need to be examined in particular where two persons work in a farmyard at the same time because a relatively high number of accidents occur in this situation, examples here would include, handling of livestock and operating tractors. In order to protect older workers it is important to identify and remove hazards for those who are slower to react.

FARM SAFETY FOR CHILDREN AND YOUNG PERSONS

The Health and Safety Authority has issued a new code entitled a *Code of Practice on Preventing Accidents to Children and Young Persons on Irish Farms* dated 3 September 2010. This code replaces the earlier code published by the Authority in 2001 on the same subject. It applies only to on-farm activities and their potential for harm to children and young persons. Between 1996 and 2009 forty-three children and young persons died as a result of farm-related accidents. The principal causes of these fatalities were crushing by farm machinery, contact with other farm machinery and drowning in slurry or water. This code applies to all children and young persons whether employed, visiting or family members.

The code defines a child as a person under 16 years or the school-leaving age, whichever is higher. A young person is defined as being between 16 and 18 years. The code identifies situations where accidents are most likely to happen, identifies tasks too hazardous for children and young persons, and gives practical advice to prevent farm accidents. In many cases, children and young persons will assist with farm tasks without being classified as employees, because a farming workplace is often also the family home. For that reason persons other than employees must be considered in any safety planning in assessing risk from farm-related hazards.

Any tasks carried out on a farm by minors must be supervised by an adult, and any instructions given must be clear and fully understandable. Minors should not be permitted to carry out any task until their suitability for doing so has been fully assessed. A safe and secure area must be provided for children to play, which must be away from dangers such as farm machinery and slurry pits. Children under the age of 14 years should not be permitted to operate tractors or other farm machinery. Riding as a passenger on a farm tractor is only permitted where the child is over 7 years and the tractor is designed and fitted with a passenger seat complete with appropriate seatbelt. All machine operators must ensure that minors be kept away from areas where machines are operating. If a minor enters an operating area, the operator should stop the machine and report the matter to the employer.

Deaths of minors on Irish farms result from asphyxiation including drowning in accidents involving slurry tanks, sheep dipping tanks, open wells, grain stores or silos, irrigation ditches and streams. All possible steps should be taken to prevent access to these areas by minors: secure covering and fencing can be used where appropriate, all entrances to silos or grain bins should be kept locked, and finally, materials should be stacked in a way that prevents children from entering areas otherwise inaccessible to them – this is the best possible way of reducing falls from heights by children. Falling objects can be a source of great danger to children so it is imperative that all goods be securely and safely stacked. Where for example bales, pallets or timber are stored, take adequate precautions to prevent child access. In addition, free-standing walls should be checked regularly for safety, as in the past, children have been crushed by the collapse of such walls.

Animals do not need to be aggressive to seriously injure or kill a minor, and for that reason the most effective way of preventing accidents is to keep minors away from animals or to allow contact only under the supervision of an adult. Even when accompanied by an adult, children should not be allowed into the pens of the following animals: bulls, boars, stallions, rams, stags, female livestock with newborn young, or any other livestock known to be aggressive. Particular care must be taken when animals are initially released from a building after being housed for a period of time, and minors should not be permitted to participate in these activities. There may be sound reasons for encouraging minors to have contact with animals, such as educational or developmental goals. In these cases, access to cows, sows, mares, ewes, does and other female animals under the direct supervision of an adult may be allowed. It should be noted that animals carry diseases called 'zoo noses', including Orf and E. coli 0-157. Orf causes skin lesions, and E. coli may cause serious illness or even death. The following precautions must be taken: ensure a regime of regular hand-washing and discourage children from putting their hands in their mouth after contact with farm animals.

It is essential that all minors be prohibited from handling chemicals including detergents and dairy cleaning agents. Whilst no evidence exists to suggest that children are at more risk from dusts than adults, it is unlikely that minors will have the maturity to use face masks when in dust areas, so therefore it is advisable to restrict children from entry into these areas. Fire is always a hazard and checks must be carried out to ensure that children are not playing in the immediate vicinity of flammable materials. Fires may occur from natural causes or from children setting fire to the flammable materials.

In conclusion, the code notes that its terms are not exhaustive and many other activities may cause hazards on farms. It notes that farmers have a responsibility to assess work activities by minors and to decide whether such activities are suitable for them, bearing in mind the level of adult supervision available and the level of competence demonstrated by the minor.

Source: *Code of Practice on Preventing Accidents to Children and Young Persons* issued on 3 September 2010, under Section 8 of The Health Safety and Welfare at Work Act 2005 and Part 6 of the amended Health Safety and Welfare at Work (General Application) Regulations 2007, (S1 number 732 of 2007) Part 6 Sensitive Risk Groups.

FARM VEHICLES

Farm vehicles and machinery cause the highest proportion of farm deaths, 48 per cent between 1998 and 2005, 87 people including twenty-three children died as a result of vehicle and machine use during the period 1998 to 2005. They accounted for 58 per cent of all child farm-related fatalities during the same period. Statistics for 1998 to 2005 show that 49 per cent of the victims were crushed, 20 per cent were struck, a further 20 per cent were pinned under and 10 per cent fell from vehicles. When the machine operation element is excluded, vehicle operation accounted for 56 per cent of all deaths.

Those operating machinery need to be competent, in particular in identifying potential hazards in use. Training must emphasise the need for both care and concentration in operation. The operator's handbook should be consulted as it gives a comprehensive guide to the safe use and maintenance of the machine to be operated. The following situations have been found to cause the majority of accidents with farm vehicles:

- driving errors due to lack of control or speeding
- falls from the vehicle

- being run over by a moving vehicle
- being crushed or trapped under a collapsing vehicle
- overturning vehicles
- being crushed between a hydraulically mounted machine and the vehicle.

Tractors are lethal weapons and need the utmost care in their use:

- passengers should not be carried anywhere on a tractor or inside the cab unless that tractor is fitted with a seat approved by the manufacturer
- a cab or safety frame to the safety standard of the Organisation for Economic Co-operation and Development must be fitted, look for corrosion on the frames of older tractors
- ensure that the tractor can be started by the key and that the engine stop control is effective
- ensure that the cab floor is kept clear to allow for safe use of the brakes and clutch
- brakes must be in working order, balanced and interlocked, except when used for field work; it is essential that the handbrake be functioning properly
- ensure that the power take-off (PTO) can be turned on and off and that the PTO shield be kept in place at all times
- ensure that the hydraulics be functioning properly
- tractor and trailer latch points must be free of wear
- do not leave the tractor seat while the engine is running
- tractors must be fitted with mirrors, lights and indicators as required by the Road Traffic Acts when in use in a public place.

Tractor Safety

A recent publication by the Health and Safety Authority entitled *Tractor Safety and You* sets out in simple terms the precautions that need to be taken in order to operate farm tractors and associated machinery safely. The code begins by asking farmers to consider in advance all those who may be at risk from the use of machinery. The categories that must be considered with particular care are the elderly and young children, these being the categories of people considered to be most at risk. Fatigue and lack of proper supervision of young drivers are seen as major safety concerns. Work should only commence after the five-minute check for safety recommended in the code has been completed. This check includes the inspection of tyres, lights, mirrors, brakes and oil levels, and cleaning of windows to ensure proper vision and of the tractor floor to avoid any possibility of control pedals jamming. Competent drivers will always follow a safe operating system of work, which includes driving at the correct speed, having regard to prevailing working conditions, being fully conversant with the use of all tractor controls, using the safety belt, ensuring that the passenger, if carried, is secure and stopping whenever you sense danger. Using the safe stop system will eliminate most farm-machinery-related accidents, six simple steps should be followed: 1) stop at a safe place; 2) apply the handbrake; 3) disengage; 4) lower implements; 5) switch engine off; 6) only then remove the key and dismount from the tractor.

Factors that contribute to the overturning of tractors include: gradient, speed, loads carried, lack of operator's experience, mechanical condition of the tractor and quick or sharp turns. If the tractor is about to overturn, do not attempt to jump clear; it is best to stay in the cab and hold on to the steering wheel.

All-terrain vehicles, better known as quad bikes, are used increasingly in farming and forestry operations. In 2005 12 per cent of farms used one. Both fatal and serious accidents have occurred involving the use of these vehicles, and the causes of accidents include:

- lack of training or experience
- carrying a passenger or an unbalanced load
- tipping on a bank, ditch, rut or bump
- a steep slope combined with other factors such as the condition of the surface or conditions of loading
- towing excessive loads using equipment without its own braking system.

It is essential that training in the correct operation of the vehicle be obtained before use. Personal protective equipment including a helmet must always be worn.

HYDRAULIC OIL HAZARDS

Pressurised hydraulic oil can cause the loss of a limb due to gangrene. This can occur where an oil leak comes into contact with the skin and the enormity of the pressure (2,000 to 2,500 PSI) causes the oil to penetrate the skin and then the bloodstream. Never place a finger over a leak in any hydraulic system. Never touch or rub a damp oil patch on a hydraulic hose as this could trigger a high-pressure leak. Work only on those hydraulic systems from which the pressure has been released. In the event of even the smallest quantity of oil being forced under the skin, seek medical assistance from the casualty department of a hospital.

OTHER FARM MACHINERY

Approximately two hundred incidents occur annually involving the use of machinery and equipment that cause serious injury, those at risk not only include the operator but also those in the immediate vicinity of the operation.

One common cause of accidents is the use of chainsaws. Chainsaws should be fitted with an on/off switch that is clearly marked, a chain brake incorporating a front hand guard, a safety throttle, a chain catcher, a rear hand guard, an anti-vibration system, an exhaust system and a chain cover for safe transportation. Chainsaw operators should have an adequate tool kit, personal protective equipment, safety helmet, gloves with protective guarding, safety boots, suitable eye and ear protectors and a first-aid kit. It is essential to carry out proper chainsaw maintenance and to consult the supplier's handbook carefully. When operating a chainsaw, grip it properly using both hands, with the left arm straight before cutting to avoid kickback. Never begin cutting with the upper half nose of the chainsaw, do not cut material above shoulder height and do not run the engine slowly at the start or during a cut.

Several fatalities have occurred from kickback, which happens when the tip of the guide bar of a running chainsaw comes in contact with an object causing violent upward movement of the saw. This can result in serious head and facial injuries. Keep this part of the chainsaw away from objects.

LIVESTOCK

Approximately 25 per cent of farm accidents are livestock-related, one-third of which are serious and result in a hospital stay. Serious accidents occur mainly in the following circumstances:

- crushing by farm animals against fittings or buildings
- goring by bulls in fields
- separating animals
- releasing trapped animals or loading animals.

Plan your work carefully to reduce the frequency of animal handling. When designing facilities for livestock, safety must be of paramount importance. Farmers are legally required to ensure that all buildings are safe, both for their own use and the use of others, such as veterinary surgeons and artificial insemination (AI) technicians.

Special attention must be paid to the collecting pen, which must be big enough to take the largest number of animals in that group on the farm. A forcing pen is a funnel to the chute and must be over five metres long (a chute of nine metres can hold six cattle). All pens and chutes must be made from a smooth material to avoid injury. One side of the chute should be capable of being dismantled should an animal go over on its back. A crush is used to hold and release an animal and its gates should be adjustable and easily operated. Dispersal pens retain animals until they can be herded back to the fields.

When dealing with bulls:

- do not treat a bull as a pet
- ring at ten months
- consider disposal if the bull is aggressive
- use suitable chains and leading ropes when leading from the pen
- two responsible persons should always be present
- walk at a slow pace, keeping the head of the bull up
- consider the merits of artificial insemination
- all young stock bulls should be dehorned
- bull handlers should be in the 18 to 65 age group, fit and properly trained in farm work
- young children must not be allowed to enter a field where a bull is running
- maximum use must be made of fields to which the public do not have access
- all gates and enclosures must be secured
- safety signs must be erected at all entry points
- aggressive bulls should never be allowed with the herd
- two handlers must always be present to separate the bull from the herd
- bulls are protective of their herd and great caution must be exercised in separating them
- housing for the bull should be designed to allow the stockman feed the bull without entering the house.

SAFE HANDLING OF CATTLE

In November 2010 the Health and Safety Authority issued an updated information sheet on the safe handling of cattle. In this guide, the Authority sets out a number of golden rules in handling cattle including having a planned escape route in advance of working with cattle, understanding cattle behaviour, making sure that all cattle handlers are agile, if using bulls ensure they are docile, maximising the use of artificial insemination, watch for warning signs of aggression in cattle and cull the aggressive animals, and during handling try to keep cattle calm. When dealing with cattle, use protective clothing and well-designed facilities with surfaces kept clean at all times, and carry out regular checks on all facilities. It is important to note that neither elderly persons nor young children should be involved in dealing with cattle, elderly persons because of a potential lack of agility and children and young persons because of their inexperience in dealing with animals, and in the case of young children, their lack of appreciation of the dangers posed by such animals.

SAFE USE OF CHEMICALS

Chemicals used in farming may be divided into four categories:

- fertilisers, fuel, oil, paints and wood preservatives
- acids
- pesticides
- veterinary products.

Most of the first group of substances are chemically inactive but some are flammable and may sensitise skin. Avoid inhaling the fumes of older paints in particular because of their high lead content. Red oxide is an example of this type of paint.

Acidic substances such as formic and sulphuric acid are chemically active, the principal hazard being corrosion injury to skin and eyes. Inhalation or ingestion would cause internal disorders. Bleaches and caustic soda commonly used in commercial cleaners react violently when in contact with acids and will result in the release of toxic gases, so it is very important to store acids and other chemical compounds separately.

There are approximately two thousand pesticides on the market, including herbicides, fungicides, insecticides and rodenticides. More than 80 per cent of these products are not subject to Department of Agriculture control as they were on the market prior to the introduction of controls in 1988. The greatest danger arises from handling pesticides as they tend to be target-specific, and in order to achieve adequate control a number of these products need to be used together. Mixing the pesticides increases the danger of skin contact and inhalation.

Veterinary products must be licensed by the National Drugs Advisory Board, which also investigates the adverse effects of products on humans and animals. Having proper handling procedures when administering to animals is the key to safety, so consider a veterinary surgeon for difficult procedures. Once proper care is used, chemicals should not pose a health and safety risk, though self-administration is a hazard associated with veterinary products.

ELECTRICAL ACCIDENTS

Yards, outhouses and fields are high-risk hazard areas from an electrical standpoint due to the wet environment. Portable equipment together with extension cables and overhead power lines are the main causes of electrical fatalities. Electrical accidents occur mainly for the following reasons:

- the plug contains a loose earth connection
- equipment is connected without a proper plug or socket
- unsuitable domestic-type plugs are used
- temporary joints are used, taped and untaped, on extension leads
- portable equipment such as infrared lamps are connected to lighting circuits
- amateur improvisation and repairs are carried out
- incorrect fuses are used
- use of faulty equipment and installations
- frayed insulation causing galvanised roofs of outhouses and steel uprights to become live
- erection of buildings or the stacking of materials under or near power lines
- operating high-rise machinery under and in the vicinity of overhead power lines.

Fuses and miniature circuit breakers are used to protect the circuit when a fault occurs, but they will not protect either humans or animals from electric shock.

Some sensible precautions are to:

- use either a miniature circuit breaker or a fuse to protect the circuit
- use only the correct type and rating
- not replace a fuse or circuit breaker with an increased size
- use a main fuse or circuit breaker to protect the entire electrical installation
- label clearly for ease of identity
- protect against automatic start-up at the end of a power cut by using under-voltage protection.

If unsure about installations always check with a competent electrician.
To prevent electric shock from portable equipment, farmers should:

- fit residual current devices
- test monthly by pressing the test trip button
- use 110 volt supply for smaller items of portable equipment
- keep all connections in good condition and replace cables when frayed
- only join cables with cable couplers
- use a maximum 25 volts' supply for portable lamps in confined or wet conditions.

Only use industrial-type plugs and sockets (IEC 309). They are colour-coded as follows:

- 24 volt is mauve
- 110 volt is yellow
- 220 volt is blue
- 380 volt is red.

Plugs and sockets must have keyway coding to prevent a mismatch, for example connecting a yellow plug to a blue socket; be appropriate to the voltage of the equipment used; and be of sufficient capacity. The same criteria apply to cable couplers.

It is essential to earth all safety devices such as fuses and circuit breakers in order to allow them to work safely and efficiently. Farmers are advised to have all such circuits tested by a competent electrician.

Electric welders should be supplied from separate circuits. Plugs and sockets should have a minimum capacity of 32 amps. Conductor cable must be connected to the work piece by a proper clamp.

WORKSHOP SAFETY

Farm workshops should be built using fireproof materials such as concrete, steel and fireproof sheeting. Solid walls should be constructed to support shelves and anchor benches. Doors must be of a suitable size to accommodate machinery. Floors should be finished to wooden float standard to achieve the best grip on concrete floors. Attend to spillages immediately to avoid slippery floors. Leave sufficient working space around machinery. Keep benches and fixed machinery in the one work area. Vehicle inspection pits must be covered when not in use. Adequate lighting is essential, as is regular waste disposal.

To prevent fire:

- never store fuels, oil, paint thinners, paints or grease in the workshop, keep in a purpose-built store
- a fire extinguisher, fire blanket and buckets of sand must always be readily available
- never store or use petroleum in enclosed areas where petrol fumes could build up
- use only strong, leak-proof containers for petroleum products, clearly marked and with a vapour-tight stopper
- use only steel bins to store cleaning cloths or greasy paper, fit with tight lids to avoid the possibility of spontaneous combustion
- note that airborne dust, especially in grain stores, can ignite and cause an explosion so the use of industrial cleaners and good ventilation is essential
- a strict policy of no smoking must be observed in farm workshops.

Electrical installations on Irish farms must comply with the National Rules for Electrical Installations. These are issued by a government-sponsored body known as the Electro-Technical Council of Ireland. An annual check of these installations by a competent electrician is required.

All lifting equipment should be fully tested before use and should never exceed the safe working load, which must be clearly marked on the apparatus.

Safety with tools involves:

- when storing tools, cover all sharp edges
- when sharpening tools, move the hand away from the blade to avoid injury
- never use a worn disc on a mini angle-grinder
- only persons trained in their use should use grinding machines with abrasive wheels as these have been known to break and fly
- guards to machines must be properly fitted.

Workshop health hazards include: petrol that may cause dermatitis with the possibility of skin cancer, diesel oil and greases, solvents/thinners, antifreeze and dust. Avoid skin contact with petrol and solvents. Keep the workshop well ventilated. Remember to use eye and ear protection where necessary.

Remember when working with batteries that the sulphuric acid in batteries causes serious burns. Always charge batteries in a well-ventilated area and keep them well charged. Ensure in the use of jump-leads that the clamps of both grip leads are firmly connected to the battery electrodes and never touch them as this will lead to a heavy electric charge.

Be extremely careful in cutting barrels if traces of flammable material remain as this can cause an explosion.

Have compressors checked annually by a competent person as a compressor may explode due to a crack in the compressor tank.

Only qualified persons should use welding equipment. They should wear a good quality face shield or goggles, non-synthetic clothing and welding gloves. Avoid inhaling welding fumes by ensuring the area is well ventilated. Ensure when in use that oxy-acetylene sets stand vertically and are secure. Do not allow either oil or grease to get on the cylinders. Ensure flashback arresters are fitted. Use a brush to apply soapy water to any suspected leak in a joint.

SILAGE-MAKING

Safety during silage-making calls for advanced planning and good organisation during harvesting. Contractors cut about 75 per cent of all silage so coordination is needed between farmer and contractor. Both have corresponding duties under the Safety, Health and Welfare at Work Act 2005.

During field operations, remember:

- to examine exits to public roads to see if visibility can be improved
- to use safety signs and bollards as necessary to warn motorists
- only experienced operatives should carry out silage-making activities
- overturning on steep brows is a major cause of accidents
- to assess risk before deciding to cut on a slope
- cutting at slow speed with an empty trailer reduces the risk of overturning
- to design silage systems to suit the terrain
- on slopes, use side-mounted equipment, dual wheels, four-wheel-drive tractors and trailer braking systems.

Children should not be present when silage making is ongoing.

FARM SAFETY STATEMENT

Farmers employing three or more persons are legally obliged to prepare and review annually a safety statement based on a risk assessment of the farm (Section 20 of the 2005 Act). It is helpful to list the work activities and then assess the hazards attached to those activities, these will change according to the seasons and for that reason it is necessary for farmers to examine their activities at different times of the year. When work activities change it is necessary to reassess existing safety arrangements, control measures and adequate supervision are imperative.

Prevention/control measures include:

- erecting a childproof fence around slurry pits
- using glyphosate herbicide instead of parquet-based herbicide
- providing training and supervision
- providing adequate notices of hazards
- providing personal protective equipment
- planning work to avoid rushing
- child supervision – in this regard a safe play area in sight of the dwelling house should be provided and all children should be informed of the dangers on the farm
- ensuring machinery is switched off before any maintenance work is carried out
- training all farm workers in manual handling techniques.

FARM HEALTH

BACKACHE

Backache is mostly caused by poor lifting techniques. Avoid lifting if possible. If the object cannot be mechanically lifted, obtain assistance or subdivide the load. Check the padding on the tractor seat before use to reduce vibration.

BREATHING

Asthma is more common than farmer's lung, and it is frequently due to the same mixture of moulds and other organic dusts. When you contract asthma your bronchial tubes narrow making it hard to breathe and causing both wheezing and coughing. Inhaling spores from mouldy hay, grain and silage causes farmer's lung: about six hours after breathing in the spores, flu-like symptoms develop. These symptoms clear usually after not more than eight days, but repeated exposure can result in lung damage. A somewhat similar condition arises in mushroom workers from the spores of the mushrooms.

Preventive measures include:

- reducing dust levels by hosing down the area with water
- opening all shed doors
- in high dust areas, wearing masks fitted with an exhalation valve for more comfort
- avoiding creating mists and sprays as far as possible
- if mists and sprays cannot be avoided, wearing suitable personal protective equipment
- avoiding skin contact with chemicals.

DISEASES TRANSMITTED FROM ANIMALS TO HUMANS

Weil's disease is a very serious disease caused by the contamination of stagnant water with the urine of rats; the disease causes both liver and kidney disorders. A less serious form of the disease is leptospirosis hardjo, which is a quite common disease passed to humans by cattle drinking contaminated water through their urine. The symptoms are akin to a bad flu.

Orf is a viral disease in sheep, especially lambs. Avoid contact with sheep with a rash around the nose or mouth and as a precaution always wear protective gloves. In humans, orf causes a swelling on hands and face that develops into blisters.

Enzootic abortion causes abortion in ewes and is a major health hazard for pregnant workers.

Lyme disease is transmitted to humans by ticks. After the bite an expanding red ring appears around the bite area, this is often linked to flu-like symptoms. Treatment is a course of antibiotics.

To avoid brucellosis, take precautions with all infected animals and in all cases consult your doctor if you feel you may have been contaminated by chemical substances or if you feel you have a lung problem.

Transmission of bovine TB takes place by drinking non-pasteurised milk from reactor cows.

SLURRY-RELATED HAZARDS

A greater threat is posed by drowning in slurry tanks than by exposure to slurry gases, so it is therefore important to protect against persons, especially children, falling into slurry pits. Covered tanks should have adequate manholes and a grid underneath that a child cannot easily remove. A wall or fence of at least 1.8 metres in height with locked access gates should surround all open tanks. When slats are removed, temporary covers or guard rails should be used to protect the opening.

Decomposing slurry produces a mixture of dangerous gases including methane, carbon dioxide and hydrogen sulphide. Hydrogen sulphide is poisonous both to humans and animals. All or any of these gases can replace air and cause suffocation.

Hydrogen sulphide is a clear gas with a smell akin to rotten eggs. Lack of smell, however, is not an indicator of the absence of the gas as the human sense of smell is lost where there exists high concentrations of it. The maximum safe exposure limit for this gas is fifteen parts per million – this means that the concentration in the air measured over a fifteen-minute period should never be higher than fifteen parts per million and indeed levels should be kept lower if possible. It should be noted that gas levels as high as 2,000 parts per million have been recorded at slat level, such a level would cause rapid death.

Gas release from slurry is greatest:

- within the first fifteen to thirty minutes of mixing
- when slurry effluent is added
- when slurry has been stored for several months
- when slurry is mixed in deep tanks
- when slurry is mixed in cold water.

When working with slurry observe the following guidelines:

- never agitate slurry in still air conditions
- remove all stock from buildings or adjacent to tanks
- open all available ventilation if indoors
- two people at least should be present
- keep children away
- never stand over or near hatch access when agitation is in progress
- stay out of the building during the first hour of agitation
- avoid rigorous agitation in confined areas
- do not allow slurry to rise beyond 300 millimetres of the cover or slats
- the gas mixture can be highly flammable so avoid the use of naked lights
- a full face mask with independent air system needs to be used. It protects against levels of up to one per cent hydrogen sulphide for up to thirty minutes, face masks without independent air will not suffice as they afford no protection against the gas.

Buildings should be designed to allow for agitation and removal from the outside, ensure that tanks are large enough to hold the slurry for the winter months. This obviates the necessity of emptying the tank whilst stock are still housed. Both agitating and emptying machinery must have a safe and efficient access to the tank.

If possible never enter a tank; work should be done from the outside. If entry is absolutely essential, a safe method of doing so must be devised. Consider forced ventilation and testing the atmosphere of the tank before entry, and use of suitable breathing apparatus. A harness should be worn attached to a lifeline under the control of two responsible adults outside the tank. Similar precautions are needed for other confined places such as grain silos.

NOISE LEVELS OF SOME FARM OPERATIONS

The Noise Regulations 2006 require that action be taken either to reduce the noise level or to provide hearing protection when the level reaches eighty-five decibels. Examples of the noise levels of farm operations include:

- angle grinders and chainsaws: 110 decibels – wear hearing protection at all times
- dry sows feeding: 100 to 110 decibels – ear protection must be worn
- tractor on full power without cab: 90 to 100 decibels – ear protection needed
- one metre from tractor at PTO speed: 90 decibels – ear protection advisable
- inside tractor with cab: 80 to 85 decibels – hearing protection advisable.

It is important to note that the decibel is based on a log scale, this means that a three-decibel increase in noise doubles the potential of hearing damage and a ten-decibel increase is ten times more damaging. Normal conversation is at thirty decibels and a radio in a domestic dwelling is usually at sixty decibels.

Once the eighty-five decibel threshold is crossed, hearing protection should be worn at all times when in contact with the noise source. The 2006 Noise Regulations require special measures to be taken in addition to the wearing of hearing protectors where the noise level exceeds eighty-five decibels. These would include a legal requirement either to quiet the source or to isolate it.

To reduce exposure to noise:

- when buying new equipment, ask for data on noise levels
- maintain machinery properly

- keep doors and windows of tractor cabs closed if fitted
- site control panels and work areas away from high noise areas if possible
- automatic feeding systems in piggeries reduce the need to enter during feeding when noise reaches a peak
- use sound barriers.

Personal ear protection includes:

- ear muffs (if worn, the cushion seal must be replaced every six months and the headband should not be stretched unnecessarily as this reduces effectiveness)
- ear plugs are equally effective (cleanliness is essential to avoid ear infections, and correct insertion is essential so follow instructions on use carefully).

SUMMARY OF FATALITIES AND OTHER INJURIES ON IRISH FARMS, 2008–2009

Construction and agriculture continue to have the highest rates of fatalities from work-related accidents. Despite this trend, the agricultural sector saw a drop in fatalities from fifteen in 2008 to three in 2009. For year end 2009 a total of 6707 non fatal accidents were reported to the Health and Safety Authority of which the Agriculture sector accounted for 84. Whilst the number of incidents reported appears to be small, especially when compared with the manufacturing sector, which reported 1,175 incidents in 2009, farm-related injuries or illnesses tend to be of a more serious nature, for example crushing by animals or machines, or falls into slurry pits. The drop generally in reportable incidents from a high in 2007 of 8,747 to the figure in 2009 of 6,707 can perhaps be explained by the fall in work activity during this period.

REVISION QUESTIONS

1   Outline in brief the legal duties of farmer employers under health, safety and welfare legislation.
2   What steps must be taken in farming to protect the health, safety and welfare of farmers and employees aged over 65 years?
3   Outline the principal safety rules to protect children in farming.
4   List the situations that have been found to cause the majority of accidents with farm vehicles.
5   List the four principal categories of chemicals used in farming.

6   What is leptospirosis?
7   List the hazards associated with farm slurry.
8   What type of materials are recommended for use in the construction of farm workshops?

REFERENCES

Esso, Teagasc, the Farmers Journal and the Health and Safety Authority (1994 and 1999), *Farm Safety Handbook*, Dublin: Health and Safety Authority

Farm Safety Action Group (2003), *Farm Safety Plan 2003–2007*, Dublin: Health and Safety Authority

Health and Safety Authority (2006), *Code of Practice for Preventing Injury and Occupational Ill Health in Agriculture*, Dublin: Health and Safety Authority

Health and Safety Authority (2009), *Code of Practice for Preventing Accidents to Children and Young Persons in Agriculture*

Health and Safety Authority (2010), *Tractor Safety and You*, Dublin: Health and Safety Authority

Health and Safety Authority (2010), *Safe Handling of Cattle on Farms*, Dublin: Health and Safety Authority

Health and Safety Authority (2010), *Summary of Workplace Injury, Illness and Fatality Statistics 2008 to 2009*, Dublin: Health and Safety Authority

Health, Safety and Welfare at Work Act 1989

Safety, Health and Welfare at Work Act 2005

Safety, Health and Welfare at Work (Control of Noise at Work) Regulations 2006

10
Occupiers' Liability and Insurance

This chapter addresses two important issues: the legal duties imposed on the occupiers of premises in regard to those persons who enter those premises; and insurance. Legislation introduced in 1995 sets out in clear terms the duty owed by occupiers to persons entering their property. It establishes two categories of duty owed to entrants. First is a duty of reasonable care owed to entrants who are categorised as visitors. Second is a duty not to disregard recklessly the safety of two other categories of entrant: the recreational user and the trespasser. Turning to insurance, the chapter explains what insurance is, how it may be obtained, the duties of the insurer and the insured, and the different types of insurance, including occupiers' liability insurance, professional indemnity insurance, self-insurance and public liability insurance.

OCCUPIERS' LIABILITY

The common law in the area of occupiers' liability divided persons entering the property of another into four separate categories:

- contractual invitees
- invitees
- licensees
- trespassers.

The duty of care owed by the occupier to a particular entrant depended on which category at law that person belonged to. Occupiers' liability law had not been affected by the decision of the House of Lords in Donoghue v Stevenson that the manufacturer of goods owed a general duty of care to the ultimate consumer of those goods. The view of Lord Atkin in that case, that a duty of care was owed, by those engaged in any activity likely to injure or damage, to anyone likely to be adversely affected, had not permeated occupiers' liability law, the existing law being too deeply seated.

Court decisions of the modern era, such as Purtill v Athlone Urban District Council and McNamara v Electricity Supply Board, both decisions of the Supreme Court, stretched the limits of categorisation in order to achieve what the court perceived as justice. In both these examples the court allowed young trespassers to be categorised as licensees in order to succeed in their respective claims for damages. The decision in the case of Foley *v* Musgrave Cash and Carry appeared to espouse a view that a duty of care to all entrants was owed by the occupier, however this was not followed in subsequent decisions.

The term occupier is defined in broad terms, it embraces both land and buildings and includes all persons in lawful occupation of land, and has been held to include such diverse places as a platform, grandstand, ships in dock, scaffolding, pylons, cars and aeroplanes. It would appear however that ordinary negligence principles apply to moving vehicles; it is simply a matter of control and occupancy. In the High Court case of Keegan *v* Owens and McMahon, nuns promoted a carnival in a field that they were permitted to use, but management of the event was in the hands of a committee. The nuns' gardener, who had been requested to help after work with the event, had his hand seriously injured after he came in contact with a nail protruding from one of the swings. His action against the nuns for negligence failed on the basis that they did not exercise sufficient control over the event to be legally classified as occupiers.

Ireland's Law Reform Commission examined the area of occupiers' liability against a background of pressure for change, mainly from the farming community, which had increasingly become subject to claims from persons either crossing a farmer's land or using it for recreational purposes, this problem was most acute in areas of outstanding natural beauty such as the Burren in County Clare. The question of access to national monuments had also begun to cause problems. The Commission received submissions from many interested sources and its proposals in this area formed the basis of the Occupiers' Liability Act 1995.

Under the 1995 Act, an occupier owes a duty towards three classes of entrants:

- visitors
- recreational users
- trespassers.

Section 3 of the Act provides that the duty owed to visitors will be to take reasonable care that they and their property do not suffer either injury or loss by reason of any danger existing on the occupier's premises. With regard to the other categories, the duty is to prevent injury or loss by intentional or reckless acts.

A number of definitions are provided in the Act. Damage is described as loss of property and injury to an animal. Injury includes loss of life, physical impairment or mental disability. Danger means a peril that exists due to the state of repair of the premises. Entrant when used in relation to this Act means a person who enters premises and is not the sole occupier.

Section 4 sets out a number of considerations that a court should take into account in determining what constitutes reckless behaviour towards an entrant under the Act:

- whether the occupier knew or ought to have known of the danger
- knowledge on the part of the occupier that persons were present in the vicinity of the danger
- whether the danger was one for which protection should have been provided
- the burden placed on the occupier to remove that danger
- characteristics of the premises and the desirability of maintaining open access to the premises
- conduct of the entrant
- the nature of any warning given
- whether the injured person was alone, unsupervised or accompanied by another.

An occupier may modify his/her duty to entrants, and this is normally achieved by posting notices to that effect in a prominent position at the entrance to the premises. Section 5 of the Act provides that such modification must be reasonable and that the entrant must be informed in advance of entry. The occupier cannot reduce his/her duty below reckless or intentional disregard of the safety of entrants. This legislation does not change the law governing self-defence, defence of others in one's company or defence of property. The concepts of concealed and unusual danger, part of the common law in this area, have been replaced in this Act with dangers the occupier knew or ought to have known of.

MINORS

With regard to persons who have not reached the age of eighteen, the basic duty the occupier owes may not in substance be different from that owed to adult entrants. A court in determining liability, however, will be required to have regard to such factors as extreme youth and the ability of a particular age group to appreciate danger.

VISITORS

A visitor is a person who enters the premises of another in a lawful manner at the invitation of the occupier or with the permission of the occupier or a member of his/her family.

RECREATIONAL USERS

A recreational user comes onto the land of another for the purpose of carrying out a recreational or sporting pursuit. Two issues are of crucial importance to this category. First, if the occupier provides a structure for the use of the recreational user the law imposes a duty of reasonable care as to the maintenance of that structure. Second, the duty does not extend to stiles, ditches and gates that are not primarily provided for the recreational user. A local authority providing swings for use by children in a public play area would owe a duty of reasonable care as to the maintenance of those swings.

TRESPASSERS

A trespasser is at law a person who enters the land or buildings of another without permission, express or implied. The duty owed under the Act to recreational users is extended to this category. It is important to note that criminal trespassers are owed no duty by the occupier unless the court, in the interests of justice, decides otherwise.

INDEPENDENT CONTRACTORS

Section 7 of the Act provides that an occupier will not be liable for the negligence of independent contractors provided he/she used reasonable care in ensuring that a competent contractor was employed.

INSURANCE

Insurance is a legally enforceable agreement existing between two legal persons, its principal factors being:

- the existence of an insurable interest
- the principle of utmost good faith.

In order to establish the existence of a contract of insurance, it must be shown that one party to the contract assumes the risk arising from an uncertain future event, over which neither party to the contract has any control. Under this agreement one party, described as the insured, must have an insurable interest in the event insured against and must pay the agreed sum, called the premium, to the other party to the agreement, described as the insurer. The insurer is legally bound to pay a sum of money to the insured if the uncertain event occurs. The contract must bind both parties to the agreement and the ordinary rules of contract law apply. In order to have an interest that the law recognises, the insured must lose as a result of the happening of the uncertain event insured against.

It must be made crystal clear in the contract that the insured has the right to payment on the happening of the uncertain event insured against, a right to a discretionary payment is not sufficient. In the British case of the Medical Defence Union *v* Department of Trade, the Court of Appeal held that the members of the Medical Defence Union did not have a legal right to payment because the union was not an insurer as it retained a discretion with its members as to whether in the event of a claim it made payments or not.

In summary, insurance may be defined as an arrangement whereby one party called the insurer, in return for a payment called a premium, undertakes to pay, on the happening of an uncertain future event, a sum of money or its equivalent in kind; as a general rule payment is made in money.

PROPOSAL FORM

The properly completed contents of the proposal form will be the basis of the future contract of insurance. A contract of insurance, unlike other contracts, is a contract of absolute good faith, for that reason a person seeking insurance cover must make full and frank disclosure of all material facts relating to the insurance sought. Full and frank answers to all questions contained in the proposal form will satisfy this legal requirement. Persons seeking insurance may with safety assume that the insurance company does not require any information additional to the questions posed in the proposal form. Where large insurance cover is being sought, a proposal form may not be used and cover may be granted verbally based on the insurer receiving sufficient information concerning the insurance sought.

The completed form constitutes an offer in contract law, which may be either accepted or rejected by the insurer. When the insurance contract comes into existence is decided by the circumstances, the rules of offer and acceptance in the law of contract apply but it appears that once an insurer issues a letter of acceptance as a general rule he/she cannot withdraw the offer (this appears to be a qualification of the common law rule of contract that states that an offer may be withdrawn at any time prior to valid acceptance).

Utmost Good Faith

As the completed proposal form is at law the basis of the insurance contract, any misrepresentation or untrue statement made in a proposal form will go to the very root of the contract. Even in the absence of a proposal form, the insurer must still be informed by the insured of all material facts pertaining to the risk insured. Because an insurance contract is of absolute good faith, full and frank disclosure must be made of every circumstance that would influence a prudent insurer in determining whether to accept the risk and if so, the level of premium required to cover the risk insured.

In Aro Road and Land Vehicles Limited *v* The Insurance Corporation of Ireland, the Irish Supreme Court decided that the test of what is reasonable is to be decided by the tribunal or court hearing the case. In the Aro case the disclosure of a criminal conviction imposed more than twenty years earlier was held not to be a material fact and therefore it was unreasonable for the insurer to require disclosure of this fact.

The requirement of full and frank disclosure is no longer necessary once the insurer has accepted the proposal of insurance and a contract comes into being. The duty of disclosure arises again at the next insurance renewal date. Examples of material facts in insurance contracts include:

- previous claims history
- previous convictions of the person seeking insurance cover
- the existence on site of potentially dangerous materials.

There is no need to disclose the following details:

- facts the person seeking insurance cover is not aware of
- any fact that reduces the risk covered
- any facts previously disclosed to the insurer
- any facts that the insurer has waived his/her right to knowledge of.

Insurable Interest

The Life Assurance Ireland Act 1866 provided that the insured must have an insurable interest in the life assured. Marine insurance legislation also provided that an insurable interest was required in both ship and cargo policies. In Church and General Insurance Company *v* Connolly and McLoughlin the defendants were members of a committee that leased premises on behalf of a youth club and that had insured the premises against fire. Subsequently the premises were destroyed by fire, but the insurers claimed that the defendants had no insurable interest in the premises destroyed and refused to pay on the policy. Basing their decision on the property rights of a lessee, the High Court took the view that the defendants had an insurable interest as they were responsible for paying rates on the premises and for their care and maintenance whilst in possession. The fact that no legal rule exists that states that a tenant is responsible for damage to a building unless expressly stated to the contrary appears to have been overlooked by the court in this instance.

The principal requirements of an insurable interest are: there must be some property interest, life or limb capable of being insured, one of the aforementioned must be the subject of the insurance and the insured must have a legally recognised relationship with the subject matter insured. Examples of where the law recognises that such a relationship exists include:

- the registered owner of a mechanically propelled vehicle
- liability for the commission of a tort by the insured
- a creditor has an insurable interest in the life of his/her debtor.

The subject matter of the insurance must be capable of being identified and must exist at the time of taking out the insurance.

EXPRESS CONDITIONS IN INSURANCE CONTRACTS

An express condition is included in the policy of insurance either in writing or orally. A distinction must be made here between warranties and conditions. A warranty is defined under Section 33(1) of the Marine Insurance Act 1906 as a promissory warranty by which the assured undertakes that some particular thing shall or shall not be done or that some condition shall be fulfilled, or whether he/she confirms or denies the existence of a particular state of affairs. Section 33(3) of the 1906 Act provides that a warranty as defined must be strictly complied with, if the warranty is not so complied with then, subject to any express provision in the contract, the insurer is discharged from all legal liability from the date of breach. Many non-life policies will contain terms that are described as warranties but that strictly speaking do not fall within the definition of warranty set out in the 1906 Act, examples of such terms would relate to the use of naked flames or where burning and/or cutting takes place.

In the case of Lec (Liverpool) Limited *v* Glover, the British Court of Appeal was asked to interpret such a term, the issue for legal cogitation was whether the presence of an assistant satisfied the condition of the presence of a firewatcher. The Court of Appeal held that the assistant was part of the task on hand and that nobody envisaged that his primary task was to watch for the outbreak of fire. Thus, the court found that the insured was in breach of the condition that required at least one employee in addition to those engaged in cutting the material to be present to see that no outbreak of fire occurred. It is important to note that breach of such a condition does not give the insurer the right to avoid the policy but simply to deny liability arising from the breach.

Section 33(1) of the 1906 Act, which applies to both marine and non-marine policies, has the effect of terminating the policy immediately the insured is in breach of a warranty and no further claims may be made on that policy. Insurers are relieved from liability here even where the loss suffered by the insured has nothing to do with the breach of warranty. In order to avail of a breach of warranty the insurer must void the contract; it is not sufficient simply to refuse to meet the claim. Warranties are simply promises either to do or to refrain from doing certain things. Courts will interpret warranties strictly, for example an insurance policy contained the following warranty: 'the machinery of the insured, his plant and ways are properly fenced and guarded and otherwise in good order'; this was held to apply only to when the policy was taken out.

CONDITIONS PRECEDENT

Where the liability of the insured person depends on a condition in the contract of insurance then such condition is described as a condition precedent. The legal effect of such a condition is that if a breach of that condition occurs the insurer may dispute liability. For example, a policy that provides indemnity for theft or fraud will invariably contain a condition that the insured must inform An Garda Síochána of any such crime and take all reasonable steps to ensure that the accused is prosecuted for that offence, if these steps are not taken by the insured then the insurer can simply refuse to meet any claim arising from this occurrence. Examples of conditions precedent in insurance contracts include:

- a clause allowing for alteration of the risk which allows for disclosure to the insurer of any alteration in the risk insured, this duty usually ends when the contract of insurance comes into force
- under a claims condition the insured is legally obliged to give notice to the insurer within a specified time including details of injury and damage suffered, in the case of road traffic accidents the time allowed is 48 hours.

A proviso will be included in the conditions section to the effect that if these conditions are not complied with no claim will be payable.

CONTRIBUTION CLAUSES

A contribution clause provides for more than one insurer of the risk insured. Where more than one insurer covers the same risk, each insurer will pay in proportion to the cover it grants. For example, where two insurers cover the same risk and each covers 50 per cent of that risk each will be responsible for meeting 50 per cent of that claim. The vast majority of insurance policies either contain a contribution clause or do not permit contribution clauses. The following requirements must be met:

- the insurance cover provided by each policy must have a common subject matter
- the loss suffered must be common to both policies
- the same interest must be covered by all policies
- all policies must be legally enforceable.

INDEMNITY

Indemnity can be described as the bedrock of insurance. It provides that the insured must be placed in exactly the same position as he/she was prior to the incident occurring in so far as a sum of money may achieve this objective. The methods of indemnity are: cash replacement, repair and reinstatement. Reinstatement can be said to arise in two contexts: the reinstatement of a partially damaged property to its original state, and the rebuilding as new of a completely destroyed property.

Indemnity may be modified; for example, to take account of new fire regulations in the replacement of a partially or completely destroyed building. Most policies of insurance are in fact indemnity policies and mean that the indemnor (insurer) will stand in the shoes of the insured in respect of the matter insured; the reality being that the insurer will often settle claims with claimants without consulting the insured because under the law of indemnity they are the insured for the purpose insured. It is in fact the practice of insurance companies to settle claims, particularly those arising from road traffic accidents, without any consultation with the insured. This is a matter that persons seeking insurance cover should make themselves aware of.

AVERAGE CLAUSES

Should the sum insured be less than the value of risk at the time of the loss, the insured will be considered their own insurer for a proportion of the loss. It is crucial that insured persons insure their property to cover its current replacement value as the amount payable on destruction of a property will be the amount insured or its replacement value whichever is the lesser. Under the law of insurance it is the responsibility of the insured to make sure that his/her property is fully insured; the insurer has no legal responsibility in this regard. Even where insurance companies increase property valuations by a percentage each year this still does not lift the legal onus for obtaining adequate insurance cover from the shoulders of the insured.

The Construction Industry Federation issues guidelines on a yearly basis setting out the replacement cost per square metre for which a certified builder in a particular area will replace a property. A sum must also be included in the insurance to cover site clearance.

NON-INDEMNITY INSURANCE CONTRACTS

Life assurance and personal injury policies are included under the heading of non-indemnity insurance contracts. The reason why these are non-indemnity policies is that it is impossible to establish the cost of a human life or a limb of the body. For that reason no legal restriction exists concerning the issue of indemnity in this type of policy, insurers will endeavour however to keep the amounts insured within reason.

SUBROGATION

The doctrine of subrogation gives the right of one person who has indemnified another to stand in the shoes of that person and avail of the rights that person has to claim against a third party. This doctrine may only be exercised once the insurer meets the claim submitted by the insured. Most insurance policies will contain a general condition to the effect that once a claim has been discharged by the insurer he/she has the right to claim against the third party.

PROXIMATE CAUSE

An insured person must be able to demonstrate that the loss suffered was covered by an insured peril. The test to be applied is whether the loss was caused proximately by the peril insured against. If the loss was caused by the risk insured against, further damage caused to mitigate the loss will be covered, thus damage caused by the fire services in extinguishing a fire will be covered. An intervening event must not interfere with the original cause, if it does a new cause exists. If, for example, a fire occurs and theft occurs in the course of that fire, theft is now the proximate cause. Another rule that arises in this context states that where human failure is competing with a natural element, for example where a storm occurs and adequate precautions are not taken to secure the property, the failure to take adequate precautions will be the preferred proximate cause.

PUBLIC LIABILITY INSURANCE

A general liability policy will indemnify the insured for damages and the costs involved in defending any legal action taken against the insured within the terms of the policy cover. The insurer here as a general rule will take over the defence of the action but the insured will still be named as a third party in any legal proceedings. It is well-established law that in funding the defence of proceedings taken against the insured, the insurance company are acting lawfully.

A general public liability or products liability policy is intended to cover the legal responsibilities for personal injury, including death, damage to or loss of property and the financial loss flowing from the incident. Insurers traditionally have attempted to confine financial loss to that occurring as a direct consequence of the peril insured. Insurance as a matter of tradition has been confined to uncertain events occurring causing loss or injury, as a consequence here claims arise in the law of tort or private wrongs whereas loss arising from trade transactions occurs in the law of contract and is generally regarded as uninsurable.

All policies are subject to a limit of liability, this is the maximum amount payable in compensation to third parties. Cover will usually extend to investigation and legal costs above the limit of liability. Policies will only cover the legal responsibilities of the insured, therefore payment will only be made in the event of a tort occurring which may be litigated against the insured. There are four types of liability policy:

- general liability policy
- employers' liability policy
- product liability policy
- professional liability policy.

General liability policies cover loss of or damage to property of persons arising from the activities of the insured. Expressly excluded from this policy are liabilities to: employees acting in the course of their employment; arising from defective products; and for professional advice given.

A clause that is common to all four policies is the reasonable precautions clause. Under this clause the insured is obliged to take all precautions that are in the circumstances reasonable both to prevent accidents and to maintain premises in a safe condition. In Frazer v Furnan, Lord Justice Diplock said the obligation that arises under a clause of this nature simply means that measures must be taken to prevent dangers that are likely to cause bodily injury. Reasonable, he said, meant what was reasonable as between the insured and the insurer having regard to the commercial purpose of the transaction and that the insured must not refrain from taking precautions he/she ought to take because the risk is insured.

The difference between employers' and public liability insurance is that an employer's liability is confined to individuals with a contract of service with that employer, whereas public liability refers to all those who otherwise render services. There exists in Irish law no legal obligation on employers to ensure a basis of compensation from which employees may be compensated for actionable torts. In Sweeney v Duggan, Judge Barron said that there existed in common law no general duty on the employer to protect the economic well-being of his/her employees and that no statute exists in Ireland that compels an employer to take out employers' liability insurance.

This matter is an increasing worry for employers facing potential claims for compensation from employees for which resources have to be found. For that reason the provision of adequate liability insurance cover is essential. The subject matter of employers' liability insurance is the amount of damages the employer can pay his/her employees in respect of accidental death, injury or disease caused during the period of cover of the insured. Such a policy would contain the following provisions:

- indemnity against payment of damages and legal costs as a result of the negligence of the employer; the Irish Business and Employers Confederation (IBEC) recommends a ceiling of €12.7 million
- coverage of a defined state, Ireland; those employed outside the jurisdiction may also be covered where that employment is temporary
- a condition that the insurer be notified of all accidents and incidents
- an exclusion clause.

Some policies will cover trainees, those on work experience and even self-employed persons working on the insured person's premises. Any exclusion clause in an insurance policy must be carefully studied as it is in this area that most disputes arise. Some common exclusions include demolition, pile driving, quarrying, use of explosives and loading and discharging vessels.

IBEC has issued the following guidelines for employers' liability insurance:

- full disclosure of the activities of the organisation
- all material facts are required to be disclosed
- all changes in the risk insured must be notified to the insurer
- the wording of the policy should adequately cover the activities of the organisation
- all exclusions must be checked with the insurer
- all locations where business is conducted must be covered
- all health, safety and welfare activities must be covered
- all company directors and members of senior management must be covered
- activities of a unique nature must be covered.

Public liability insurance, as a general rule, will cover two fields of activity. First, risks occurring from the ownership and/or management of business premises. Second, risks arising from the activities of employees and/or agents of the insured to third parties. The following conditions apply in the operation of public liability insurance:

- the insured must not admit liability or settle any claim without the insurer's specific consent
- the insurer will usually place a limit on payment in respect of any one accident or incident
- the policy will specify the claims procedure to be followed.

It is important to note that both product liability and professional negligence are outside the scope of general public liability insurance and separate cover would be required in both instances.

The Liability for Defective Products Act 1991 imposes strict liability, that is liability without fault, on manufacturers and suppliers of defective products in respect of loss or injury suffered by the purchasers of such products. The Act provides for only very limited defences to a tort action and for that reason it is important that insurance cover be sought to cover this particular liability.

Those who give professional advice need to obtain professional liability cover because whatever the written terms of the agreement between professional and client the common law imposes on the contract a duty that the professional perform his/her work with reasonable skill, care and diligence. Any doubt that a duty in both contract and tort is owed by the professional to his/her client was removed by two decisions of the Irish Supreme Court, Finlay *v* Murtagh and Wall *v* Hegarty.

IBEC's guidelines for such insurance recommend:

- having the same insurer and public liability insurance as a claim may arise under both headings from the same accident
- be fully aware of the implications of any excess clause
- insure the indemnity of all directors, senior managers and first-aiders
- it may be necessary to discuss insurance cover for independent contractors with the insurer
- all activities likely to expose the insured to claims should be covered
- no admission of liability or promise to pay should be made without the express consent of the insurer
- the policy should exclude property in the personal custody or control of the insured.

SELF-INSURANCE

Self-insurance refers to a situation where the organisation will either finance its own losses in the event of liability occurring or avail of a deductible. In the latter case, the insured will agree to pay either the first €100,000 or €1 million and an insurer deals with liability over that amount. If an organisation decides to self-insure, it should first take expert advice as to how it can finance any losses occurring and it must take the following factors into consideration:

- provide sufficient funds to manage any claims arising and to create a reserve fund for cases outstanding
- specific measures, such as the provision of expert medical treatment, are essential to discourage claims
- a claims management team must be established to advise on claims arising
- all employees must be made aware that the organisation does not carry conventional insurance cover
- all claims should be settled sooner rather than later
- systematic training of management in the costing of accidents, investigations and court appearances is essential.

REVISION QUESTIONS

1   Define any two of the following terms of the Occupiers' Liability Act 1995: 'visitor', 'recreational user' or 'trespasser'.
2   Under the Occupiers' Liability Act 1995, what is the law pertaining to minors and criminal trespassers?
3   What is the significance of the proposal form in the law of insurance?
4   What is meant by utmost good faith in a contract of insurance?
5   Describe subrogation in the law of insurance.
6   Define insurable interest in the context of a contract of insurance.
7   What is meant by indemnity insurance?
8   Describe the type of insurance cover that an employer would obtain on taking out public liability insurance.
9   What is self-insurance?

REFERENCES

Aro Road and Land Vehicles Limited *v* The Insurance Corporation of Ireland, 1986 Irish Reports, p. 403

Church and General Insurance Company *v* Connolly and McLoughlin, unreported decision of The High Court, 1981

Donoghue *v* Stevenson 1932 Appeal Cases, p. 562

Finlay *v* Murtagh, 1979 Irish Reports, p. 249

Foley *v* Musgrave Cash & Carry, unreported Irish Supreme Court, 1985

Frazer *v* Furnan, 1967 Volume 3 All England Reports, p. 57

Keegan *v* Owens & McMahon, 1953 Irish Reports, p. 267

Lec (Liverpool) Limited *v* Glover, 2001 Lloyds Reports, p. 315

McMahon, B. (1995), 'Occupiers' Liability Act 1995', *Solicitors Gazette*, December

McNamara *v* Electricity Supply Board, 1975 Irish Reports

Occupiers' Liability Act 1995

Purtill *v* Athlone Urban District Council, 1968 Irish Reports

Sweeney *v* Duggan, unreported decision of The Irish Supreme Court, 1997

The Medical Defence Union *v* The British Department of Trade, 1979 All England Reports

Wall *v* Hegarty, 1980 Irish Law Reports Monthly, p. 124

11
Health and Safety in Childcare

CAROLINE QUINN WITH REVISION BY ANN FANNING

The focus of this chapter is on children's health. The prevention of infection is vital to health and particular emphasis is paid to the ways in which infection can be spread, along with the precautions that can be taken to prevent such spread. Vaccination against specific infections is recommended and the immunisation schedule for Ireland is detailed. Childcare workers are responsible for the health of all children in their care. However, determining ill health in babies can be challenging and guidance is given on when to seek medical aid for the very young. While the cause of sudden infant death is unknown, there are particular risk factors and these are described in the final section.

ROUTES OF INFECTION

The ways by which infection may be spread are referred to as the routes of infection. Modes or methods of infection transmission also carry the same meaning. The main routes of infection include:

- *airborne or droplet*: spread is via moisture droplets in the atmosphere. Examples include influenza, the common cold, measles, mumps and tuberculosis. The risk increases with sneezing, coughing and talking
- *food and water*: contaminated water is responsible for the spread of diseases such as cholera, typhoid and E.coli. Food-poisoning organisms include salmonella, listeria and clostridium botulinum
- *direct and indirect contact*: when an infected person touches another person the infection may be passed on, for example infectious mononucleosis (glandular fever), herpes simplex (cold sores), impetigo and chicken pox. Alternatively, infections can be transmitted via fomites or inanimate objects (things), for example athlete's foot and hepatitis A
- *blood and bodily fluids*: HIV/AIDS and hepatitis C are bloodborne diseases and can enter the body through a cut in the skin. Other bodily fluids include faeces, urine, saliva and vomitus; these do not provide any great risk for HIV or hepatitis C transmission, however toothbrushes may be a source of contamination and should be stored separately.

Infections such as rubella, chicken pox and HIV can be spread transplacentally (from mother to baby during pregnancy)

- *animals and insects*: animals can be a source of disease through bites or via food, for example rabies and tuberculosis. Tropical diseases such as malaria are spread by mosquitoes and sleeping sickness by the tsetse fly
- *soil*: many organisms can be dormant in soil or dust and become activated when entering the body through a cut or when ingested, for example toxocariasis (parasite found in the faeces of dogs and cats). Tetanus can also be spread via the soil
- *sexually*: specific sexually transmitted infections include gonorrhoea, syphilis, herpes, genital warts and chlamydia. Spread is via sexual fluids (semen and/or vaginal secretions).

BREAKING THE CHAIN OF INFECTION

In order for infection to spread a sequence of events occurs. This is known as the chain of infection. First, the source (infected person or animal) spreads the micro-organism (germ) into the environment. This can be a bacteria, virus, protozoa or fungus. Second, the micro-organism is transferred to another individual (host) via a route of infection. That individual then becomes infected and the whole cycle begins again. This chain of infection must be broken to prevent the spread of infectious disease.

An exclusion policy is one whereby infected persons are prohibited from attending school/the workplace for a period of time. The time limit will be determined by the specific infection and the symptoms of the individual. Therefore exclusion periods vary greatly. The purpose of exclusion is to prevent the infected person from spreading infection into the environment, thereby safeguarding other persons from becoming ill. Workplace exclusion policies can determine what illnesses are to be included. If in doubt, local doctors or area medical officers with the Health Service Executive will be able to offer advice.

Conditions which may be included in an exclusion policy are, for example:

- *bacterial meningitis*: exclude until recovery
- *chicken pox*: exclude until blisters have crusted over
- *conjunctivitis*: exclude until eye discharge has stopped
- *diarrhoea and vomiting*: exclude until symptoms have ceased
- *hepatitis A*: exclude for at least seven days after symptoms of jaundice appear or until recovery is medically certified

- *impetigo*: exclude until antibiotic treatment has been commenced
- *measles*: exclude until recovery is medically certified
- *mumps*: exclude until symptom-free
- *parasitic infestation* (head lice, scabies, thread worms): exclude until treatment has commenced
- *rubella*: exclude until symptom-free
- *tuberculosis*: exclude until medically certified
- *whooping cough*: exclude until recovery is medically certified.

It is not necessary to exclude those with HIV, hepatitis B or C. Children or adults who are displaying signs or symptoms of infection in general should if at all possible be excluded from public places until symptom-free to prevent the spread of that infection.

Personal Hygiene

Hand-Washing

Hand-washing is the single most effective method of preventing cross-infection. However hands must be washed effectively to prevent the spread of infection. The hands harbour millions of micro-organisms, many of which are healthy. Hand-washing will not sterilise the hands but will prevent infection from being directly or indirectly spread by touch. Nails should be kept short to encourage cleanliness. Fingernails should be rounded and toenails should be cut straight across.

When washing hands:

- always use warm running water; cold water is a deterrent to spending a sufficient length of time washing; running water ensures that potential disease-causing organisms are flushed away rather than remaining in a stagnant pool
- use of liquid soap is better than a bar of soap; bars of soap are a breeding ground for infection as the same bar is used by many people; bars of soap also remain in tepid pools of water, further encouraging the growth of infection
- hands should be rubbed in a lively manner with all areas washed, including the backs of hands, thumbs, between the fingers, palms, wrists and fingernails
- it is not usually necessary to use a nail brush unless visible dirt under the nails is hard to remove
- hands should then be rinsed to remove all soap, again under warm running water

- individual towels, cloth or paper, should be used to dry the hands fully
- hand cream can then be used to prevent the drying out of the skin.

Hands should be washed:

- before eating or preparing food
- after visiting the toilet
- after changing nappies
- after outdoor activities
- after handling pets/animals
- after using a tissue to sneeze, cough or wipe a nose.

USE OF GLOVES

Disposable gloves are essential personal protection equipment for childcare workers. Under the duties of employers in the Safety, Health and Welfare at Work Act 2005, gloves should be provided in crèches, daycare centres, schools and any other type of childcare placement. Gloves should be worn when changing nappies, toileting children, wiping noses, cleaning up bodily fluids and when dealing with cuts and scratches. They should be worn once only, changed for each child and disposed of hygienically.

TOOTHBRUSHES

Toothbrushes are for individual use only. All food debris should be washed off toothbrushes after use. They should be stored in an upright position after use which allows the brushes to dry. Bristles from different toothbrushes should not be allowed to touch. It is recommended that toothbrushes be replaced every three months.

TISSUES

Disposable tissues should be used to wipe noses, and when coughing or sneezing. This will prevent airborne micro-organisms being dispelled forcibly into the environment. They should be disposed of hygienically after use and hands should be washed.

HAIR CARE

Hair should be washed at least once weekly and inspected for the presence of dandruff and head lice. If these conditions are present they should be immediately treated with an appropriate solution. Hairbrushes are for individual use and should never be shared; this will help to prevent the spread of head lice. Brushes should be cleaned and washed on a weekly basis. Black curly hair is naturally dry and the daily application of oil is recommended to prevent the breakage of hair.

PERSONAL CLEANSING

The average person produces 500 millilitres of sweat daily. When sweat is exposed to air it produces an unpleasant odour. From an infection control perspective, the natural micro-organisms present on the skin are attached to skin scales and may be a source of infection when shed into the environment. While those natural flora are not harmful to the carrier, they may be a source of infection to others. Therefore daily showering is an essential element in breaking the chain of infection. Likewise, given that skin containing micro-organisms is shed onto clothes, clothes should be washed/cleaned after wearing even when dirt is not visible.

Dry skin should be moisturised to prevent cracking, as cracks in the skin harbour micro-organisms providing a source for infection. Black skin requires particularly intensive moisture.

VENTILATION

Adequate ventilation, whether natural or artificial, is essential to prevent the spread of airborne infection. Fresh air dilutes the concentration of micro-organisms in the environment thereby minimising risk. Simply opening windows can be sufficient. However care must be taken if any person suffers from asthma as pollen and dampness are trigger factors. Weather and pollen count checks will guard against problems here.

Artificial ventilation and extraction systems should be well maintained and inspected regularly for faults. While endeavouring to improve air quality, ventilation systems can conversely be a source of infection, for example legionnaire's disease. The legionella bacteria thrive in stagnant waters that accumulate in vents and ducts and then spread via the ventilation system into the environment.

FOOD HYGIENE

Strict food hygiene is necessary to prevent food poisoning. All food surface and storage areas should be kept spotlessly clean. Hand-washing facilities must be provided for anyone in the workplace involved in the preparation, storage, cooking and serving of food. Raw and cooked foods should not be stored together or prepared on the same surface. All food should be used within its best before date. Perishable food such as dairy produce, meat and fish should be stored in a fridge under 4 degrees Celsius. Meat should be thoroughly defrosted before cooking and should then be fully cooked. Heat food once only – never reheat leftover food.

GENERAL HYGIENE MEASURES

Washable toys should be washed once daily in hot soapy water, wearing gloves to prevent drying of the skin. Alternatively toys can be washed in a dishwasher. Non-washable toys should be used by one child only and stored separately to other toys.

Books and newspapers can be a source of infection. Washable books should be used by young people whose immune systems are still developing.

All surfaces including furniture, worktops, floors, toilet areas, sinks, etc. should be cleaned daily. Smooth floor areas such as tiles and wood are easier to clean than carpets. All carpets and rugs should be professionally cleaned regularly.

Sandpits should be covered when not in use to prevent soiling by animals. The toxocariasis worm can survive for years in sand and can be carried by unwormed animals. Sand should be washed regularly and changed as necessary.

Rubbish bins should be sterilised regularly and lined with an appropriate bag. Black bags are sufficient for daily household and workplace waste. Bags should be tied up after use and left for collection by a waste disposal organisation. Waste should not be allowed to accumulate as it will attract flies and rats. Flies can spread food poisoning and rats carry leptospirosis (Weil's disease).

CHILDHOOD IMMUNISATION

Immunisation is the most reliable and cost-effective way of preventing specific infections. The purpose of any immunisation programme is to provide immunity against an infection. The risks from having certain infections greatly exceed the risks of side-effects from immunisation.

Immunisation is usually delivered with a vaccine. A vaccine is a prepared substance which stimulates the production of antibodies. The antibodies are specific against the pathogens (disease-causing agents) causing the infectious disease and are produced by white blood cells. The antibodies remain in the body and protect the child against the disease. Vaccines consist of active ingredients (inactivated or weakened pathogens), preservatives and stabilisers. Most vaccines need to be given many times to build up lifelong protection. It is safe to administer many vaccines on the same occasion as even an infant's immune system can respond effectively to this practice.

The present Irish immunisation schedule is set out in Table 11.1. It is important to note that immunisation programmes may vary from country to country.

Table 11.1. Irish Immunisation Schedule

In Ireland, all the recommended childhood immunisations listed in the timetable are free of charge.

Age to Vaccinate	*Type of Vaccination*
At birth	BCG tuberculosis vaccine (given in maternity hospitals or a HSE clinic)
At 2 months Free from your GP	**6 in 1:** Diphtheria Tetanus Whooping cough (Pertussis) Hib (Haemophilus influenzae B) Polio (Inactivated poliomyelitis) Hepatitis B **PCV:** (Pneumococcal Conjugate Vaccine)
At 4 months Free from your GP	**6 in 1:** Diphtheria Tetanus Whooping cough (Pertussis) Hib (Haemophilus influenzae B) Polio (Inactivated poliomyelitis) Hepatitis B **Men C:** (Meningococcal C)
At 6 months Free from your GP	**6 in 1:** Diphtheria Tetanus Whooping cough (Pertussis) Hib (Haemophilus influenzae B) Polio (Inactivated poliomyelitis) Hepatitis B

Age to Vaccinate	Type of Vaccination
At 6 months *(continued)*	**Men C:** (Meningococcal C) **PCV:** (Pneumococcal Conjugate Vaccine)
At 12 months Free from your GP	**MMR:** Measles Mumps Rubella **PCV** (Pneumococcal Conjugate Vaccine)
At 13 months Free from your GP	**Men C** (Meningococcal C) **Hib** (Haemophilus Influenzae B)
At 4–5 years Free in school or from your GP	**4 in 1:** Diphtheria Tetanus Whooping cough (Pertussis) Polio (Inactivated poliomyelitis) **MMR:** Measles Mumps Rubella
At 11–14 years Free in school	**TD:** Diphtheria Tetanus
At 12 years (1st year second level school) *Girls only* Free in school	**HPV:** Human Papilloma Virus

Will immunisations still work if my child doesn't get them at the right time?

Yes. Most of these vaccines can be given at any age, and a child who misses one injection in a course of injections does not have to start again. The vaccines already given will still work and your child will still develop protection. Just ask your GP.

If you have any queries or concerns about vaccines please contact your GP or local health office.

CONTRA-INDICATIONS AND SIDE-EFFECTS

There are very few reasons for not immunising a child. Children who suffer from epilepsy, asthma, eczema, were premature, had jaundice and/or are on antibiotics should be immunised normally. Given that the MMR is an egg-based vaccine, those children with a severe egg allergy will need to be closely supervised during and after the delivery of the MMR. However, it should still be given. If a child is pyrexial (has a high temperature), it would be advisable to wait until the child's temperature returns to normal (37 degrees Celsius) before immunising.

All vaccines carry potential side-effects, but most of these are mild. Occasionally severe reactions may occur. If parents or caregivers are worried they should contact their local doctor or practice nurse for advice. Side-effects may be classified as local or systemic. Local side-effects indicate a reaction at the site of the infection and can range from mild to severe redness, soreness, swelling, itching and burning. A lump may be palpable for a number of weeks. Systemic side-effects refer to reactions throughout the body and again can be mild to severe. They include a low-grade fever, rash, nasal drip, cough, inflamed eyelids, swelling of the salivary glands, diarrhoea and feeling 'off form'. Very rarely, a child may have a convulsion or encephalitis. There is no evidence to support a link between immunisation and brain damage or autism. However there is a risk of severe side-effects from infections if a child is not immunised.

UNIVERSAL INFECTION CONTROL PRECAUTIONS

Universal infection control precautions are recommended to prevent the spread of infection, in particular bloodborne diseases such as HIV/AIDS and hepatitis C. These infections can enter the body through a cut in the skin or through the eyes. Precautions include:

- covering all cuts or scratches with a waterproof dressing
- using disposable latex gloves when handling any bodily fluid
- washing hands after contact with bodily fluids

- wearing disposable plastic aprons if there is a possibility of contact with bodily fluids
- using protective eyewear such as goggles if there is a danger of blood splashes
- if a needle-stick injury occurs: encourage the wound to bleed, wash with soap and water, cover with a waterproof dressing and note the name and history of the original recipient
- if eyes/mucous membranes are splashed with bodily fluids: wash out with saline and report to a local hospital
- when a spillage of bodily fluids occurs: wear protective gloves and an apron, seal off the area, soak up excess fluids with disposable towels and treat the whole area with bleach and water in a 1:10 solution, leaving the solution in place for a few minutes. Dispose of materials as clinical waste. Clean the area again with the above solution.

INFLUENZA A (H1 N1)

Preventing the spread of germs is the single most effective way to slow the spread of influenza (flu).
You should always:

- use tissues to cover your mouth and nose when you cough or sneeze
- place used tissues in a bin as soon as possible
- ensure that everyone washes their hands regularly with soap and water
- clean surfaces regularly to get rid of germs

If you think you have flu, please avoid close contact with others, stay at home and seek medical advice by phoning your doctor or the Flu Information Line.

ANIMALS

While animals can bring pleasure to individuals and families, they can also be a source of infection. Even family pets can be hazardous if not properly cared for. Animal-based infections that can spread to humans include:

- toxocariasis, which causes asthma and blindness, can be found in the faeces of cats and dogs. It can be prevented by three monthly worming treatments. Children should not be allowed to play in areas where dogs have soiled. Dog owners should clean up after their animals. Hands should be thoroughly washed after handling animals

- Lyme disease is a bacterial infection carried by ticks which can infest dogs
- Leptospirosis or Weil's disease, a bacterial infection carried by rats, can cause liver damage. It generally only affects those who work outdoors or with sewage and it is very important for such workers to cover as much skin as possible with clothing and to cover all cuts with a waterproof dressing
- Toxoplasmosis is a protozoan infection and is carried by cats. It is particularly dangerous to the pregnant woman as it can cause blindness, hydrocephalus or intellectual disability in the child if transmitted in early pregnancy. Contact with the faeces of cats should therefore be avoided by pregnant women.

In general, any illness in an animal should be professionally treated by a vet. Litter trays should not be in the vicinity of children. All areas should be kept free of animal faeces. Any pets should be dewormed and receive the appropriate vaccinations. They should be inspected regularly for the presence of fleas and treated accordingly. Compliance with the legal requirements in the Control of Dogs Act 1986 and any amendments to same is essential for dog owners. Any queries can be directed to a local vet or the office of the Irish Society for the Prevention of Cruelty to Animals (ISPCA).

SOIL

A number of infectious agents are present in soil. These include tetanus, a bacterial infection which affects the nervous system and that is most likely to enter the body through a cut. Prevention is possible by receiving the tetanus vaccine. It is also important to keep any cuts or wounds covered.

SEXUAL SPREAD OF INFECTION

As sexually transmitted infection during pregnancy can affect the foetus, it is advisable that precautions be taken to limit the risk of contracting such an infection, prior to and during pregnancy. A number of steps can be taken to prevent the spread of sexually transmitted infections (STIs). These include:

- having one sexual partner for life
- use of a condom when having oral or penetrative sex

- disposing of condoms hygienically after use; condoms are for one use only
- inspect condom after use and seek medical aid if a tear has occurred.

If an individual is unsure of a sexual partner's past medical history or if they have had more than one sexual partner, attendance for a medical check-up at a local doctor's surgery is recommended. This will ensure prompt diagnosis and treatment of any infection. Some STIs can be asymptomatic, for example chlamydia and gonorrhoea, so therefore self-inspection may not be sufficient to establish that infection has occurred.

THE UNWELL CHILD

A child's daily caregiver will know how that child appears when healthy and can therefore easily identify when the child is ill. Young children often present with the symptoms of minor illness, for example nasal drip or a slightly raised temperature. Occasionally certain symptoms may indicate a more serious disease process which requires medical attention.

The following signs and symptoms are indicators of illnesses which require medical aid:

- fever of 39 degrees Celsius or above or a high fever for more than twenty-four hours
- persistent, prolonged coughing, or coughing which is accompanied by a whooping sound at the end of a bout of coughing
- dyspnoea (difficulty in breathing)
- cyanosis (bluish discolouration of the skin and mucous membranes)
- green or blood-stained sputum or nasal discharge
- discharge from the ears
- yellow pus around the eyes
- yellow discolouration of the skin and whites of the eyes (jaundice)
- pale-coloured, greasy, foul-smelling faeces (may be due to malabsorption)
- dark, brown-coloured urine
- diarrhoea and vomiting
- loss of appetite
- symptoms of dehydration (dry mouth, dry loose skin, sunken eyes, depressed fontanelles in young babies)
- dysphagia (difficulty in swallowing)
- enlarged glands
- high-pitched or weak cry, less responsive than normal, or more floppy
- unusual rash

- yellow discharge from a scab on the skin
- complaints of persistent pain anywhere in the body
- complaints of a stiff neck and/or photophobia (aversion to light)
- regression to younger behaviours.

Action to take when a child is unwell:

- if the child is with others, he/she should be separated from them
- a caregiver should remain with the child at all times to reassure and monitor the condition
- parents should be contacted and if necessary medical aid should be sought
- take the child's temperature if a fever is detected. A high temperature in young children may predispose a febrile convulsion, therefore it is important to instigate cooling measures if the temperature is 38 degrees Celsius or above. Paracetamol is an effective antipyretic, but it should only be given by a parent or if a caregiver has parental permission. All medication given should be recorded. Removing clothing and sponging a child with tepid water is an effective method of reducing a fever. A baby can be placed in a bath of tepid water. The room should be well ventilated and fluids given to prevent dehydration
- placing a child in cold water to reduce a fever will cause intense shivering (rigor) which serves to raise temperature and is therefore counter-productive
- note all signs and symptoms and record them
- always be kind and caring: an ill child is less independent than normal and a gentle approach will help him/her feel more at ease; help may be needed with certain activities such as feeding, personal cleaning, dressing and toileting
- wash hands after contact with an unwell child, especially prior to working with other children
- report progression of the illness along with medication records to parents and/or a doctor.

SUDDEN INFANT DEATH

SIDS or sudden infant death is also known as cot death or crib death. The term refers to the sudden or unexpected and unexplained death of a child, usually less than twelve months, but it can occur up to two years of age. The incidence of SIDS in Ireland is decreasing and there has been a drop by more than two-thirds since the 1980s. Four out of ten deaths in infants aged between one and twelve months are attributed to SIDS. The National Sudden Infant Death Register shows that the rate is 0.7 per 1,000 live births. The cause of SIDS has not yet been determined, but a number of risk factors have been identified, including:

- overheating
- parental smoking
- sharing parents' bed
- prematurity
- bottle feeding
- winter
- being male
- low birth weight
- lying the baby in a prone or side position
- general malaise a few days prior to death
- absence of routine soother use
- sibling death from SIDS.

The following guidelines have been developed to reduce the risk of SIDS:

- babies should be placed on their back to sleep with their feet to the foot of the cot and blankets placed under their arms, the 'back to sleep' position
- give up smoking; the risk of SIDS is higher if the mother smokes during pregnancy and if the baby is exposed to cigarette smoke, indeed the risk increases with the length of exposure
- room temperature should be maintained at 18 degrees Celsius. Babies should never be given hot water bottles, electric blankets or placed adjacent to a direct heat source such as a radiator. Avoid the use of duvets, blankets and cot bumpers. 'Honeycomb' or cellular type blankets are appropriate. The temperature of the abdominal (tummy) area is a good indicator of the core body temperature. Signs that a baby may be overheated include sweating, rapid breathing and agitation. Never cover a baby's head
- do not share a bed. Babies should sleep alone in a cot in the parents' room for the first six months. SIDS is a much greater risk for those babies who share their parents' bed; overheating is a probable cause here. The risk further increases if the parent is a smoker, has consumed alcohol or drugs or is simply exhausted. Consideration should also be given to the practice of allowing babies to sleep with a parent on a sofa – this is unsafe

- seek medical help for an ill baby. If a baby's health is causing concern, he/she should be taken to the local doctor where prompt treatment can be given and fears allayed
- breastfeeding may be protective, as may routine soother use.

REVISION QUESTIONS

1 Identify the main routes of infection.
2 Briefly describe the chain of infection.
3 What is an exclusion policy?
4 Why is hand-washing important?
5 Explain the relevance of ventilation in infection control.
6 What immunisation schedule is currently in use in Ireland?
7 Enumerate five possible side-effects of vaccines.
8 Name the steps to be taken when a needle-stick injury occurs.
9 Identify those signs and symptoms of illness which indicate the need for medical aid for a two-year-old child.
10 What are the risk factors for cot death?

REFERENCES

Control of Dogs Act 1986
National Sudden Infant Death Register
Safety, Health and Welfare at Work Act 2005

Index